The
Aesthetic
Character
of
Blackness

THE AESTHETIC CHARACTER OF BLACKNESS

Sounds Like Us

Jemma DeCristo

DUKE UNIVERSITY PRESS
Durham & London
2025

© 2025 DUKE UNIVERSITY PRESS
This work is licensed under a Creative Commons Attribution-
NonCommercial-NoDerivatives 4.0 International License,
available at https://creativecommons.org/licenses
/by-nc-nd/4.0/.
Designed by A. Mattson Gallagher
Typeset in Arno Pro and Degular
by Westchester Publishing Services

Library of Congress Cataloging-in-Publication Data
Names: DeCristo, Jemma, [date] author.
Title: The aesthetic character of blackness : sounds like us / Jemma DeCristo.
Description: Durham : Duke University Press, 2025. | Includes bibliographical references and index.
Identifiers: LCCN 2025009910 (print)
LCCN 2025009911 (ebook)
ISBN 9781478032588 (paperback)
ISBN 9781478029212 (hardcover)
ISBN 9781478061403 (ebook)
ISBN 9781478094531 (ebook other)
Subjects: LCSH: African American aesthetics. | Aesthetics, Black—Philosophy. | African Americans—Music—Philosophy and aesthetics. | African American art. | Critical race theory. | Arts and society—History—20th century.
Classification: LCC BH301.B53 D437 2025 (print) | LCCBH301.B53 (ebook)
LC record available at https://lccn.loc.gov/2025009910
LC ebook record available at https://lccn.loc.gov/2025009911

This book is freely available in an open access edition thanks to the generous support of the University of California Libraries.

*To the Black/
Trans/Palestinian/
Unhoused Struggles
for Liberation*

*& to the tented
streets, alleyways,
tunnels, &
undergrounds that
home them*

Contents

Preface   ix
BLACK ART AGAINST BLACK PEOPLE

Introduction   1

1   Emancipating the Spaces   31
of Sonic Capture

2   More Nearly Members of the Family   67
THE UGLY HISS

3   Ma Rainey's Phonograph   103

4   Music Against the Subject   133

5   Sounds Like Us   167
ON BEAUTIFICATION

Coda   207
SELF-DEFENSE AGAINST DENSITY

Acknowledgments   211
Notes   213
Sources   245
Index   261

Preface

BLACK ART AGAINST BLACK PEOPLE

I don't see how things can get better for black musicians, until they get better for black people.

Archie Shepp, in "Vibrations: Archie Shepp Interview + Lecture"

Vanished from our cities. There are no longer any ghosts who can remind the living of reciprocity

Michel de Certeau, *The Practice of Everyday Life*

On Friday, May 29, 2020, four days after George Floyd was executed by Minneapolis police, a discordant collective rearranged Oakland's downtown into a brilliant cacophony of black rage. During the week following these uprisings, a compendium of important yet insufficient collective projects resurfaced: organized abolitionist teach-ins, robust mutual aid networks, and self-defense trainings. These practices partially revitalized endogenous approaches to sustaining black lifeworlds that had been simultaneously expelled from and appropriated by Downtown Oakland's last two decades of city beautification.

 Long before that May night, Oakland had been populated by small pockets of raucous black musical venues and blues dives, black public street culture, and black queer cruising points that the city had all but modulated into a lucrative silence.[1] By early 2020, the combined din of these black sounds paled in comparison to the bombast of perpetually in-construction luxury condos and tech offices and official city art events that were brought in to beautify the area. These state-sanctioned noises became the standard against which black sounds and black life would be policed through noise ordinances and other measures that orchestrated black displacement. Certified city art events like the monthly Oakland Art Murmur were, I contend, a crucial part of this system of antiblack policing and displacement. Elsewhere called art crawls, these officially permitted events cleared Oakland's streets of an unproductive and too-loud black peopling they would later aestheticize and market as part of Oakland's official culture to facilitate building those uninhabited luxury apartments. The manageable blackness of the Art Murmur humanized the dominance of the encroaching empty real estate. The novel coexistence of black art in the Murmur established the myth that the condos had not destroyed the lives of the people whose neighborhoods they now occupied. Even more insidiously, the dominance of vacant housing, built primarily to prevent black life from living here, further assured that those it had displaced were not only unable to fight back, but that they could be made to work for and beautify the very real estate valuations that displaced them. The black art of the Murmur made it seem like black people could be commissioned to beautify and make more valuable their own violent eviction. This book is about the deceptive violence through which the voluminous sounding of black life is hushed into the aesthetic character of an art murmur.

The coy, almost-apologetic sonic figure of a "murmur" of art is an essential aesthetic vessel with a long history. This low rumble ferries the noisiness of black life into the sociability of a world directed against it, a world the rebellions of 2020 dared to imagine overthrowing. Leading up to those anarchic May nights, Oakland city officials had spent decades colluding with multinational real estate development agencies to construct a landscape of sanitized cultural productivity. The art murmur was a refined melody scored by the long eradication of boisterous black world-making. Lucrative concert venues, chartered art schools, and exorbitantly priced music bars all coincided with the construction of the Art Murmur, replacing more intramural black sonic cultures. For decades, this black sounding had been referred to in local publications as "violence," "gang activity," or "noise."[2] These imaginative justifications facilitated both the extermination of black life by real estate and police and the resurrection of black culture in and as the aesthetic character of a more acceptable and official blackness of the Art Murmur. The displacement and antagonism of black life and black people took place through black art, not without it. The core argument of this book is that the black work of art and the black artist attain value by regulating black life into the value-making project of an art "murmur." I offer the genealogy of a form that achieved this violent process. This book is an argument against the value-making process that is the black work of art and the black artist, which acquire their regulative aesthetic function through consuming and antagonizing black life. This book is a critique of us becoming works of art.

Art Is After Us

In the weeks following that lively May night, a more insidious and deceptive art murmur emerged. The broken bank windows and cacophony of riotous crowds was quickly remixed and amplified into a series of eye-level commemorative murals that began popping up in June 2020 under the broader slogan of "Black Lives Matter." The innumerable shouts, conversations, and collaborative and improvised strategizing that echoed throughout the streets those rebellious nights and beyond had been refined and transposed into an official arrangement. City monies again quickly flowed into the coffers of recently founded black arts nonprofits, and even into the pockets of some struggling black artists too, to "turn Downtown Oakland into an art gallery," as a social media post by a participating group boasted.[3] The noisy and anarchic black compositions of the previous week were hushed into another art murmur. The antiblack world that had inspired the resistant sounds and sentiments in the murals was not undone but reified through these representations. Nothing so noisy, so rowdy, and so unofficially black would threaten the peace and quiet of this empty real estate anechoic chamber ever again, they promised.

The value of the aesthetic is not just in the art it proffers but also in the creative world-making it holds back and restrains. Some of the artists and groups who built this new "art gallery" were of course transplants whose faux-graffiti aesthetic had been crafted in far-flung art schools. However, just as many who made this new murmur were black artists born and raised in Oakland who had witnessed the decades of gentrification and state-sanctioned antiblack violence I described above. As the variety in the slogans of the murals—"End All Racism," "Black Lives Matter," "Defund Oakland PD," and "We Can't Breathe"—suggest, some merely espoused an aimless anti-racism and many seemed genuinely to advocate for the abolition of the police (see figures P.1–P.4). Yet no matter how different the backgrounds or how radical the political content of those murals was, a new police was re/formed through the black work of art. The absorbing and pacifying function of the aesthetic could justify almost anything so long as it could keep the productive capacities of antiblack world-making in place and restrain the force of anyone and anything fighting against it.

Streets that days earlier had reverberated with righteous black rage were now awash in the sonic circulation of the city's normal; a muted museum we could once again only operate in accordance with some scripted authority of rights and privileges. A once-defiant presence that had peopled in the void of Oakland's downtown buildings disappeared into the ephemera of official political murals that simultaneously memorialized and killed the ongoing revolt. As if confessing their own aspirationally temporary presence, these murals appeared on the transitional façade of nailed-down plywood protecting the fragile glass of mostly empty real estate. Stores, banks, businesses, and tech offices and their abundant interiors were defended from a recurrence of the noisy mischief of the previous nights. A janky piece of plywood covering the window of a recently opened yoga studio said "We Can't Breathe." Across the street in massive relief, more plywood murals shielding the fragile lobby windows of vacant luxury condos shouted, "End All Racism," "Black Lives Matter," and "Defund the Police," each one screaming at street level while massive banners from above still advertised luxury real estate: "Now Leasing," a terrifying echo chamber disguising a world raised against us.

These murals simulated a shout, a breath out, as if they were us sounding. Much like the Art Murmur before them, they aimed at amplifying our

P.1 (*opposite left*) "End All Racism" message on luxury condo under construction in Downtown Oakland, October 8, 2020. Photo by the author.

P.2 (*opposite right*) "Black Lives Matter": another anti-racism message on a luxury condo in Downtown Oakland, October 8, 2020. Photo by the author.

P.3 (*above*) "Defund Oakland Police Department" mural on the window of an empty condominium in Downtown Oakland, October 8, 2020. Photo by the author.

P.4 (*right*) "We Can't Breathe" message on plywood protecting yoga studio windows in Downtown Oakland, October 8, 2020. Photo by the author.

voices while obliterating us. Quite deceptively, these murals were not for us; they were against us. They were for the protection of empty buildings we could never live in. They were banks that flourished from making our communities, homes, and lives unlivable; stores that we, like Banko Brown, could never shop in without being followed, harassed, arrested, and murdered.[4] These black representations expressed an affliction that cohabitated with Oakland's arting. Our resounding and our imaging increasingly liberate the aesthetic; they do not liberate us.

As you move through this public "art gallery" and its absorbing images and slogans, you never needed to look up at the force of the real estate bearing our echoes. You could almost forget that you were walking in a built environment that nurtured only defensive architecture. The whispered world of emergent condos, the noise ordinances they ushered in through their construction, and the noise complaints made from inside their space of private protection had found a new value they could never have attained without our help. The exorbitant values of the real estate that had displaced black people could now hide in plain sight in the mere aesthetics of black life, for the shouts of these murals were meant not to protect us by building a different world but to maintain the current one that is killing us. These murals were conscripted to be bastions for the onslaught of luxury condo lobby windows, radical slogans commissioned to shout "please, don't break our glass (again)." This book thinks in broad ways about what it means for black art to be the surface of a luxury condo's "please." What does it mean that something called black art can live and resound in a world where black people cannot? What does it mean to turn the intentionally evacuated interiority of these condos—of this world—which is always waged against black life, into the plentiful surface that stages our aesthetic value?

The apparently reflective surface of the empty condo glass and the professed depth of the resounded black slogans of the murals are not opposites, and the moment I outline here make this uniquely clear. Both center on the reflective and regulative function of the aesthetic I track in this book, which developed primarily in the late eighteenth and nineteenth centuries. The aesthetic is driven toward creating "that which pleases universally," and any passersby should want to see themselves in this globally ubiquitous reflective surface of luxury.[5] The pleasing and pleases of these black murals reify the inclusive speculative capacity of the luxury condo glass; you can't shatter the surface of a world you see yourself progressively reflected in. To the extent that forcefully wielded hammers or wayward rocks and parking sign posts shattered this illusion, the successive frescoes offered a restorative or corrective. The surfaces of the new murals offer a heavily managed and curated black imagination in which "seeing and hearing ourselves reflected in" ensures that we will not fight back; we will never trouble the rapidly expanding surface's integrity.

The emptiness of behind the glass and the plentitude of the flamboyant surface converge in what they hold back. This is the aesthetic I analyze in this book. While the extraction of industrial black labor has been substantially eliminated from US urban centers of production since the 1970s, the black imagination (which is tucked within that modality too) remains a plentiful resource for propping up the racial capital of this luxuriated aesthetic order.[6] Like the empty condos built to prevent any poor people from living there, black imaginative labor is no longer about the life it can produce or sustain; it is about the life it can confine, guard against, police, and hold back for the production, expansion, and protection of racial finance capital. Black artistic capacities hypostatized in these murals and in other such official culture become verisimilar with the endless emptiness of the condos they are enlisted to protect. Both sites are conscripted to defend the infinite site for the accrual of value. In many ways, this overlapping empty space is the central preoccupation of this work.

I argue that the roots of subjectivity granted to the black artist and the black work of art emerged largely to animate and protect this antiblack abyss of value production in racial capitalism. I begin with the contemporary moment of how black sounds of rage, coordination, collectivity, and rebellion became murals and memorialization to anchor the genealogical journey of the aesthetic character I map in this text. Yet the problem of the aesthetic I unfurl goes back to the discovery and appropriation of black sound as black music in the nineteenth century. Countering the prominent emphasis on correcting, expanding, or beautifying black representation that conflates its improvement with the enrichment of black life chances, I aim to understand how the life of black representation has long been and is increasingly designed to displace and regulate black life. The void of black displacement animated by the black work of art, I argue, is not just about producing art but also about arresting black imaginative capacities to maintain the productive faculties of that antiblack world. The arresting reflective surface of the black work of art and the depths of black life and sounding it extracts from and traverses unite in an aesthetic character that can beautify the constraint and captivity of our imaginations, making the unmaking of this world seem ugly. This aesthetic houses us so long as we remain only a "please" in their ideal world, in which there is still black art and there are still black art opportunities but there are no more black people.

The Art of Exposure

Part of this monograph comes out of my experience and disillusionment as a black musician and artist during the last decades I have referenced here in the Bay Area, playing, making, and attending shows in increasingly empty rooms. Spaces that once reverberated with black laughter, contentious shouts, banter, and all kinds of carrying on were increasingly hushed by the displacement of black life. The benefits for the black artist were an artists' residency in this emptiness, a room of one's own that several black people used to live in. Black musical performers and visual artists ingratiated themselves in order to access bigger, more official, and more luxurious spaces, no longer just playing in the emptiness but playing the emptiness too. It is easy and important to blame the albatross of venture-capital-fueled tech and real estate development that went hand in hand with the antiblack state policing practices, but black artists and the black work of art played their part too.

Over the years I gradually discovered that for many black artists the desire for a "platform" and the need for representation and to be represented too often operated as a conveyance for power's imaginative faculties, even or perhaps especially when cloaked as some kind of "resistance" or "resistant practice." I watched and confronted many fellow black artists in the Bay Area who justified making work that adorned, and to varying degrees consciously legitimated and defended, the conceptual aegis of real estate projects, wealthy private spaces, gentrifying public enclaves, and even the lobbies of tech offices. The directives and market aspirations of all these entities sought to police, imprison, displace, exploit, and drive toward the brink of death the very poor and working-class black people these artists claimed their work addressed and celebrated.

Their reasons for selling out were rarely monetary—none of them then were compensated anything approaching an impressive sum. They were often instead "paid in exposure." How being exposed constitutes something like being paid and something like having one's needs met is part of that empty space I have alluded to, the empty space that keeps expanding through the black work of art. This void is the essence of black representation, and this is the void I seek to think through and criticize in this work. I pursue the aesthetic in this work to understand how the black work of art makes us more sociable to the antiblack world instead of making a world that is more hospitable to us and our needs.

A century ago, during the Harlem Renaissance, W. E. B. Du Bois referred to this very predicament as the "deadly bribes" of the black work of art and the black artist: "I will say that there are today a surprising number of white people who are getting great satisfaction out of these younger Negro writers [and artists] because they think it is to stop agitation on the Negro question . . . and many great colored people are all too eager to follow this advice; especially those who weary of the eternal struggle along the color line, who are afraid to fight and to whom the money of philanthropists and the alluring publicity are subtle and deadly bribes."[7] This problem has only gotten worse. Du Bois's language of "deadly bribes" makes overt an always latent subterfuge within not just the form but also the circulation and practice of black art. The deadliness of the bribe seems both the precedent and the afterlife of the black work of art. This black aesthetic labor mimics or prefigures the dead labor Marx famously entombed in the commodity form that was wielded against the life of its producers by making little means of life for them and everything for the lifeless futurity of capital. This deferral of our endogenous needs for the needs of representation is synthesized in the regulation of our needs that alienate us from our living. This aesthetic labor, which I call the black work of art in this book, is unique not just for how it produces products or artworks but also for how it imaginatively restrains and constrains us.

Often black artists are "paid in exposure" or representation because the implicit currency of black art emerges from its negation of an imaginative abundance we already share and operate in among each other—and that we could share much more with each other. The "fight" for the world we need and want is what the aesthetic entices us into fleeing. The stakes of black art's ploy, both the abundance of the black life it draws from and the currency of the "fight" (or to use a term with which Du Bois is more commonly associated, "problem") it admonishes are indeed deadly. We are not just memorializing our fallen kin as cultural totems on commemorative murals, we are arming and aiding the institutions that are killing us. This book hopes merely to spark the realization that we need to steal back our lives, our living, our work, and our needs from this fantastical investment property in which our only occupation is its defense and not ours. It is never real beyond our constant paranoid defense of it. This is an immense task that this work hopes to imagine and think us into collectively.

Introduction

this is about songs
about when they happen about
pieces and absences
of connection about for no reason

this is about practicing
any gap any short for the jump
this is about going about
years with the live fragment

singing it over
and over for years learning its meaning
only accuracy   not an aesthetic
only as the most

maybe empirically correct song

    Ed Roberson, "the puzzle in bundles"

Mirrors ought to think a bit before
reflecting images

    Jean Cocteau, *The Blood of a Poet*

It is impossible to grasp what the black work of art is and what it does without understanding its origin in the invention of black music in the nineteenth century. Black music was not simply a category describing the music-making practices of enslaved black people and their descendants; it was a project of aesthetic refinement that sought to humanize and regulate the soon-to-be-manumitted for the racist society that had enslaved them. Rather than thinking exclusively about the positive content and expressions black music proffered, which largely guides how it was studied by nineteenth- and twentieth-century scholars and writers, I situate "the slave society's" aestheticization of black music as part of an emerging form for restraining and regulating black life and resistance.[1] I trace the regulative function of the black work of art and the black artist alluded to in the preface to the mid-nineteenth-century development of black music. How black music became a point of aesthetic regulation is best understood through its earliest and most vocal nineteenth-century exponent, Frederick Douglass.

In some of the most influential lines of his widely circulated *Narrative of the Life of Frederick Douglass, an American Slave* (1845), Douglass composed the form of black music I am concerned with in this book. Douglass's book profoundly transposed the noisy creativity fashioned by the "slave community" into the manageable aesthetic character of a song. While he was not a trained musician and while he has not been regarded in scholarship as an artist of any sort, Douglass's reproductions of enslaved black sonic practices inspired the first serious studies, recordings, and capture of black music.[2] He wrote, "The hearing of those wild notes always depressed my spirit. . . . To those songs I trace my first glimmering conception of the dehumanizing character of slavery. I can never get rid of that conception. Those songs still follow me to deepen my hatred of slavery, and quicken my sympathies for my brethren in bonds"[3] Through his authorship and the circulation of his public persona—and here, through his ability to translate relatively inscrutable black cultural forms into representations accessible to and intended for white audiences—Douglass became an early (and important, if rudimentary) exemplar of the black artist.

I single out Douglass's use of quintessentially aesthetic terminology such as "song" and "character" to signal how a shift was taking place. The activities of the enslaved were being deceptively refined and granted a representational quality to justify their living and continued existence "after slavery" to the very society that still held black folks in bondage. This emerging aesthetic justification was quite novel in Douglass's oeuvre. He offered an occupation and use value for the soon-to-be-manumitted by re-forming the sounds of the enslaved as a source of value that could live beyond the increasingly maligned model of plantation labor and rule. Through his account and the accounts of black artists that followed, this book traces how black music, black song, and (later, in the twentieth century) the black work of art materialized as a justification for sociable black life to be plucked from the brutality of enslavement and racist oppression. I argue that this aesthetic rationalization of black cultural practices provided a way for the slave society to extract value from and install management within black life. Liberated from bondage, black music was freed to revivify and beautify the imagination of the slave society during and after manumission. While black music represents the supreme object of rationalization for this aesthetic character in the nineteenth century, the chapters of this book trace how in the twentieth century, this logic expanded into related forms through what can be called broadly black art. It was not just black music, but a burgeoning conception of the black work of art that emerged from black music, that carried out this aesthetic regulation.

After all, these aesthetic concepts of "song" and (humanizing) "character" differ markedly from the more overtly violent sonic figures that feature prominently in Douglass's *Narrative*: the crack of the whip, the screams of torture and beatings, or the infamous sound of his Aunt Hester's scream, about which Saidiya Hartman and Fred Moten have famously argued.[4] Yet his account of black "song" allows us to trace how black aesthetic labor and the black work of art arose through the waning of the slave plantation and the persistence of "the dehumanizing character of slavery," as Douglass termed it. The positive humanizing character of black music was extracted directly and reactively from the brutalized "dehumanizing character of slavery." But equally, this humanizing character derived from the inscrutable black life within the evasive and resistant operations of the slave community and its "wild notes." The songs of the enslaved, following Douglass's narrative, came to form the official language of "black music."

In *The Aesthetic Character of Blackness*, I focus on how black life, in all its unwieldiness, was administered through the aesthetic formation of "black music." Many studies have emphasized the liberatory expressions realized through the loosening of black music from the plantation. However, I complicate what black music's putative discovery liberated. I offer initial skeptical quotation marks around the term "black music" to assert the distinction between the upheaval of black life Frederick Douglass glossed and appropriated and the contemporaneous language of musical and aesthetic refinement and humanization into which that life was being mixed, compressed, and mastered down as music. I think through the far more complex, often dialectical, process wherein the liberation of black forms is in no way reducible to, and may even be weaponized against, the liberation of black life. Black music and the black work of art would prove just as essential in contesting the intrinsic value of the enslaved commodity form during chattel slavery as they would in reimagining the kind of value that can be extracted from and mobilized against black life "after slavery."

The mid-nineteenth-century "discovery" of black music created a cultural gold rush for the free world. Instead of a precious metal, Douglass had smuggled a uniquely expressive content that would establish a new industry and a new investment in the humanization of the enslaved and soon-to-be-manumitted. As John Cruz's ethnomusicology of the nineteenth-century study of black music affirms, Frederick Douglass's writing was the catalyst for the antebellum and postbellum rush to study, write, capture, preserve, and reproduce black music.[5] The contents and forms of expressions excavated from black music would vary over time, of course, but in this book I provide a partial genealogy for the form of their capture, consumption, and regulation. By building an aesthetic frame for black music, Douglass aimed to dispute the earlier "counterfeit" culture of the blackface minstrel stage whose aim was to justify keeping black folks enslaved by denying their capacity to produce proper dignified human culture and governance. The notion of "black song" was understood to offer a counter to this denigration. Black music would propose a positive liberating expression, a generous act of humanization, re-sounding an imaginative space of escape for black sounds from slavery that mirrored Douglass's own flight rather than a re-formation of captivity by and for the free world. A generation later, texts that began to formally and explicitly champion the idea of black art and the black artist would draw upon Douglass's framing of black music as liberating black expressions from the bonds of antiblack oppression. Seminal works such as Du Bois's *The Souls of Black Folk*, Alain Locke's *The New Negro*, Ralph Ellison's *Living with Music*, Albert Murray's *Stompin' the Blues*, Amiri Baraka's *Blues People*, and Samuel Floyd's *The Power of Black Music* all owe some of their emphasis on the liberatory power of black cultural forms' expressive capacities to Douglass's framing.

My interest lies in what the slave society or the free world were "getting" from the alleged liberation of black music and what had to be regulated or extinguished among black folks to ensure such a product. I challenge the progressive framing of black music and the black work of art that is both implied and explicated within an emphasis (sometimes exclusively) on it as liberatory expression casting off captivity. Rather, I show how implicit within the refinement of black cultural expressions is a regulative aesthetic justification of black life as a source of value production.[6] The receptive aesthetic terms Douglass used to reproduce black sounding ("character" and "song") invited outside consumption of black cultural practices in a way which—as I discuss in chapter 1—ironically resembles the minstrel stage he wished to contest in its total reliance on the justificatory. Douglass was clearly operating under a still-enduring naïveté that Henry Louis Gates Jr. would espouse some 150 years later: the idea that "the only way that you can fight a representation in art that you don't like is to create new art, to create more art, to surround it."[7] The work of creating "new [black] art, more [black] art" to surround the "bad" is part of the postmanumission value production and labor I track in this book. Through the aesthetic, black folks have been made to work on justifying black life and black productive capacities to a society that will only ever use such justifications to arrest them, repress them, and put them further to work.

I argue that the property of enslaved labor's impending re-formation required new value-making sites and capacities that would be powerfully fashioned through the black work of art. This black work of art formed from a world in which black sounds and collective creative practices were metabolized as mere expressions of and pleas for our supposed humanity, as errant shouts in need of refinement, or as reflections exercised against our living. I do not claim that the black work of art, or black "cultural production," fully supplanted or replaced plantation production or labor.[8] Quite to the contrary, I argue that black music fleshed out a new material frontier that would become the quintessence of the aesthetic regulation and production of the imagination. I situate how the slave society that emerged from manumission needed the aesthetic justification of black folks in order to persist and expand. I move through and beyond the framing of black music as a source of "pleasure" or "enjoyment," importantly theorized in Saidiya Hartman's *Scenes of Subjection*. I assert that it was not just an affective economy, but an aesthetic or imaginative economy that black folks' music and artistic labor built for and against the slave society.

I do not pay short shrift to the black cultural even though I deemphasize the sentiments or "feelings" Douglass highlighted. My claims about how aesthetics arrested black life are guided by just how revolutionary and terrifying slave revolt and unmeasured black cultural practices were and can still be to the slave society when they evade official legislation and value production.[9] The secret dances, the too-noisy policed black gatherings, all the inartistic modes of "stealing away" that destroyed the property in enslaved labor time became subordinated to and sublimated within more official aesthetic labor out from slavery as song. Douglass's refinement of black song importantly prefigures the capture, commodification, and reproduction of black sound and the black recording artist through formal phonographic technologies by several decades. This drives my emphasis on Douglass's oeuvre, for without his aesthetic modeling we would not have the form of material reproduction that is black music and the black work of art, whether that is the artistic refinement that blunted the property-destroying force of graffiti in post-1960s New York City—playfully but pointedly narrated in Charlie Ahearn's 1982 *Wild Style*—or the infamous arrest of black improvisatory composing under the name of "jazz" or the pacifying murals with which I opened this book. The threat of slave insurgency, times of black rebellion, and even forms of deviant unregulatable black life are antagonized by the representations that surround black folks and demand from them their aesthetic justification.

The imagination of the slave society is the material site from which black aesthetic justification is forged and reified. The imagination of the soon-to-be-manumitted, who were for the first time granted such a sentience, and the imagination of the world into which they would be liberated became a new site of speculation for the expansion of racial capitalism. The imagination may sound like a nebulous object or site to draw a whole method and set of problems around. However, aesthetics in the West has long taken the imagination as its supreme object of rationalization and regulation with just such an emphasis. The Kantian project and its Schillerian variation inform part of my analysis here, because they clearly shaped Douglass's relatively contemporaneous outlook and the formation of the black work of art. The laws placed around, the justifications asserted through, and the judgments decreed over imagination surrounded Douglass's terms for reproducing black sound in the free world. Archie Shepp used the phrase "the plantation of the mind" to describe the imaginative site for the "regularizing" and regulating of black life without the overt sound of the whip and its countering liberatory violence.[10] The legislation of the imagination produces as impactful a material reality and set of effects as we might commonly reserve for the traditional "displays of mastery" that governed the slave plantation.[11] My book participates in such a tradition and approach of aesthetic thought, and I take the imagination as a serious and shifting site of inquiry. If the plantation functioned as both a productive container for black labor and a symbolic limit for black cultural practices—as overtly illustrated in the minstrel stage—then the imagination represents a new frontier for black folks' production, speculation, and exploitation.

I invoke the imagination of the slave society to situate how the re-formed exploitation of manumitted black folks was justified to the free world and how the embrace of the free world's re-formed exploitation was justified to manumitted black folks through the aesthetic. Again to invoke Frederick Douglass's quintessence as the black artist, we can see overtly both his justification of the sounds of the enslaved to the free world and his own imaginative justification of the free world through black sounds. The free world for Frederick Douglass was a mostly quiet place where black song and its attendant form of labor were but a contained reverberation. Later in his same narrative, Douglass spoke of his disembarkation in New Bedford, Massachusetts, remarking, "There were no loud songs heard from those engaged in loading and unloading ships. I heard no deep oaths or horrid curses on the laborer. I saw no whipping of men; but all seemed to go smoothly on. Every man appeared to understand his work, and went at it with a sober, yet cheerful earnestness, which betokened the deep interest which he felt in what he was doing, as well as a sense of his own dignity as a man."[12] The relative tranquility of the free world bore a striking resemblance to the fantasy of a quiet white suburb or gentrifying neighborhood, where the value-making processes of production and consumption are hypostatized in private property as their quietest and most agreeable form for racial capital's luxuriation. The only acceptable site of ruckus noise is consigned to the privation of imagination and the tolerated compliant drone of enabling manual labor. The loud music blaring slightly from headphones or private parlors is reflective of "the private life that regulates the consumption of art in the nineteenth century" and beyond.[13] The consonant obedience, efficiency, and sociability of free labor and the free laborer in building such spaces of privation was augmented by the dissonant sound of enslaved labor. Black song, freed from being heard as an ungainly public spectacle of the slave coffle and transposed into an aesthetically captured "song" by the imagination, would beautify free labor. The imagination of the slave society to which I referred is not just a capacity from without, not just a beautified whip coming from outside that drives black value making but also a compulsion from within the formerly enslaved as espoused by Douglass. Black music's initiation into the imagination became the site of a new material process of exploitation and regulation.

Black music is the "raw material" from which black life would produce value through justification. I move away from and critique the common scholarly framing that black music is a mere adjunct to the abolitionist movement's successful war of propaganda. Frederick Douglass and his white comrades in the abolitionist movement emphasized vehemently that they were ridding the world of one form of oppressive black labor and life, as Douglass suggests in the passage above. Yet this book tracks how a new frontier of black labor was also created from aesthetic re-formation of slave labor in black music and culture. This new or re-formed black work was created through the sublimation of black song. I enrich and expand Sylvia Wynter's framing of the nineteenth-century extraction of black music: "Black culture, black music in particular, became an original source of raw material to be exploited as the entertainment industry burgeoned. Once again blacks function as the plantation subproletariat hidden in the raw material."[14] This black "raw material" was mined for the restructuring and liberation of the slave society's imagination through this newly legislated aesthetic character.

The transportation of these black sounds to the free world through the space of imagination is an explicit invocation of the power of the black work of art to beautify free labor and the reproduction of the free world. The argument that whites extracted "empathic identification" from black songs is only part of the story.[15] Freeing black sounds from the bondage of enslaved labor liberated them into new and expanded sites of speculation and aesthetic labor. Black music is a contrapuntal force that justified the quiet productivity and value of the free world—of the slave society. The value of black sounds and the loudness of black life was not exclusively an aspect of their form and value under bondage. Just as black song was successfully making slave labor ugly and dehumanizing under Douglass's conducting, it would equally be enlisted to beautify the free world. As I argue in this book's first chapter, many of the very same sounds of black labor would attain a potent formal social character, shifting not just their signifying value as distressing or unpleasant but also the form of their hearing, recognition, and consumption and the worlds they produced and beautified. It is black song that makes the sound and suffering of free labor seem "smooth," for black sounds can and must be driven toward or made more sociable to the telos of labor and life that awaits them as the freedom of the shore. Black music is reflected in Douglass, as is the black work of art, to make black life work anew, for something new, in Gates's words, and not necessarily for itself.

I focus on the aesthetic in this work because it is not the enslaved who would be freed with emancipation, but the aesthetic imagination of the slave society that would be liberated through the capture and reproduction of black music. In this book's succeeding chapters, I discuss the newly "gifted" private property of the imagination of the recently manumitted; what would more overtly expand as the private and domestic property in black music through the birth of the recording industry and the black work of art. Building from the extensive and supportive work done on the quiet Victorian prose of the nineteenth-century slave narrative and the scholarship on the public prominence of antebellum and postbellum black music, I aim to understand how black song and the black work of art circumscribed and continues to constrain the bounds of black sociability. This will require a more focused and instructive breakdown of my terms that illuminate the organization of the book's chapters as well as the title, *The Aesthetic Character of Blackness*. I will begin with a more in-depth treatment of the aesthetic that guides my definition and use of the concept in this work.

The Aesthetic, Bounded by the Shore

Aesthetics is not a liberation of our living but a liberation of forms through the restraint and constraining of our living and our imaginations. Intending its original usage, I assert that aesthetics is a regulative force crafted to make black folks more sociable to the world instead of making the world more hospitable to black life. My stance here complicates the common attributions of Frederick Douglass's nineteenth-century artistic endeavors as well as those that motivated much of the history of black aesthetics I track in this book in the Harlem Renaissance and even to a degree in the Black Arts Movement. This is why I seek to challenge the conflation of aesthetics with subjective feelings or expression. To the extent that the aesthetic produces our liberatory expressions, it manages them through and against us for the beautification and liberation of the free world over and against us.

The aesthetic imposes a kind of "small mastery" on or over our imaginations. I pull this term "small mastery" from Sylvia Wynter, who locates such an idea originally within the blackface minstrel stage whose re-creation of the plantation emerges from and admits that "all could not be equal masters; one could be a small master," adding that "[there was] the need to be master in order to experience oneself as the Norm, as human."[16] Wynter's stance, re-sounded in Eric Lott's book about minstrelsy, *Love and Theft*, is often only applied to blackface minstrelsy and racial masquerade. I, however, thread this notion of "small mastery" into my analysis of the very aesthetic form that was raised in protest of minstrelsy's romantic reification of black bondage: black music. As Douglass's framing suggests, aesthetics emerged to beautify (white) restraint and capture of black folks from without and from within. Distinct from, yet related to the sound of the whip echoing in the open field or the servant's bell ringing across empty rooms, the imagination becomes an expanded site for the maintenance of the "lawful external relations" of aesthetics.[17] In its modern formulations and institutions, aesthetics is about formal restraint and being held back, of being internally arrested in and by our imaginations.

The aestheticization of black music and the black work of art becomes a conflicted site for this restraint of the imagination. As I have noted, black sound was framed as troublesome contraband or paltry excess of black nature cum racial pathology. Slaves sang or made noise to affirm their amenability to their bondage, the minstrel stage and proslavery proponents would famously declare. Once liberated from enslavement, these sounds were sublimated to "the formal condition" of participating under the "lawful authority" of the newly available "civil community" of the slave society or the free world, first in the humanizing prose of slave narratives like that of Frederick Douglass, then in the pages of songbooks for proponents of the nineteenth-century abolitionist movement, then in the inquisitive logbooks of early ethnomusicologists.[18] Soon they were committed to the brittle grooves of early mass-produced records. Aesthetics offered and imposed a new mode of self-regulation for the recently manumitted. Part of this self-regulation stemmed from its positive and beautified assertion within the eighteenth- and nineteenth-century traditions of the aesthetic rooted in a willful character conceived from the shores of freedom, to reference Paul de Man's referencing of Kant's metaphysics or equally to reference the nautical portions of Frederick Douglass's own flight from enslavement to the northern shores of New Bedford, Massachusetts. Black music is not just composed of fugitive expressions, it is also composed of spaces and points of arrival through which new forms of power and captivity are fashioned.

Aesthetics open a new space of speculation in and against black life through the imagination. The imagination becomes a battleground but also a resource for the liberation of the slave society through the self-regulation of black people. Aesthetics are central to the world we hold up in having our imaginations held back and holding our imaginations back. This is a valence of how Saidiya Hartman frames black folks' inauguration into the free world during Reconstruction in terms of "self-mastery" that was implanted in and over the enslaved. Self-mastery, Hartman asserts, is a marriage of "the will and the whip"; that is, "a willing submission to the dictates of former master, the market and the inquisitor within." Hartman concludes that such exigencies effectively "bore a striking resemblance to the prostration of slavery."[19] Though by no means stated in Hartman's oeuvre, an expansion of the resemblance of black self-mastery to slavery, or "the slave" itself, has become prominent in black study over the years. And indeed, "a return to slavery" or re-formation of slavery would be the widely stated worry of black aesthetic thinkers such as Du Bois and Alain Locke just a generation or so later. My emphasis on aesthetics complicates this pervasive economy of resemblance, however. Aesthetics is important for my argument because its modes of management are quite distinct from slavery but still creatively antagonize black life. A new frontier, new territories, and new spaces of speculation emerge through the imagination that, as Douglass's "song" and "character" suggest, are not quite reducible to the whip.

The "small mastery" over the imagination is not just an exogenous invention of white outsiders and eavesdroppers but an endogenous production that emerges from and through black music and the work of the black artist. The imagination is not something that just happens to or is enacted on black folks, it is an asymmetrical yet shared site of production and extraction. This again sheds light on my initial investment in Douglass as a kind of early black artist (a form I will expand upon shortly) because he articulates and defends this still relatively exclusive province and property of the black aesthetic imagination. Douglass also complicates, even in his perceived exceptionality—an exceptionality which I discuss further in chapter 1 and which will be liberated and expanded to others—the idea that it is not a perpetual metaphysical victimhood that ensures blackness's aesthetic regulation but a kind of regulative "human activity" (where the humanity of that activity must itself be humanized).[20] Indeed, eighteenth- and nineteenth-century aesthetics is rooted in this promethean power that Douglass enacts to give life to forms without subjectivity.

This vivification of form, which I will shortly define as our "aesthetic justification," dwells in the imagination. As the opening of this book suggests, black aesthetic justification is housed far more than black people are. In fact, it displaces us to attain its luxury; it lives better than us and beyond us, producing a form of futurity without and then against us. I invoke aesthetics because in this book I am most interested in the kinds of life that animate these empty spaces: the domestic space of the mid-nineteenth-century parlor piano, the spaces of the phonographic record's grooves, the empty belly of the phonographic cabinet, the uninhabited life of the law of genre, and the depopulated neighborhoods bearing massive black murals. These are the specific spaces that characterize each chapter of this book. These are the spaces Douglass would fill with black music and the black work of art would build up and defend. These spaces are not just defined by their metabolization and consumption of black music but by their capture and reflection of our sounding-image back at us, as us.

No matter how loud they are perceived to be, the dominance of black representations always carries this silencing and constraining subterfuge. The benefit of aesthetics' property in things marks their "separation from all society" such that society can be rendered as pure instrument of the aesthetic.[21] I frame the aesthetic as instrument to emphasize that it is not only the extracted or appropriated content that is dangerous, but even more so its weaponized form. We no longer need black life when we have murals reflecting its presence as the reprieve from it. This quieted space of reprieve from "the fight" Du Bois described early, the height of which Kant simply calls "luxury," makes us intimate with the quietness of these empty rooms against the noisy intimacy with each other.[22] Only aesthetic values are animated here. In black song Douglass could imagine a free world that was without and even against black life. In the placid life of the free world, he more perilously illustrated the pursuit of a life beyond the slave community or its presumably freed variants. This life of forms freed from the demands of their living has a name in aesthetics: beauty.

No doubt any reader of traditional aesthetics has noticed how glaring the absence of beauty has been from my definition. This is intentional. Most eighteenth-century conceptions of aesthetic thought started or ended with beauty because beauty is often described as the telos or goal of aesthetics. But this is part of the problem I critique. I define beauty throughout this work as a looming nonrelation. Beauty is an intimacy with concept alone. To make this clearer, nothing lives under beauty but judgment and justifications. I oppose this living to black life, through which beauty is so readily and violently channeled and smuggled. Black life is instrumentalized for the sake of creating this beauty. The beauty from the shore that Douglass found in the hush and murmur of the free world's distinctly oppressive labor was an escape from enslavement as well as an escape from the aimless noisiness of the slave community. What sound, what work, and what life cannot be teleologically driven to the beautiful must wash out in the wake of Douglass's arrival on the shore. This journey, what I will elsewhere through the writing of Black Arts Movement theorist Dingane Goncalves call "the plucking of the beautiful," is the grounding of the aesthetic. This book invokes Douglass's journey and indeed the journey of many black artists to think about the practices that prop up, suffocate, and drown before reaching beauty's ashore.

The aesthetic encourages us to stay shore-bound, to never swim out to each other and get wet, never board the ship and fight with and for each other, and never drown together and become the ocean. This is the restraint the aesthetic places on the imagination and how its form afflicts black life. In exchange for each other, we are given willful artists and artwork that keep us out of the fight. I am bound to and enlivened by a conception of black-being-together-as, that imagined force of the inside of the hold, of the slave community, of the storm inside the ship in the storm that only gets sung as a song from those who swam to the shore.[23] Blackness's differentiation from this ocean is part of and productive to the legacy of the aesthetic I track in this book. I invoke the aesthetic to understand what worlds it keeps us from tearing down and making rather than the works it produces or captures. Part of this restraint emerges from how the administrative function of the aesthetic bears down upon black folks with an apparent saving power, both re-forming and far away from the sound of the whip or the screams of brutalized black kin. In the aesthetic we are differently shipped, but too often we imagine ourselves to be or aspire to be similarly shore-bound. We are surrounded by the blockade of this shoreline, looking at and not enclosed by each other and our needs. While this may seem beyond the purview of what is traditionally defined in aesthetics, it has everything to do with the voyage from "the dehumanizing character" of slavery to the shores of humanization that Douglass and black music navigate.

Blackness, the Humanizing Character

Humanity and its humanizing character were not needs or reveries crafted from the imagination of the enslaved. Humanization had to be shaped as an aesthetic or imaginatively constrictive project. Humanization was a form, a sociable character, that would attempt to bound the imagination of black folks from without and from within for the benefit of the slave society. The shore of humanization that Frederick Douglass arrived at, to which he brought black song, is a limit concept. This limit concept of humanity requires the aesthetic regulation of black life and black sounds to expand its bounds. Humanization itself needed to be humanized, and black music and the black work of art would be an essential conscript of humanization's avant-garde. As part of the professed goals of the Garrisonian abolitionist movement in which Douglass participated, black humanization was enlisted to expand humanity's authority and force. Ultimately, I theorize how humanization is sharpened through its metabolizing of and expansion through black cultural forms; becoming a weapon wielded against black life. Black music is the first and most prolific hinge for humanity's violent cultural re-formation.

It is nearly impossible to overstate the centrality of Frederick Douglass to the humanizing character of black music. The emerging and conflicted space Douglass occupies as an early articulation of the black artist is central for forming the limits of the aesthetic regulation he proffered through the humanizing character of black music. Instead of narrating Douglass within a putative or given system of bondage, I want to highlight the "structuring antagonism" through which the emerging postemancipation order required Douglass's escape to be framed as the liberation of humanizing character of blackness in order to reimagine and expand the imaginative bounds of the value-making processes of the slave society.[24] I start the first chapter of this work, "Emancipating the Spaces of Sonic Capture," with an audiovisual drawing of Frederick Douglass created by the white abolitionist Jessie Hutchison Jr. to grace the cover of a widely circulated abolitionist songbook in the 1840s. As reputedly the most imaged black person of the nineteenth century in the West but also the most prominent exponent of black music, Douglass is a central figure in liberating this giant art project that I call the aesthetic character of blackness over much of the world. However, I focus less on Douglass as a figure of enslavement and instead think about him more as a figure of escape and arrival, one who finds himself initiating yet ensnared in emerging cultural modes of captivity through the aesthetic regulation he helped bear forth.

Under the threat of its disappearing value production in the plantation, black life became ominously formless, something demanding of aesthetic regulation to shape it. Early aesthetes such as Friedrich Schiller confessed that such a terror drove the legislative power of aesthetics: "As far and as long as [man] impresses a form upon matter, [man] cannot be injured by its effect; for a spirit can only be injured by that which deprives it of its freedom. Whereas he proves his own freedom by giving a form to the formless."[25] Against the threat of this unstructured ocean of black living, aesthetics fashion the lifeboat to ferry the sociable world through the impasse of black life. It is more often the liberal Lockean tradition that is (rightly) criticized for the ascetic individuated boundaries it asserts, the endless locking away of life it imagines as liberation. I identify an equally potent and deceptively perilous anti-relationality in the aesthetic humanization of black music. Aesthetics is central to determining what constitutes this formless, purposeless life of the slave community it must be wielded against: "Where the mass rules heavily and without shape, and its undefined outlines are forever fluctuating between uncertain boundaries, fear takes up its abode; but man rises above any natural terror as soon as he knows how to mould it, and transform it into an object of his art."[26] We can hear Schiller's quote as if echoing through Frederick Douglass's head when he converts the black life and sound of the slave community into the manageable aesthetic character of "song."

I push against the affective, progressive, and liberatory framing of the abolitionist movement's agitprop that reactively argued for black song as a liberatory expression. Instead, I consider how black song was a novel site of aesthetic regulation of the imaginative practices of black folks. This is a critical juncture to start from because the metabolization of black song and black culture in the abolitionist movement paved the way for its early exploitation in the phonographic recording industry and its relatedly expropriated life in ethnomusicological scholarship just a generation or two later. I link the two often-contrasting realms of the aesthetic (and its modes of humanization) and the technological reproduction that follows it through the discovery of black song Douglass proffered. The modern promethean power of aesthetics, the godlike creativity that even the most resolute critics like Nietzsche would embrace and extol, is a self-asserting power to dominate the open sea. Douglass's journey and the scholarship in and discovery of black music it inspires offer a form for expanding into this terrifying expanse. Friedrich Schiller's words again resound, "As soon as he upholds his independence toward phenomenal nature, he maintains his dignity toward her as a thing of power."[27] I touch upon the fears of the dark and unknown black life that drive such a power-grab through the humanizing command of aesthetics and how such fantasies and material realities are mined through black music.

I resituate the limits of the humanization offered through the aesthetic in terms of conflicting relationships of force to free the enslaved. The aesthetic justification of the enslaved arose to negate and delegitimize the use of liberatory violence as well as other forms of unlawful resistance that ironically bore similar symbolic standing to black music's frequent contraband status. Instead, humanization became a force that was visited against that unwieldy watery tumult of black creative practices, especially those that never aspired to the representability and governance of an art. I read this fear of force as something that eighteenth- and nineteenth-century aesthetic thought, relatively contemporary to Douglass, was grappling with. Kant, Schiller, and indeed much of the enlightenment tradition—even Nietzsche—would pose aesthetics as an edifying defense against force and or an equivalent realization of it ("as a thing of power") yet beyond the mere effects of force, being above the fight, being beyond the whip, and never being in it or under it but always being its beneficiary. Paul de Man translated Schiller's thinking (referencing Kant's epistemological figure of "a broad and stormy ocean"), stating: "It's better not to be on the boat that's being tossed up and down, it's better to stand on the shore and see the boat being tossed up and down, if you want to have a sublime experience."[28] It is hard not to imagine the black life inside the hold in de Man and Schiller's tossed-about ship as that which the aesthetic, always shore-bound, is necessarily and endlessly raised against. The practices of that shipped and oceanic life, all its complicated and antagonistic togetherness, is not just a symbol, but a set of practices, ways of living, surviving, fighting, and revolting that aesthetics must prevent. Black life, especially during and immediately following manumission, threatens to make more of the shore into the ocean. The practices and potency of black imagination had to be regulated, reined in, and redirected to the humanizing aesthetic. The liberatory violence, the labor organizing, and the ungainly life of the enslaved formed unsettling and "uncertain boundaries"—the unshapely mass, the ring shouts, all the kinds of noise of black life and the terror it can unleash—that had to be sublimated to a manageable aesthetic "character" for the slave society.

By staking out the humanizing capacity of black music in the nineteenth century, I challenge not just the budding development of genre but of music itself as a modern regulative project. Music was, simultaneous to Douglass, being rigorously formalized as both the most essentially human and the earliest stage in a people's "development."[29] This is why music can quintessentially humanize or ferry the justification of black humanization to the slave society. Just a decade before Douglass's framing, Hegel wrote that "music . . . which is concerned only with the completely indeterminate movement of the inner spirit and with sounds as if they were feeling without thought, needs to have little or no spiritual material present in consciousness. Therefore musical talent announces itself in most cases very early in youth, when the head is empty and the heart little moved. . . . After all, we have seen very great virtuosity in musical composition and performance accompanied by remarkable barrenness of spirit and character."[30] For Hegel, because they bespeak a lack of development, the "barrenness" of music's "spirit and character" alluded to an abundance of what Wynter called "raw material." The value of black music to the slave society was that it offered a newly formless clay for outside hands to mold and tame black life through. Black sounds would be transposed into the speculative site of humanity's primitive accumulation and development. The fullness of black music's sentimentalization, its fullness of feeling and presumed emptiness of thought, are understood to be a product of the dehumanizing character of slavery. The late nineteenth and twentieth centuries marked the contestation of this argument of black cultural vacuity. Scholars ranging from Anténor Firmin to Melville Herskovitz countered the notion that the Middle Passage and the brutality of the plantation were so total that no putative fullness of African or syncretic culture remained. But these were also responses to Douglass and related mid-nineteenth-century invitations to sculpt the alleged formlessness of black life through black music and culture.

Arguments of black cultural vacuity were and are part of a ploy to impose an austerity logic on black life that can be regulated through the aesthetic. In Douglass's framing, black song emerged initially as a dehumanized counter to the coordinated internal systems and actions of enslaved black people's revolt, music-making practices, care, mutual systems of support, and complex choreographies of movement and dance. These practices were washed away under the brush of emptiness and abjection. Concomitantly, black song was then projected as the fertile territory of the expansion of humanization. The uncertain boundaries of black life and sound are frightening until they can be evacuated into the quiet, dignified contemplation of the imagination as a site of voluminous labor and production. Beyond mere "purposeless form," the form of black music needed to be granted out from its emptiness a plentiful purpose in its distinguished capacity for humanization.[31] It was a new and emerging neighborhood to be gentrified, a fresh and fertile frontier to be tilled with the refined implement of black song.

The Dehumanizing Character of Blackness

In the early chapters of this book, I argue that humanization itself must be humanized and that black music has been an essential conscript of humanization's avant-garde. I am not arguing that black music humanizes black people. The form of de/humanization is itself extraneous to the brilliantly unwieldy worlding practiced by black folks under and out from bondage. We do not and have never needed such a limited category to imagine or practice our liberation and our relation. It is the slave society's de/humanization that I analyze here. The contingent reproduction of enslaved humanity is grounded by the aesthetic as an allegedly civilizing power, a power wielded by this aesthetic character that will ferry the slave society toward liberation on the precipice of its very collapse. For Saidiya Hartman, enslaved humanity emerged emblematically through the violent scenes of subjection detailed in Douglass's narrative. Such scenes risk reifying "the spectacular character of black suffering," leading Hartman to query: "What does the exposure of the violated body yield?"[32] But how black folks and especially the black artist (whom I will define shortly) were conscripted to humanize and expand the slave society becomes far more complicated than the spectacle of abjection.

I distinguish my own argument and concerns here from Hartman's position in that it is not merely through the symbolic, the abject, or the "exposed" that a new form of regulation arises. I do share an attention with Hartman to the violent construction of and the perils of representation of humanization. However, I tend to focus on the more ambient and mundane sites of its imagination and rationalization. It is the imagination through which the justificatory power of this aesthetic character of blackness became a new site for the expansion and enforcement of the slave society, beyond the impact of the whip. This beautified captivity constructed a new imaginative force of antagonism against black life that was re-formed and proclaimed as the free world. As Douglass's own celebration from the shores of the oppressive silence of free labor attest, this aesthetic imposes a forceful limitation on how black life might be imagined beyond bondage and racist oppression. Dehumanization functions equally as a limit concept that is stuck in a dialectical dance with the humanization I described above. I engage dehumanization for not only formal reasons but to avoid any totalizing romanticization that might be misconstrued in my defense of black life. Black life is not a positive resolution against de/humanization. Black life is a site for which the regulation of de/humanization must be raised as a formal law. My aim is not to offer a positive or romantic rendition of black life so much as it is to understand the aesthetic formalized against it.

In chapter 2, "More Nearly Members of the Family: The Ugly Hiss," I engage slavery's "dehumanizing character" through George W. Johnson, both his childhood as an enslaved black musician and his adulthood as a freed black recording artist. In Johnson, I illustrate a unique traversal of formal black musical capacity captured within or as slave property in order to aesthetically regulate black musical capacity in early sound recording and cultural production. The dehumanizing specter of the minstrel stage, which Douglass largely implicitly reacted to, is fascinatingly overt in Johnson. The passing late-nineteenth-century fascination with Johnson as a novel object of the recently invented phonograph emerges out of the mid-nineteenth-century study that rationalized black music from Frederick Douglass's charge and the virtual disappearance of the formal blackface minstrel stage. These warring cultural oppositions were synthesized to socialize and ingratiate the phonographic machine to the domestic life of the free world. Although the formal dehumanizing sentiments and figures of Johnson's career differ, his work created or was used for a similar site of domestic privation as Douglass. My argument in this chapter is that the aesthetic character of blackness is what ferries across this oft-championed surface of sonic technological reproduction and progress.[33] Johnson's career illustrates the increased prevalence of mastery as self-possession, extending from Douglass, but it also discloses its overt aesthetic limitations. Ultimately, I contend that formally, Douglass's humanization was no different than Johnson's (more overt) dehumanization and that the two merely synthesized the bounds of the slave society's aesthetic or imaginative limit through black music.

Although I do not focus exclusively on black suffering, a related emphasis on representability or making representable guides the arguments I lay out in this work. How black life is made into a representable aesthetic character that polices our imaginations is my primary interest. A common contention by some readers of this text will be that I do not pay enough attention to the fulsome and "inartistic, irreducibly socio-aesthetic, life," the peopling, that precedes and exceeds aesthetic regulation as blackness, as official black music and art.[34] However, I grant frequent and intentionally opaque space and reference to what I refer to as the powerfully illegible assemblage of black life and its sounding. My invocation of black life loosely encompasses a peopling whose theorization is always being enacted in practice and that certainly does not need the temporary governance of a well-intentioned study to recognize it. It is my fundamental position that this paraontological relation of black life should remain unknown and is extraneous to the understanding of any order of "thought," lest I merely repeat the prurient and extractive justifications of Douglass's aesthetic, lest I aspire to be the very black artist and produce the black work of art that I criticize throughout this book.[35]

Black Music, Our Aesthetic Justification

As I have been arguing, black music and the black work of art arose out of bondage as the form of justifying black life to the slave society. Justification was the material or the "how" of this aesthetic. Black song emerged as both a material point of our unscripted being together and a surface that provided our aesthetic justification beyond us and against us. Black music became more than errant intracommunal "wild notes" of relation. It became more than its internal language laboratory that might manifest as an inscrutable force on the oppressor who, largely denied such a resistant and excessive meaning and world-making capacity, could be generated by the enslaved. Under Douglass's conducting, black music achieved something that was intended to justify the being, meaning, and value of the enslaved and the soon-to-be-manumitted. It justified black folks to those who had already created meaning and value in them through the invention and protraction of enslaved black labor.

In each chapter of this book, I show how, in differing ways, black aesthetic justification became a new kind of labor. To understand and conceptualize the framing of the slave society I offer in this book, I invoke Nietzsche's famous and contemporary nineteenth-century terminology of "aesthetic justification." However, I invert Nietzsche's proclamation and reframe it as a terrifying decree for black life under bondage and after manumission: "We have our highest dignity in our significance as works of art—for it is only as an aesthetic phenomenon that existence and the world are eternally justified."[36] Aesthetic justification is not a point of reverence for black life but a burdensome yoke and a terrifying decree. Black musical theorists as varying as W. E. B. Du Bois, Langston Hughes, Duke Ellington, Ralph Ellison, and Albert Murray have proffered arguments for an essential liberatory freedom espoused in black musical forms. I analyze and situate some of these arguments within the justificatory framework I have theorized by paying particular attention to how a quest for the sociable and the beautiful stalks and restricts their imaginative framing of black life. I argue not for black music as influential content but as essential to the form of the justificatory in the West. My treatments in chapter 3 of blues artist Ma Rainey and my treatment in chapter 4 of Dorcas Manfred, the volatile protagonist of Toni Morrison's novel *Jazz*, oppose a kind of messy and bickering black relationality to the justificatory framework that theorists such as Alain Locke were increasingly placing around black life during the Harlem Renaissance. I theorize what many black music scholars are uneasy about considering: how black music has justified us from without and from within to the imagination of the slave society and to our imaginative practices with each other.

The interiority projected into, as opposed to the interiority lived as, black music was a forum for the debate of black will and sentience during the mid-nineteenth century. The space of black song was used to invent and measure the capacity of the newly liberated to participate in the "elegant social intercourse" of the allegedly free world.[37] Schiller asserted that "though need may drive Man into society, and Reason implant social principles in him, Beauty alone can confer on him a social character."[38] The emerging social character of black folks had to be coercively sculpted and extracted from the raw material of a burgeoning enslaved humanity. Hartman argues that it was through "the pageantry of the coffle, stepping it up lively on the auction block, going before the master, and the blackface mask of minstrelsy and melodrama" that black folks were granted a "restricted sentience."[39] The driving force behind this patronizing bestowal of consciousness produced a valuable and sociable form of black life that could be molded to re-form and benefit the slave society, integrating black life into it rather than letting black life remain outside it—or worse, threatening to undo or overthrow the social character of the slave society. Black song aspired to offer a flirtation with reason through its aesthetic resounding of a black sociability. This black sociability would expand or be used to expand the slave society. The formerly enslaved were to be beauty's vanguard.

Black aesthetic justification, fomented by Douglass, reached a vital cresting point during the Harlem Renaissance under the patriarchal stewardship of aesthete and philosopher Alain Locke. In chapter 3, "Ma Rainey's Phonograph," I demarcate the bounding of the black imagination, which takes its most intensified turn under Locke's proclamation that aesthetics needed to produce a sociable value affirming of a black social that could precipitate gendered black class division. As a contemporary counter to Locke's patriarchal model of aesthetic regulation and cultural production, I engage a series of performance routines by the black queer blues artist Gertrude "Ma" Rainey. Such fleshy and playful performances were, I argue, the primary transgression against which Locke's law of the aesthetic was raised. Through these performance routines and Rainey's broader repertoire, I offer a critique of the epistemological tenets of the privation and domestication of black music through sound recording, racial pathology, and the development of official black culture as a response to the racist yoke of minstrelsy represented in George W. Johnson's rise. In the period 1923–1925, Gertrude "Ma" Rainey carried out an elaborate quasi-burlesque performance routine in which she sang while hidden inside a giant phonograph. This routine precisely referenced and troubled the legacy of black sounds and black performing bodies and their conflicted forms of capture and embodiment through sonic technologies, racial normalization, and gendered domestication. I build on black trans/queer blues scholarship by Angela Davis and K. Allison Hammer that argues against the patriarchal straightening of the black cultural that occasioned its ascension and regulation. Rainey's performance quite literally disrupted and disturbed the aesthetic justificatory values Locke was attempting to impose on and through black life and music.

The model for the black artist that Locke, and to a lesser extent Du Bois, proffered during this time was rooted in their capacity to initiate black aesthetic justification. Aesthetic justification privileges a relation with black life's capacity to produce a justifiable representational outside rather than the fleshy black queer world of intracommunal meaning that Ma Rainey espoused. Typically, aesthetic justification is born by the willful subject of the black artist that is affirmed by the aesthetic justification they realize.[40] This justificatory power is realized not just through beautiful works but even more importantly through the work, capacity, and duty to beautify the world. Representational technologies that were making black life more audible and visible during the Harlem Renaissance, effectively intensifying the exposure Frederick Douglass had enacted a generation earlier, expanded this power and demand of the justificatory. So while Nietzsche sent the justificatory to save a humanity from its purely technological rationalization, black women blues artists exposed the peril of this aesthetic justificatory force. Black queer women blues artists such as Rainey ultimately challenged the regulatory representational framework that beauty installs in and against black life.

Although Nietzsche's aesthetic justification granted art a saving power, this chapter and others show that no matter how exalted and dignified the aesthetic could be, art will be wielded as a weapon against us. Thus, my focus is on the danger of the black work of art for black life. While many imagine the black work of art as a way to evade the slave society's moralism and jurisprudence, I follow Sylvia Wynter in exploring how the idea of the black work of art is every bit as annihilating and regulating.[41] Beauty is not the law, but it becomes law-like. For Alain Locke, this was quite simply the value of the black work of art. I argue that in this view, the black work of art attains its value from beautifying the violence of black class division, justifying black life as a necessarily classed patriarchal social, and restraining black folks from imagining it can be anything else.

In chapter 4, "Music Against the Subject," I confront the legal character of the black work of art in the Harlem Renaissance's emerging genrefication of "jazz." I formally link and metaphorize the genrefication of jazz with the dignified regulation of the black social during this period. I analyze Toni Morrison's novel *Jazz* as emblematic of the attempt to construct a dignified black social through the aesthetic regulation of black life as genre. I look at genre and narration as two related modes of aesthetic capture and ensnarement: as essential forms for legislating black life and restricting its imaginative possibilities. I focus on how *Jazz* counters earlier and contemporary arguments that black music and art ought to create a sociable black character for representation. I analyze the novel's wayward and chimeric main character Dorcas Manfred and the photographic collection that inspired Morrison's writing of the novel, James Van Der Zee's *The Harlem Book of the Dead*. Through these works I think about how wayward and unjustifiable forms of black life evade and contest the aesthetic capture of the black work of art and its aesthetic justification.

The cultural clerics of the Harlem Renaissance will revel in the litigious implications of this black artist and the power of black aesthetic justification. The black artist as a new emissary of the race, to again paraphrase Henry Louis Gates Jr., will be vested with the power to create the "good" black representations that can drown out the "bad." The justificatory form of the world the black artist ushers in will emphasize representation, dignity, class division—beauty. The Harlem Renaissance valuation of the artist lies in the promethean power of the humanizing character of aesthetics in which the artist's creative capacity counters the prevailing godly prowess of emerging mass representational technologies (the photograph, the phonograph, film, mass-produced print media, and early radio), all of which are suddenly and rapidly producing all these "bad" depictions of black life. In response, Nietzsche proclaims, the artist "feels like a god. . . . Man is no longer an artist, he has become a work of art."[42] The conflation of black life with black aesthetic character expands during this period, not just from without but from within. If the social can be permeated by the violence of racist aesthetics, it is the Harlem Renaissance that launches a counteroffensive of black aesthetic justification. In black aesthetic justification, the dignity of black "social character" transcends the mere "semblance character" of the work of art by being tasked to relate to and contest the mere "legal character" of black folks in the law, by making more regulations for black living, more beautiful justifications to dominate black life.[43] The black work of art in form will prove black sociability. The black work of art is not merely a representation, it is a legal practice for the world without and a police power that is re-formed for the world within.

Aesthetic justification grants the musician or the artist an aesthetic power to transcend their mere legal rationalization. Harkening back to Frederick Douglass's thinking, we can already glean the seeds of such revelations, for he invoked the music making of enslaved black folks to transcend their legal status and standing as property by imposing and embracing the law of aesthetics. Douglass and participants in the abolitionist movement believed that black music and culture could counter the law's justification of black slavability. Yet I analyze the underside of this power, for this also means that black music's aesthetic prowess must be a greater justificatory instrument than the knives and hatchets of Nat Turner, the rifle and secretly quilted maps of Harriet Tubman and participants in the Underground Railroad, or the fists Frederick Douglass used to defend himself against his master, Covey. Black art thus fantasizes a kind of freedom neither as property nor as wanted poster, as something beyond the fight and enmity which these imply. It is not just that aesthetics must work on "the cold heart" of the law's rationalization; aesthetics must work on us too.[44] The black artist and the black work of art dull the point and deviate the trajectory of a well-aimed tip of the spear.

The Black Work of Art

The terms "black art" and "black artist" will no doubt conjure as many expectations about this text as they do disagreements with my framings. My stance in this book is that the black work of art becomes the justificatory form of black life to the slave society. The black artist is an agent of this process. Black music and the black work of art re/form enslavement but they do not themselves replace slave labor. The process, I will argue throughout this book, is much more dialectical. The black artist is not a slave. This is crucial—and to a degree obvious in Douglass's own nebulous standing with respect to enslavement at the time of his capture of black music. To adopt such a flattened argument, that the black artist is a slave, would obscure the flexibility of how the domination over black life must be fashioned again and again. Power must be aestheticized; it must be beautified to be expanded. So while black art is not slave labor, it must construct a kind of work that I have referred to throughout as "the black work of art." What black art and the black artist—presaged in Frederick Douglass—will work is the imagination of the slave society. It is within this framework (and guided by a long history of black aesthetic thought) that I situate the black artist and the black work of art in this book.

Despite any inherited assumptions by the reader who might dispute my framing, I must assert fundamentally that what constitutes "black art" and "the black artist" has always been a point of inquiry and open contestation within the circles of those who theorize black art. *The Aesthetic Character of Blackness* extends and participates in that open inquiry. From early scholarly approaches to the question by W. E. B. Du Bois and Alain Locke to Black Arts Movement theorists such as Larry Neal and Amiri Baraka (LeRoi Jones) to the contemporary critics like Fred Moten, Darby English, M. Charlene Stevens, and the late, great Greg Tate, this process of inquiry is an indispensable part of the formalization of black art and the black artist. In this study I attempt to locate black art and the black artist within a long history of the management of black life and of making blackness more sociable and more valuable to the slave society formed through and after manumission. However, this book is not in any disciplinary or scholarly sense an art history of black art.

I do not offer a canon of black art genres or forms. I in no way champion or display a pantheon of great black artists. My avoidance of a strict art historiographical study is not accidental. Black music's hallowed place within broader black cultural formations immediately complicates what sound studies scholar Jonathan Sterne refers to as the "visual hegemony" of the aesthetic in modernity.[45] I assert a genealogy in this text wherein black music gives way to and is endlessly sublimated in the creation of black aesthetics and the aestheticization of blackness. Black sound and black sounding thus remain a variable yet critical component of my arguments even in my treatment of "the visual." So while I am guided partially by the multidisciplinarity of sound studies, this text is also not only or entirely a sound studies text.

The critique of visual hegemony within sound studies is important to disarming the authority of traditional art historiographical approaches, which are often dogmatically centered on the visual. However the importance of black music globally, socially, conceptually, materially, and beyond, especially within our varied cultural formations, is self-evident and so central to the construction of the black artistic that "visual hegemony" never quite materializes. My position is grounded in the arguments and the ethos of contemporary scholars such as Fred Moten, Ashon Crawley, Nathaniel Mackey, Aldon Lynn Nielsen, Herman Gray, the late Richard Iton, Alexander Weheliye, Fumi Okiji, Carter Mathes, and many others. These contemporary scholars draw upon a longer, substantial black critical blues tradition informed by black blues and improvisatory musicians, some of whom I track here, as well as writers such as Langston Hughes, Ralph Ellison, Amiri Baraka, Toni Morrison, Albert Murray, Nikki Giovanni, and Ed Roberson, all of whom have argued that black aesthetics are irreducibly rooted in black music, particularly the blues.

My approach in this work is no more ethnomusicological than it is art historical, however. If my method is to be outlined, I would say it is more akin to Foucault's "genealogy of the present."⁴⁶ Thus, the earlier materials of this book, stretching as far back as the eighteenth century, are understood as equally "living and continuous" with the more contemporary moments I engage. More pointedly, I do not reduce black music, black art, or the black artist to a history of influential individuals. Although some populate the space of this text as individuals and figures, they are not invoked as a litany. *The Aesthetic Character of Blackness* is more a genealogy of the aesthetic regulation that "prescribes rules of exercise" by which the black work of art and the black artist is made to emerge and operate.⁴⁷ No doubt this approach will be unsatisfactory to those expecting a more historiographical or empirical project or even an approach to art approved under one distinct disciplinary regime. However, ultimately the hermeneutic I provide in the text moves primarily as a negation that is not limited to any one aesthetic form. I tend less to offer black art as a wholly positive and positivist conception and instead to situate it as a negative function of our long-standing and prevailing order of instrumental rationality, social regulation, and valuation. The black artist and black work of art chases after, polices, and apprehends our imaginations. This problem and predicament of the regulation of our imaginations has always stalked the question of what constitutes the black work of art and the black artist.

In a 1926 essay on what constitutes black art, "Criteria of Negro Art," W. E. B. Du Bois theorized the human activity of the black artist in a way that shapes and guides my understanding of it in this book. For Du Bois, the black artist is both a conveyance and an agent ruled by the synthesis of beauty, where an individuated black will is sublimated to and sifted through a collective representation of justice. Du Bois provocatively stated, "The apostle of beauty [the black artist] thus becomes the apostle of truth and right not by choice but by inner and outer compulsion. Free he is but his freedom is ever bounded by truth and justice; and slavery only dogs him when he is denied the right to tell the truth or recognize an ideal of justice."⁴⁸ As I will discuss in the book's final chapter, a counter strand to Du Bois in black art history and aesthetic thought emerges in Darby English's writing, which asserts that such a stance conflates the space of black artistic imagination with "the space of black representation."⁴⁹ While English's emphasis on the regulatory is helpful, it is black life rather than the black artist that is ultimately constricted and antagonized by the justificatory. As the opening of this book asserts, I theorize the integrity of the condo's emptiness—the fantastical room of one's own, even when bereft of black representations, preserved behind the tinted glass—as eminently linked to the spectacular space of black representation. That the black work of art is integral to protecting the glass in which the vacant space of black aesthetic imagination aspires to live, work, or have an artist residency has a great deal to do with how beauty bounds "the ideal of justice" to which Du Bois refers.

The beauty the black work of art produces is not primarily "the space of black representation" but the ideal of justice that regulates black life. I invoke the black work of art to emphasize this labor and the productivity of the justificatory over the purely representational, which can be incidental to the racial essence it often claims. I argue throughout this work that the value production of the black work of art is primarily rooted in the imaginative restraint it facilitates. Part of this restraint lies in the creative force of the justificatory. Art for Du Bois, not unlike Nietzsche, can never escape the justificatory. The question is merely what and how it justifies: "Thus all art is propaganda and ever must be ... used always for propaganda for gaining the right of black folk to love and enjoy. I do not care a damn for an art that is not used for propaganda."[50] In perhaps surprising ways in his conclusion, Du Bois partially echoed the utterly humanistic valuation of art championed in Nietzsche's notion of aesthetic justification, although he also importantly and rigorously revised this nineteenth-century inheritance. Both Du Bois and Nietzsche rejected the established and enduring hermeticism of *art pour l'art*. Instead, they ascribed to the black artist a clerical power and drive to affect the social. Yet it is not the purely individuated prowess of the artist in Nietzsche that realizes this power. The black artist is driven and sustained by an "inner and outer compulsion" that Du Bois attributes to a collective or community. It is around this sociality that an overt fissure arises between Du Bois's demand that the artist be a disciple of "justice" and Nietzsche's contention that the artist should be the ultimate model of individuation, which he argued is precisely the "limits of justice."[51]

Part of how the black artist is not enslaved is by beautifying the limits of justice. This beautification effort is something the black artist can possess to the extent that he defends it. The black work of art thus emerges as a kind of property, much like the property of labor in racial capitalism, only to the extent that it is a site of defense against the threatening egress of black life, even and perhaps especially when such life is appropriated and symbolically included. The black artist's labor of beautification occurs by working the imagination of black sounding and black life away from crime and driving it into sociable aesthetic regulation.[52] The defensive architecture of the murals and the art murmur with which I opened this book that were designed to suppress criminal black activity perfectly illustrate the black work of art and the black artist as a force of deterrence. This again recalls my framing of the aesthetic humanizing character of black music during and after manumission as a limit concept placed on and against black resistance and autonomy, including the resistance of the black sounding it was appropriated from. The contraband of black music making must be re-formed into and legislated as a new sociable law of the black work of art to be waged against the criminal.

The black work of art, like the capture of black music, prevents black life and sounding from becoming black criminality, which is to say force waged against the slave society. The participatory aspirations implied in Douglass's celebration of free labor are made explicit in Du Bois as "the right of black folk to love and enjoy." The black enjoyment that in the nineteenth century was sublimated in the purposiveness of the humanizing character of blackness reemerged positively in the twentieth century as a right. Justice and black enjoyment would litigiously comingle in the black work of art and the black artist. Black "love and joy" had to be regulated into an acceptable and dignified form of art that was surrounded by "rights," lest the dogged pursuit of slavery recapture black life. The rights in love and joy are of course incredibly abstract and alienated notions. Rather than naming and facilitating articulations of black enjoyment and need in the world, the investment is shifted over to the black work of art as the arbiter and depository of such theoretical sites of enjoyment. This move, on the one hand, leads to the infamous appropriation of black poor and working-class cultures by the black bourgeoisie. And on the other hand, this abstraction coerces and cajoles black life into a representative economy in which the black artist is not just a conveyance but an administrator of black enjoyment.

The franchise around black enjoyment is staked out through the black artist who manages the distinction between purposeless black pleasure and justificatory, justifiable, or just black enjoyment through his distribution and defense of the beautiful. This distinction between aimless or purposeless pleasure became central to the Harlem Renaissance and the Black Arts Movement, as I will discuss in the final three chapters. However, the origins of this imaginative restriction around black pleasure can be gleaned in Frederick Douglass's relegation of enjoyment under enslavement to a mere recapitulation to bondage. Douglass quite famously asserted that holidays were "the most effective means in the hands of slaveholders of keeping down the spirit of insurrection among the slaves. . . . These holidays served the purpose of keeping the minds of the slaves occupied with prospective pleasure within the limits of slavery."[53] While Douglass characterizes black art as a distraction for black social life from the reality of its oppression, in Du Bois's writing, the black artist must fashion the justificatory as a way of working black life, of making black life justifiable against its domination. Much more clearly by the twentieth century, the black work of art produces a way of, in Petero Kalulé's phrasing, coaxing black life into "being right-with," the sociable character of the slave society and with representation itself.[54]

I will expose and challenge this beautification of bondage, however, which I argue moves black life into the internalized subservience to the aesthetic character of black representation. Like the law of right, the law of beauty will manage and limit what activity is imaginable by restricting what is justifiable, what is beautiful. The aesthetic character administrated by the black artist will craft the justificatory as a related kind of repressive servitude that Douglass attributes to black music under enslavement. Ironically, this fear of a return to slavery manifests the limits within which black pleasure is pacified, but this time through the regulation of the black work of art. Woven throughout my study will be the contention that the positive property of the black work of art will be how it holds at bay a "return to slavery" by holding at bay how black folks imagine a world beyond and otherwise—the right of black enjoyment functioning as no more than a disguised regulation and domination by the apostle and concept of beauty.

In chapter 5, "Sounds Like Us," I consider the relationship between the aestheticism of the Harlem Renaissance and the revolutionary ethics of the Black Art Movement around the idea or figure of "black beauty." I consider how the seminal writings of Amiri Baraka, Larry Neal, and Dingane Goncalves and black artist collectives such as OBA-C/AfriCOBRA of Chicago and the Black Artists Group of St. Louis grappled with the relationship between beauty and ethics. I oppose the ethical practices of these groups and theorists, which were inspired by the Black Power Movement, with the emerging violent inclusion of black art as a category and force of the black beautiful, the black artist, and the black work of art most prodigiously by city beautification campaigns. My chief concern in this chapter is the terrifying reality, expanded dramatically in the 1960s but birthed in Douglass's time, that the world wishes to enfranchise more and more of black life into black art.

I conclude that the trajectory of the aesthetic leads to a world in which more and more of black life is rendered as black art. When black music and black art become our aesthetic justification, and become wedded primarily to the justificatory, they will become rigorously dislocated from that which is unjustified or hegemonically unjustifiable. The revolutionary violent, the criminal, the deviant, and the queer will become increasingly threatening to the society that black art aims to be made more sociable to. What is violently included as well as excluded in our justification is a deadly important consideration. What is policed by the "inner and outer compulsion" of the black work of art? This will be a recurring and central preoccupation throughout this text, for our art will justify us, but our life and its defense will always be crime.

Emancipating the Spaces of Sonic Capture

1

> we lost our bodies in,
> sound alone
> survived
>
> Nathaniel Mackey, "Sound and Somnolence," in *Nod House*

> The social machine of the plantation system [was] a machine whose marks and inscriptions ... colonized above all Desire.
>
> Sylvia Wynter, "Sambos and Minstrels"

Frederick Douglass's hand is pointing to the right of the frame—it's his left, but the direction and the directive only really matters for the viewer—the listener hearing his request. The sound of Douglass's pointing resonates in the space of the viewer beyond the frame: the parlor where the family piano is kept, upon the keys the meeting point where white hands could strike up concord with Douglass's outstretched arm and all the weight of movement it bears. I am describing the image that graces the 1845 cover sheet to "The Fugitive's Song," which bears Frederick Douglass's image as he stands on the bank of what is likely the Ohio River, a common antebellum dividing line between South and North (figure 1.1). The cover was illustrated by and the song was composed by Jesse Hutchinson Jr. of the internationally renowned white abolitionist singing group the Hutchinson Family Singers. This sheet music and its alluring image were crafted in commemoration of Douglass's highly publicized journey out of slavery as recounted in his *Narrative of the Life of Frederick Douglass, an American Slave*. If, as Saidiya Hartman asserts, "laboring hands [were] the synecdoche for the

1.1 Ephraim W. Bouve's lithographic rendering of Frederick Douglass for the sheet music for "The Fugitive's Song" (Boston: Henry Prentiss, 1845). Source: Library of Congress, https://www.loc.gov/item/2008661459/.

self-possessed individual," then what do we make of the pointing hands of Douglass and the space they worked and resounded?[1]

The oddly inviting nature of Douglass's pointing and the engaging stare drawn across his face cohabitate with the factual referentiality of his fugitive journey that the image is meant to conjure. He is escaping, and only you can help him. Douglass's performative double on the cover of this sheet music is not only a result of the prurient hands of Hutchinson, but also, more broadly, a product of the cajoling hands of the many white progressives who ushered Douglass's voice onto the documentary stage of abolitionism and who imagined themselves as empathically and aesthetically being able to inhabit and re-ensnare his sounding body by striking up these selective chords on the parlor piano. What did it mean and what was the value of capturing the words, songs, image, and spirit of Frederick Douglass, who was after all a fugitive?

This chapter is distantly a genealogy of Frederick Douglass's pointing. The meaning of that expanding empty space he is pointing into is a figure for this work, specifically the voices and echoes that speak in, out, against, and through the expansion of this space. Much of the discourse on the fungibility of black flesh in the form of slave property has presciently related the hinge of captive and liberated activity across a dividing line of dispossession that Frederick Douglass's imaging references here, first as a slave property, then as something else, something exceeding that symbolic inscription. The property form that Douglass's image suggests at the dawn of legal emancipation will no longer be entombed solely in the blackness of slave property, as both his fugitive status and the image's imaginary celebration of his escape suggest. On a cursory level, this is a profound affront to the integrity of a centuries-old mode of subjugated human property and all the violence of force it congeals. Douglass frequently and famously stood as a symbol of willful black autonomy freed from the legal and symbolic yoke of slavery, but this exposure also opened him up to new imaginative constructions and strictures. His journey, his movement also unearth an unsettling or irresistible temptation, for the dispossessions of black life interred in the form of property will have to be reconfigured, reimagined, recaptured, and liberated precisely through a set of imaginative exercises illustrated through his captivating flight. This is what the drawing of Douglass draws.

A new aesthetic mode of capture is formalized through the dream of abolition. Douglass's standing was not just about unjustness of the "peculiar institution" he had "graduated" from but was equally if not more about the justification of the impending frontier of judgments he entered and points to with his illustrated hand. Here Frederick Douglass stands, on a riverbank, a shore, a border between putative captivity and freedom, on a stage, both before and after the law that chases after him as a fugitive. The abundance of who Frederick Douglass left behind—what Angela Davis calls "the slave community," is disappeared against the voluminous austerity and solemnity of the endless frontier cast in the image's looking.[2] The corridors of the slave community whereby "if resistance was an organic ingredient of slave life, it had to be directly nurtured by the social organization which the slaves themselves improvised" are negated and sublimated into the singularity of Douglass as this imaginative restriction of the unseen but all-seeing listener and onlooker.[3] I am encouraging us not only to think of Douglass as a positive character representing freedom but also to think about what kinds of freedom Douglass makes unimaginable as the moment of his pointing. This futurity, or the space and temporality of where and when Douglass's hand is pointing to are clearly not the slave community that nourished him and radicalized him to escape, but the prurient and speculative gaze of the slave society he has escaped into. While it was the contention of the abolitionist movement that drew Douglass here that his sound-imaging held the potential to liberate black folks from bondage, I will assert throughout this work that this arrangement liberated representation, as our necessary justification, over black folks and against black life. Douglass's conveyance of black music is the hinge and condition of possibility for this arrangement.

I will engage Douglass in this chapter as both a figure who heralds the study of black music and someone, who in doing so, became essentially the prototype of the black artist. Specifically, I will focus on how Frederick Douglass's sounding and appearance on the stage of abolitionism and the sheet music for "The Fugitive's Song" demands that a facticity, a rationality, and an authenticity be visited upon black life as and through black music. Thus, I read against the grain of Douglass's intended claim that the liberation of black music (as an object of humanization and rationalization) serves to liberate enslaved black people. Through examination and rationalization, black music takes on the quality of a documentary object as evidence of black sentience and cultural capacity invoked largely to dispel what Douglass and later informal study of black music deemed the pure mythology of the blackface minstrel stage. Extending the argument touched upon in the introduction, I thus situate Douglass's sounding and his conveyance of black music as aspirationally enacting a double escape: from the formal labor and life regime of plantation slavery and from the confinement of blackface minstrelsy's dehumanizing character. Yet I ultimately argue that the humanizing aesthetic character through which Douglass engineers this escape and the recognition of black music becomes another kind of captivity that does not abolish enslavement but merely or mostly re-forms, reimagines, beautifies, and liberates the slave society over the soon-to-be emancipated. I track how black life and enslaved labor were also reimagined and aestheticized through the liberation of black music, forestalling a broader critique of the very society into which they were liberated. Finally, throughout this chapter and in different iterations throughout this book, I speculate as to what forms of black life and labor existed behind, underneath, and beyond Douglass's particularly regulated and sociable mode of escape. Perhaps most important, I assert that Douglass's aestheticization of black music initiated a new form of labor and value production to replace the enslaved form it aimed to escape from and abolish.

A Brand New Fact

Of the framing of his abolitionist speeches during his Garrisonian speaking tours in the North, Douglass once wrote: "I was generally introduced as "'*chattel*'—a '*thing*'—a piece of southern '*property*'—the chairman assuring the audience that *it* could speak. Fugitive slaves, at that time, were not so plentiful as now; and as a fugitive slave lecturer, I had the advantage of being a '*brand new fact*'—the first one out."[4] This totality of sentiment, despite Douglass's vehement contestation, often came to form this image of a documentary life—a life lived, sounded, and embodied as a document, as "a *brand new fact*." In her work on black performance in the nineteenth century, Daphne A. Brooks elaborates Douglass's revelation in the escape of Henry Box Brown's solitary act of self-concealed fugitivity through the mail (which was memorialized in a song) as an opaque contestation of the slave narrative's technology of revelation of the black document, the black fact, the fact of blackness.[5] The mixture of facticity and sentimentality borne by, imagined in, and lived through blackness and the captive black body became a model for the raw materiality of what was to emerge after the formal abolition of the slave plantation.

Quite infamously, white masters' claims of the cultural vacuity of black folks led to the ventriloquism of the minstrel stage. Indeed, Douglass's slave humanity, like Du Bois's later soul in the souls of black folks, is meant to recontextualize the vacuity of black folks carved by the minstrel stage into the positive possession of black culture and art. The predominant idea formalized in minstrelsy was that roughhewn black sounds could and needed to be refined into melody (however bawdy or trifling) by white performers capering through black skin. Douglass's circulation as an audiovisual object sounding the humanizing character of blackness for a mostly white audience was conscripted to counter the more parodic (de)humanization of the minstrel. The geographical supply lines of minstrelsy's proclaimed sources, the claim that songs had been smuggled up North from "way down South," mirrored the flight lines of many a fugitive slave. In this sense, the minstrel stage's trade routes of cultural currency that sought to reinscribe and extract imagined value from the contraband of black flight would be re-formed by Douglass's black music.

Just as the reality of the melodies of the minstrel stage lay in the harmonies and meters of recently immigrated European (especially Irish) folk songs from the North, so too was the sonic work of Douglass meant to signify a black re-sounding that was directly composed of white northern musical sources and primarily the domestic space of the Victorian parlors of white abolitionists. I will argue in this chapter and the next that the private consumptive spaces of re-sounding—the nineteenth-century parlor, the (white) family, the space of the imagination—mark new and differently oppressive sites that black music was enlisted to expand and re-form. These late nineteenth-century and early twentieth-century spaces of private artistic reflection and consumption emerged from a synthesis of the blackface minstrel stage's racial spectacle and the quiet domesticity of abolitionist agitprop such as Douglass's narratives and songbook. The minstrel stage is much more often discussed as the generically symbolic and ideological flailing of white mastery to maintain its grip over blackness in the face of the impending decline of the plantation.[6] And while the blackface minstrel stage is rightly seen as the cultural and material antecedent of the modern American and Western entertainment industries and American popular culture, the abolitionist movement's deepening mid-nineteenth-century fixation with implanting and extracting a manageable black humanity—a "humanizing character" at the heart of black folks and the slave community—marks a complementary and perhaps equally significant mode and site for the regulating of black life and the production of later mass-produced music and culture. Countering and complicating the common historical argument that the blackface minstrel stage is both the origin of the US entertainment industry and the white fascination with putative black culture, I invoke Douglass to invert the image of the Virginia Serenaders, a blackface minstrel troupe of white men (figure 1.2). What was the effect of putting black music in a suit, so to speak?

Much of Douglass's staging was indeed a reaction to the minstrel stage. In fact, the peak of popularity of the blackface minstrel stage coincided roughly with the emergence of Douglass's popularity as the representative political and artistic figure as well as the beginning of the scholarly study of black music he championed. Douglass's facticity as "a brand new fact" on

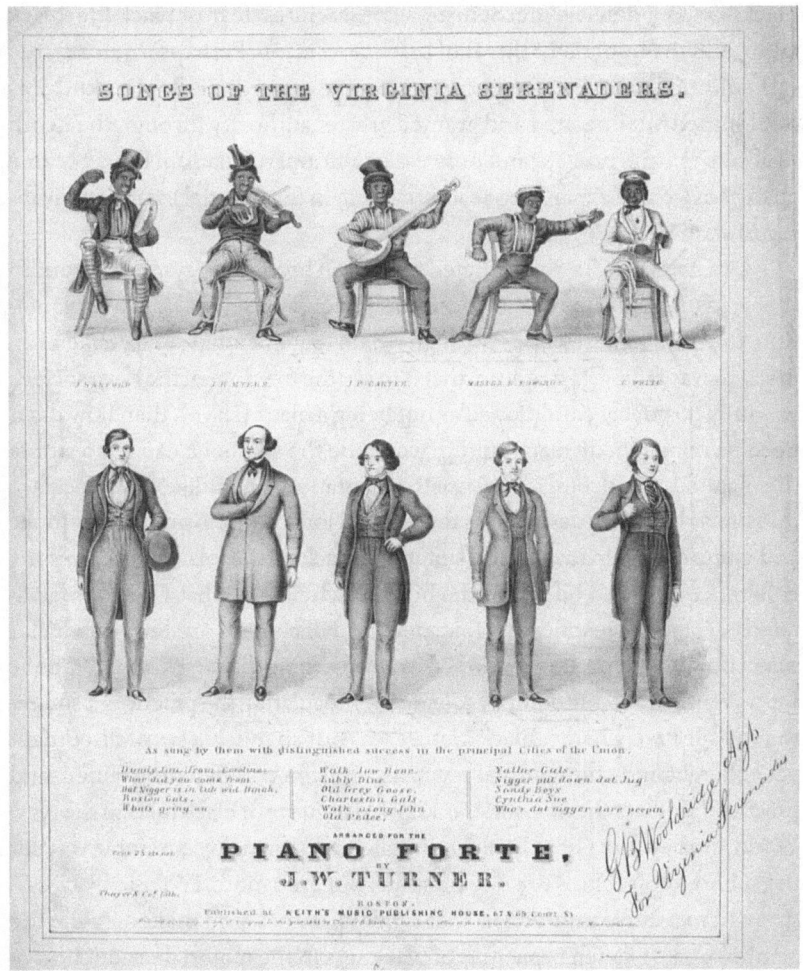

1.2 Show poster for the Virginia Serenaders. Published by Keith's Music Publishing House in 1844. Courtesy of Boston Public Library.

the stage of abolitionism was meant to counter the mythos of minstrelsy whose authority the abolitionist movement misguidedly located in its counterfeit nature rather than its reproductive currency or its conveyance of power and authority. Distinct from the image of Douglass on the cover of "The Fugitive's Song," minstrel show advertisements illustrate that the audience rarely labored under the delusion of the performers' factual blackness. Instead, they marveled at the capacity of white performers to reproduce

EMANCIPATING THE SPACES OF SONIC CAPTURE

blackness as a defense mechanism against whites' fear of black life, black labor, and the immanent threat of black revolution. Perhaps ironically, the rather limited surface of minstrelsy's power (quite literally the skin) was not blunted but liberated and granted greater authority through the depth of abolitionism's process and prowess of cultural regulation. Race became an expansive and expanding aesthetic force in the (partial) wake and waning of slavability.

Douglass's endlessly mediated figuration brought to symbolic fruition the fantastical bounds of the liberated subject precisely as the slave plantation, the prior material basis through which that liberated subject had been created, was fading. If freedom, that is to say the freedom of the slave society, was only positively conditioned as not being a black (slave), then how did it need be reimagined? Black culture would be the symbolic capital to suture the material and ideological loss of the plantation, not unlike how blackface minstrelsy had been designed as the cultural joint propping up the symbolic and cultural legitimacy of the plantation. Black music, black voice, and the coherence of such a body and the body of scholarship that Douglass facilitated became the justification for a new kind of cultural mastery, by which I mean how black culture functioned as an emerging discursive and symbolic (and eventually commodified) category for regulating the practices it sought to retrospectively name. Black culture was not so much a set of discordant yet coherent and contrapuntal practices, unnamed, differently named, and practiced as it was the not-quite-unknown language of black folks in the New World and beyond. For as Douglass implied, this unwieldy ensemble was not the sublime object he wished to translate. But even more, I refer to black culture as a regulative production that renders, names, and makes legible the symbolic value-laden capacities of blackness in the material production of the emerging slave society through the waning of the plantation.

The fantasies of proximity that were sentimentally anchored in black music were carried out formally and technologically through the fungibility of the captive body. As Saidiya Hartman notes:

> The relation between pleasure and possession of slave property, in both figurative and literal senses, can be explained in part by the fungibility of the slave—that is, the joy made possible by virtue of the replaceability and interchangeability endemic to the commodity.... Put differently, the fungibility of the commodity makes the captive body an abstract and empty vessel vulnerable to the projection of others' feelings, ideas, desires and values; and, as property, the dispossessed

body of the enslaved is the surrogate for the master's body since it guarantees his disembodied universality and acts as the sign of his power and dominion.[7]

Abolitionism's project of making enslaved black interiority capacious was not an exercise in producing nothingness but of creating something that could bear a symbolic, affective, and material fullness—excessively so: that is, the liberalization and liberation of the affective dominion over blackness as an aesthetic and imaginative space of regulation. As Hartman's writing suggests, the fantasy of mastery that inhered legally and formally in slavery had to be liberated, expanded, and ferried across (as it dredged) new waters of valuation to maintain the monopoly of its own "disembodied universality." With the partial or relative disappearance of literal whips, chains, and auction blocks, or really their re-formation and enclosure within the prison system and emerging new colonies, the re-formation of mastery required further spaces of its disguised assertion. Before the law of manumission could be realized, an imaginative space of regulation and capture had to be created. Just as the blackface minstrel stage pacified white fears of impending black emancipation or ongoing and potential black revolt, a positive space of imaginative cultural valuation was conscripted to ease this transition.

The space I am tracking throughout this work, particularly in this chapter, is the increasingly inhabited space of "the slave's" imagined interiority that is the object of the slave society's imagination. Numerous material spaces of the world emerged through this imaginative space. The open space into which Douglass points is just as much an internal psychic space, what Theodor Adorno would call much later in the twentieth century, in a fusion of Marxism and psychoanalysis, the "psychological economy of the self"; that is, a reificatory space of self-possession that arts and is arted by the means of cultural production and consumption.[8] Adorno's treatment of early reproduced music and "the culture industry" locates the spaces of social reproduction that in Marx's writing are largely designated the mere *faux frais* of capitalist reproduction as they allegedly stand as epiphenomenal to the material base of the formal labor economy. Like Adorno, I will complicate this nineteenth-century formulation, especially as it is grounded in enslaved and recently manumitted black cultural labor and production. Through and beyond even Adorno's thought however, I think through how the voluntarist labor and production of black music that emerged from its relationship to waning legal and formal slave labor enfranchised critical modes of aesthetic production and regulation. I invoke Frederick Douglass's sounding here, as in the previous section, as a figure—a character who helps concretize larger machinations of social reproduction by founding the regulative voluntarist labor of black aesthetic production.

Black song, or in the following chapter "the black voice," increasingly entered en masse the domestic and domesticating space of mastery that was once the exclusive province of the relatively few formal slave masters. Black music was thus indispensable to liberating the domestic space of mastery I will track in this chapter and the next two chapters. The liberation of the domestic space, both the psychic interiority of this "eavesdropper" and the primitive accumulatory space of the domestic sphere, are what black music liberates—not black people. In Sylvia Wynter's words, Douglass and black song—black music—help map the "wilderness of technological rationalization."[9] That is, black music and culture "[fed] the barest minimum of an affective and emotional life" that was disturbed by the rupture of the legal decline of plantation slavery and the increasing rationalization of the means of production and life. The mapping of this ominous wilderness was produced through black music as an internal source of affective relief that scholars of black culture from Saidiya Hartman to Herman Gray and scholars of black music from Greg Tate to Kofi Agawu have identified as a consumable curious and exotic romantic empathy that for black folks positively constructs, in Tate's phrase, "everything but the burden."[10] Refracting Tate's formulation of "burden" from the context of 1990s black popular culture, I would add that the antebellum and postbellum elision of black needs, which were sublimated to (white) exogenous enjoyment, facilitated a formal rationalization commonly reserved for the technological. Black music was not just an affective content but attained a formalization of the very spaces of labor and consumption.

The re-formation of white domestic space that was once attended to and built up through black subjugation requires a new imagined proximity to ferry its values across emancipation. The prurience of the cover of "The Fugitive's Song" allowed symbolic access to Douglass's fugitive body through the domestic materiality of the music reproduced. His body and sentiments were no longer only a public product of the minstrel stage but became a privatized thing that the private sheet music collector and possessor could expect access to. Within the image on this sheet music, Douglass was drawn into material supplementation with the singing voice of the white abolitionist, both the Hutchinson Family Singers, for whom the piece was composed, but also the likely white abolitionist consumer of the sheet music. The sheet music rematerialized Douglass's body and the accompanying hands on the piano struck up his sentimental interiority in some obscured consonance with the white hands of Hutchinson that inscribed it. All of this material relation was set up by the reduction of Douglass's narrative to this solitary lyrical act of escape, which became a kind of embodied document. I will expand this notion of "documentary embodiment" in chapter 3, but its tendrils can be located here in Douglass and the figure of "the slave" on the stage of abolitionism.

Douglass's geographical destination as "a graduate from the peculiar institution," may have been perceived to be "the Free States and Canada" or the "New England and Freedom" of his biographical narratives. The space also reflected the locus of Douglass's public speaking tours for William Lloyd Garrison for the American Anti-Slavery Society in the northern states and eventually in Western Europe. Illustrated by Douglass's longtime friend, the white abolitionist musician Jesse Hutchinson Jr., "The Fugitive's Song" was intended to extend the narration of Douglass's journey to freedom, earlier imagined in his slave narratives, providing Douglass's journey from enslavement and his arrival into a new captivity with a phonographic voice to sound the authority and subjectivity of its receiver, or what the twentieth century would later call a listener. The spatial trajectories of Douglass's embodiment were not meant to dwell in one physical space and reaffirm a geography from North to South so much as they were meant to undergird a sentimental landscape that requires a kind of spatial and corporeal ambiguity as the way of guaranteeing perpetual affective proximity to the formerly enslaved.[11] The freedom to which Douglass might be pointing, referenced either directly or implied in all geographical trajectories, is a new proximity, a new affective regime. Douglass's image was meant to re-sound liberal freedom insomuch as it emancipated a new material method and affective mode of capture of blackness that would be traversed by the vehicle of black culture and music. While black music is commonly framed as a content of the abolitionist movement, it is its form.

As I will set out to prove throughout this book, but especially in these first three chapters, part of black music's invention and extraction were not primarily about humanizing the enslaved as mere content to an already existent humanity but were in fact about humanizing, liberating, and expanding that dominant and oppressive imaginary of humanity. Simply put, humanity and humanization would not have been possible without the liberation of Douglass and black music; black music humanized humanity. Frederick Douglass's act of giving access to the circle of black music to an alienated eavesdropper had the effect of also producing from black life, black interiority, spaces beyond it that materialized as new modes of labor and consumption. In its simplest distillation and by Douglass's own words and sound-imaging, he reproduced black music to create spaces and material relations beyond slavery. The open frontier to which Douglass points is a (scientific) field for the rationalization of black life and culture, most overtly akin to the field of ethnomusicology and the study of black music, as I will argue in the following chapter. Supplementary to this affective domestic space of the sheet music cover, this frontier-like space that Douglass points toward furrows a newly mapped psychic and material terrain. By providing this supreme object of rationalization that is distinct from the kitsch of the minstrel stage, Douglass's black music inserts a re-formed scientific and scientistic investment in black life and labor. Indeed, as the Sylvia Wynter epigraph that opens this chapter suggests, the "social machine of the plantation system" embodied in this sheet music makes possible the later "talking machine" of the phonograph.[12] Instead of a stage, Douglass drew a circle of inquiry around black music. Beyond the mere prurience associated with the songs of the enslaved, this circle called for a penetrative entrance, an invitation into the very space into which Douglass's sound-image feigns escape.

Those from Without

Prior to Douglass's imaging on the sheet music that opens this chapter, another partial articulation of this open space emerged in Frederick Douglass's own writings, a space he framed as the (hermeneutic) social circle of black music from which its humanizing character could be extracted. This space or circle was extended continually as a site of return to a humanity that Douglass was extracting from his enslavement and that might be inhabitable and made intelligible by "those [from] without."

> I did not, when a slave, understand the deep meaning of those rude and apparently incoherent songs. I was myself within the circle; so that I neither saw nor heard as those without might see and hear. They told a tale of woe which was then altogether beyond my feeble comprehension; they were tones loud, long and deep; they breathed the prayer and complaint of souls boiling over with the bitterest anguish. Every tone was a testimony against slavery, and a prayer to God for deliverance from chains. The hearing of those wild notes always depressed my spirit, and filled me with ineffable sadness. I have frequently found myself in tears while hearing them. The mere recurrence to those songs,

even now, afflicts me; and while I am writing these lines, an expression of feeling has already found its way down my cheek. To those songs I trace my first glimmering conception of the dehumanizing character of slavery. I can never get rid of that conception. Those songs still follow me, to deepen my hatred of slavery, and quicken my sympathies for my brethren in bonds. If any one wishes to be with the soul-killing effects of slavery let him go to Colonel Lloyd's plantation, and, on allowance-day, place himself in the deep pine woods, and there let him, in silence, analyze the sounds that shall pass through the chambers of his soul,—and if he is not thus impressed, it will only be because "there is no flesh in his obdurate heart."[13]

In this immensely influential passage from *Narrative of the Life of Frederick Douglass, an American Slave,* Douglass narrates black music as tragedy, as sorrow heard and verified in "[the] understanding" by "those without." Douglass's figuration of black music launches its claims to divulging a humanistic essence, hidden in the raw material of slave life that is incidental to slave labor: woe, anguish, breaths of mortal souls, from all of which empathic identification can and indeed must be secured by those from without. First, this valuation is initiated by Douglass and then by the future and distant eavesdropper called into embodiment, both corporeally and culturally, emphasized in this passage's terminal invocation of a line from William Cowper's 1785 poem *The Task.*

Douglass ends the passage with an excerpted suasive appeal of "brotherhood" from Book II of *The Task* entitled "The Timepiece":

> There is no flesh in man's obdurate heart,
> It does not feel for man. The natural bond
> Of brotherhood is severed as the flax
> That falls asunder at the touch of fire.
> He finds his fellow guilty of a skin
> Not coloured like his own, and having power
> To enforce the wrong, for such a worthy cause
> Dooms and devotes him as his lawful prey.

How the law makes "lawful prey" of black people under bondage ought to call for the abolition of the law itself. But by decoding transatlantic enslavement as a condition of a "guilty" willful action, legal individuation (which was not properly available either before or after enslavement to black folks) became the moral and equally legalistic precondition and telos of abolition. It was as if black folks were innocent and only rendered guilty by an unfair trial that now deserved the retrial of emancipation, not merely to exonerate the soul of the enslaved (and grant them a new innocence) but to most importantly reform and exonerate the judgment and authority of the enslaving society that put them in chains in the first place.

Cowper's language in the poem secures the fantasy of an aspirationally fraternal bond, linking the intelligibility of the common white domestic sphere in which the recitation of his renowned poem re-sounded. Parlor music and then the reproduced music of the phonograph would gradually replace this space of poetic recitation and re-sounding. Douglass created the transparency of this "looking-glass" into the circle of black music by transposing the sentimentality of the poem onto the voices, sounds, and bodies of the enslaved, opening their social as a frontier of embodiment to the absented eavesdropper to their practices.[14] As Saidiya Hartman notes, the force of righteous dissatisfaction and revolt of the enslaved is insufficient as "oppositional culture" unless "sorrow rather than resistance characterizes such songs."[15] Douglass thus enacted a formal transubstantiation of the songs and sounds of the enslaved by transporting and transposing them into a more common literary affective register, both humanizing and, more subtly, formally regulating them. The sentimentality of the content rationalized the extractive function of the form, and contrary to its intent to dispute the embodied inhabitation of minstrelsy, ended up reproducing the rudiments of a new economy of regulative embodiment.

The law around the enslaved was not abolished but re-formed by the circle of black culture Douglass draws. What is rooted in empathy and a perceived call for equality would become a new aesthetic mastery. The ploy of black music's liberation through Douglass's sounding would be to produce a new figure or character against which rationalized comparisons of humanity could be made and extracted just as slavery, which carried out such a function, was being re-formed. Douglass's circle that liberated black music into understanding could not do so without the litigious establishment of a new law. It was the medium or technology that reproduced black music's haunting message of subjectification. What remained in bondage under the law, when extracted, allowed for the liberation and humanization of the law without its abolition. If this weren't the case, then the very "skin" which Cowper decried as the medium of differentiation would not have been expanded through manumission. The regulative function of colorism in fact expanded and did not contract after the emancipation of the slave society. In chapter 3, I will discuss embodiment and the registers of the skin in black women's late nineteenth-century and early twentieth-century performative repertoires. I argue that in such performances, the skin is often a barrier to the kind of penetrative suasive understanding Douglass offered here through black music. But the social life Douglass imagined through black music is the social life of "the understanding" and not the social life of the slave community that produced it.[16]

Black music's sentimental and rational figuration is synthesized through Douglass as a singular, self-possessed black artist. The black artist brings to court the synthesized justification of black life, its emotional and rational plea. As he modeled this manageable process of extraction, Douglass was transformed from the sentimental rendering of "the slave" when he presented himself as a sentience-bearing subject who could communicate the rationalization of black music. Saidiya Hartman presciently tracks the Rousseauean empathic registers of re-sounding testimonies such as Douglass's that sought to "bring slavery close" to establish a "shared sentience between those formerly indifferent and those suffering."[17] If "the slave" is brought close, then he also brings the bringing close, like the later mechanized invention of the phonograph fuses technorational justification with the feeling of its sublimely captured object, the fantasy of swimming ashore with the relief of avoiding the stormy ocean. What this new mode of captivity secures through Douglass's partial inhabitation is not the liberation of the enslaved but the liberation of judgment.

The Singular and Synthetic Judgment of the Slave

As Douglass's imaging suggests, the autonomy realized in the open space of his image and imaging is not opposed spatially or temporally to the proscriptive figure of the plantation but requires such a space as an aesthetic map for the territory of the free world.[18] This realization reveals the emerging aesthetic contingency of what the slave plantation's formal demise could liberate: a shift, not a total abolition, but a movement from one form of property to another. Just as it was during the "time of slavery," the plantation in being rendered as an escaped-from site is also continually a site that is figuratively, legally, politically, and narratively a returned-to place through the increasingly aestheticized portal of "the slave" Frederick Douglass. The singularity of "peculiar institution" and the slave lose the slave community under their legal-philosophical brushstrokes.[19] In particular, a certain kind of victimization (from which the saviorism of abolitionism will be stoked) that is invoked in Douglass's inviting sounding-image disappears the way new and active forms of aesthetic value making will take place from the symbolic liberation of this figure and this space. No living takes place in the hollow of Douglass's escape, only the productive capacities of the slave society his singular imaging makes possible.

The reality of constant slave resistance, which all defined the contrapuntal discontent of slavery's constitution, carried with it a "form of fear," as Susan Buck-Morss notes, that had yet to find a medium and technology capable of bearing its fantastical rationalization.[20] The fear that the enslaved would rebel transcended slavery's introjection of a finite number of slaves against a finite number of slavers. So great was the resistance of the enslaved that the force of fear transcended its immediate reality into an ungainly imaginary. This is the negative immeasurable paranoia provoked by the force and determination of collective black freedom that was positively defined as property in the New World. C. L. R. James reported on the incalculability of emerging slave revolt in the words of Toussaint L'Ouverture, who, speaking about the recently victorious Haitian revolutionaries, asserted, "If they [the enslaved] had a thousand lives they would sacrifice them all rather than be forced into slavery again."[21] How to reduce an army of millions and still millions more beyond who or what could be counted to the manageability of one? Still further, as W. E. B. Du Bois's seminal chronicle *Black Reconstruction* discusses, how to produce value through blackness as the potential innumerable threat of a suddenly riotous crowd? The infinite and anarchic specter of these "thousand lives" had to be regulated in a singular "the slave" on the stage of abolitionism to appease the oppressive imagination of the slave society they threatened. Thus the overbearing threat of an innumerable slave community had to be reduced to a single slave standing and pointing on a river bank; bringing with him all the rationalizations of a world wrought through his violent inclusion.

To treat Douglass as the slave, as he so often was treated, enacts a complex value-making process, a space I am calling the aesthetic character of blackness. I will attempt in this chapter to step out from behind that process in the hope of doing some pointing to it on my own. In this chapter I thus concoct a compressed and partial genealogy of the lines and boundaries that draw the positive historical and symbolic figure of "the slave," a figure that owes much of its lineage to Josiah Wedgwood's world-famous 1787 lithograph *Am I Not a Man and a Brother* (figure 1.3). Far more widely circulated than the sheet music that bore Douglass's image but sentimentally comparable to the circulation of his slave narrative and his photographic image in

1.3 Lithograph of *Am I Not a Man and a Brother?*, originally a ceramic medallion created by Josiah Wedgwood for the Society for Effecting the Abolition of the Slave Trade in Britain in 1787. Source: American Anti-Slavery Society and Anti-Slavery Office, 1837; Library of Congress, https://www.loc.gov/item/2008661312/.

the nineteenth century, *Am I Not a Man and a Brother* was reputedly the most popular representation of a black person in the West in the eighteenth century. Much like Douglass's corpus, *Am I Not a Man and a Brother* was put forth by a white abolitionist. Josiah Wedgwood, a wealthy British merchant, an early developer of what would by the twentieth century be called marketing, and the great-grandfather of Charles Darwin, created this iconic image with the intent to center liberally espoused views of a brotherhood of humanity into which the enslaved ought to be tentatively inaugurated. Humanity and the interpolation of the symbolic slave into it were undoubtedly carried out through a brand of rematerialized mastery. The inscriptive lines literally produced the sinewy body of the enslaved into which Wedgwood put such a semantically and rhetorically weighty and hence universally embodied and recognizable question: "Am I not a man and a brother?" These words, these lines, were meant to refer to a simultaneously fantasized yet precisely abstracted social context of the slave's bondage. *Am I Not a Man and a Brother* bears none of the contextual viscera or rationalized judgment of the narratives of Douglass or other formerly enslaved writers, none of the explicit abject peculiarities of the peculiar institution and none of its excavated humanizing rewards. Instead, *Am I Not a Man and a Brother* carries out a more naked, a louder and a more consumable embodiment and sound of subjection. If Douglass's sojourn offers up black song, Wedgwood's carving contributes a snippet or early sound bite.

The sound of *Am I Not a Man and a Brother* is an entirely projective space set up by the disembodied universal authority of the master's understanding of humanity. The ability to implant reason in the benighted body of "the slave"—rather than the more ominous threat of a riotous and (potentially) revolting caste of enslaved black folks—did not expose but affirmed white mastery through the ventriloquial gesture of its speaking and sounding. The ruminating harmonics of attachment resound in the rhetorical question that finds its voice solely and primarily in the voice of its receiver. The singularized body of the enslaved, this time made multiple but manageable in the hands of its (white) beholders, becomes a vehicle to answer that onlookers' own questions and hence authorize the authority of their own humanistic value construction that slavery had both materially made possible and held the barest potential to morally impinge. Hence, *Am I Not a Man and a Brother* tautologically served as verifying proof for what Sylvia Wynter calls the "infrasensory ontologized."[22] That is, the captive body could be symbolized for the senses so readily and so precisely because its fungibility had been so thoroughly rendered through the formal mechanisms of the plantation's scopic and auditory production. The space of circulation, exchange, wearing, hearing, empathizing, of drowning out, provided a space of controlled proximity to blackness vis-à-vis its aesthetic character. This pacified the phobic intrusion of revolting slaves in the holds and on the decks of ships; in fields, houses, and town squares; on the island of Haiti and on plantations across the New World.[23]

The image was widely reproduced on domestic objects like crockery and also became popular on fashion accessories. According to Clarkson, gentlemen had the image inlaid in gold on the lid of their snuffboxes. Of the ladies several wore them in bracelets, and others had them fitted up in an ornamental manner as pins for the hair. At length, the taste for wearing them became general; and thus fashion, which usually confines itself to worthless things, was seen for once in the honourable office of promoting the cause of justice, humanity, and freedom.[24]

The authority of reason, hermeneutically sealed in the echo chamber of this image, gained a new valiance in its circulation. Power and its alleged opposite were materialized as ornament. It became generalized as an articulation of aesthetic taste—a "consumer choice," a moral judgment—and this authorized the singularity of its fantastical authority. The reality that "the slave" is central to the story mastery wishes to tell itself about itself is revealed to be far more aesthetically and materially rooted than reason—as an agency for resolution and unification—would let on. The right thing to do must feel, look, and sound good; the right thing to do must be beautiful.

In his art historical description of *Am I Not a Man and a Brother*, David Dabydeen alludes to the conversion an enslaved black form initiated from that "which usually confines itself to worthless things" to something whose carving out ferries in a magnanimity that occasions its circulation and hence its value. How much value did carrying around an image of the enslaved have when your own body-servant followed you into town? Not only did *Am I Not a Man and a Brother* rematerialize any form of coinage to which it was affixed (purses, buttons, bags, coins, etc.) but, by proposing a new value in the disappearance of the enslaved from their prosthesis to their master, it reimagined and revalued the embodiment of mastery itself. Thus, while it is tempting to consign this value to the mere symbolic, this overlooks the very materiality created through the reproduction, the echoing and re-sounding of its circulation. How do we get from the materiality of enslaved black labor to the materiality of black culture and for whom and for what (value)? This is the question I am getting at with the aesthetic character of blackness.

The diminishing raw material of the plantation system as a mode of production had to be materialized elsewhere, especially the fantasized proximity to force and knowledge through which it extracted labor and through which it produced authority. As Hartman writes, "From the vantage point of the everyday relations of slavery, enjoyment, broadly speaking, defined the parameters of racial relations, since in practice all whites were allowed a great degree of latitude in regard to uses of the enslaved."[25] The circulation of *Am I Not a Man and a Brother* realized as it concealed the objectification of the (force of) the world "after slavery" as rooted in a related yet dialectically unresolved materiality of what I am calling the aesthetic character of blackness.[26] Because *Am I Not a Man and a Brother* revealed that a drawing could circulate as far and wide as the ships that were still transporting human cargo, it exposed a latent and emergent affective mastery as the new saving power of humanity, a saving power only attainable through the humanizing character of blackness.

Invoking the slave as a synecdoche for a world we do not want has significance both at the time of Douglass's sound-imaging as well as in our own time, especially within the oratory of the black radical tradition,[27] but it also has its affective and material limits, as Douglass's case illustrates in fascinating breadth. This re-presentation of "the slave" as a discursive and aesthetic object was more an attempt at the foreclosure of another possible end to the world of the slave society, the very set of projects the enslaved enacted in myriad ways before manumission. How I focus on a historical or even symbolic history of this figure of "the slave"—and this will be differently expanded and complicated in the following chapter—centers more on how and what this figure and figuration mediated and what was meant to exceed and fall away from its aestheticization. Black music, black culture, and later black art would become these focal points for the sifting and staging of the manageable and sociable character of a potentially ungovernable set of black relations.

As Jon Cruz has pointed out, within the Garrisonian tradition of abolitionism, Frederick Douglass initiated a call to white America to study the songs of the slaves as a testament and testimony to their humanity, and this provoked much of the early, albeit at times informal, humanistic scholarship on black music and culture.[28] This call exposed black music to a notoriety more commonly attributed to Douglass's slave narratives at the time, but it initiated an even more radical formal conversion that shifted black music from being an opaque and even threatening endogenous practice of the slave community into an unmediated document of black life wherein black life would increasingly be reduced to a pained and striving black humanity discernible imaginatively from without by its disembodied listener. What Daphne A. Brooks identifies as the technological properties of the slave narrative that provided "a looking glass . . . exposing the ordeals of bondage," was undoubtedly sonically transferred onto black music from the nineteenth century onward.[29]

Black music emerged as a formal sonic medium and media for the negotiation of profoundly materialized sentiments. This "looking glass" was as real as the lines that drew Douglass's sonic embodiment, a body that preceded and made possible the more formally recognized sonic technologies like the phonograph that I discuss in the next two chapters. That black life, through black music, would not just reflect an ultimate Rousseauean ideal pity but also a profound vanity of mastery propping up the civil society that viewed itself as "saving it from bondage" is part of the story I am tracking here. What the aesthetic character of blackness follows and asserts is that the re-formation of black plantation labor during and after emancipation also converted black life into a site of aesthetic justification and symbolic cultural production and extraction. To this end, this book is less concerned with making legible black music as an object of study than it is with the question of what black music makes and has made legible.

Through Frederick Douglass I am attempting to theorize the shape of this "looking glass" as a predecessor to and preconfiguration of the formal exegeses of technological media and mediation to come. The more speculative tenets of my argument in this chapter and the next are that the technological rationalization of the plantation funneled black culture into its last gasping arteries of production. Furthermore, that same rationalization, vouchsafed through the material and sentimental investments of the emerging (abolitionist) modes of humanization and aestheticization, facilitated new forms of cultural production for the slave society.[30] For as "the slave" was being made into an ugly denotation whose specific aesthetic presence and mode of regulation morally impinged upon the liberal imagination of an allegedly freed society that created it, the beauty of the humanizing character of blackness would be enlisted to humanize what was to come.

Beautifying Black Labor Through Black Song

What becomes beautiful is simply "not slavery," and what is good is simply good enough so long as it resists regressing to its increasingly mythological origins. The capacity to make black labor beautiful against black needs prospers only as it admonishes the totalizing ugliness and austerity of slavery, including the robust kinship of slave community and riotous anger of numerous slave rebellions that demanded a wholesale end to the slave society. Of course, the term "ugliness of slave labor" misnames the extractive and world-destroying violence of enslavement and by amending only the legal writ of slavability merely re-forms the material products and civilizing function of black labor. For out from under the ugliness of the sound and site of the whip, an internal instrument of discipline must be installed in the formerly enslaved.

The danger of the mythological saving function of black music is partially its capacity to beautify the grueling and alienating reality of black labor by gracing it with a moralizing function. The articulation of domination within black work is reduced solely to slave labor, allowing for beautification of black labor (once again) against black needs. The terms upon which enslaved black folks made music and the positive world they imagined is meant to be replaced by their humanization and beautification from without. Forced black labor is admonished so coerced free black labor can be made beautiful. Black work is thus sublimated to the humanizing character of the abolitionist movement such that once the yoke of slavery is symbolically removed, the work that escapes from underneath it is no longer or hardly regarded as oppressive. As Tera W. Hunter's seminal work *To 'Joy My Freedom* illustrates, the reality of black work, most especially black women's work, after manumission hardly changed.[31] Yet the aesthetic imaginary of black work, by the beautification of its regulation, had dramatically shifted from without. If black labor (once again) appears to be noncoercive, voluntary, contractual, self-regulating, edifying, beautiful, even if it still involved black folks doing the same material labor, then it beautifies the world by which it is exploited. This has eminently to do with the beautification of black work made possible through black music.

In Marx, the mythological beauty of art is only the longing for a mythological lost origin, although we could say that Douglass reaches similar conclusions. But the work of art also resurfaces in the aesthetics of work itself. Even Marx puts work in an aesthetic framing, maintaining that the subordination of work to production, especially in Adam Smith's moral theory, instills work with an ugly quality: "[Smith] is right, of course, that, in its historic forms as slave-labour, serf-labour, and wage-labour, labour always appears as repulsive."[32] Relatedly, the products or ends of "estranged labor" are divided by class: an abundance of "beauty" accrues to the bourgeoisie and "deformity" is doled out to the wage laborer. We might add that the brutality of criminalization coaxes production from the management of surplus populations who accrue neither the means of production nor, of course, the surplus production generated from the means of production.[33] The repulsive nature of slave labor was of course originally not strictly bound to the forms of production; in the caste mode of production, it was legally inscribed onto enslaved laborers and the system in which they slaved, which

1.4 "How Slavery Honors Our Country's Flag." Lithograph of procession of enslaved folks led by an enslaved musician playing a fiddle. Source: Fels African Americana Image Project, Library Company of Philadelphia (1835-02).

would be liberated increasingly into the society as race—not only gender-racialized labor, but the work of gendered race. However, during plantation slavery, black work and black song were held in equal disgust: "The coffle gang was a sight [and sound] that even proslavery Southerners found distressing and unpleasant, while abolitionists featured it as a standard object of provocation in their propaganda. The 'Song of the Coffle Gang' appeared in several antislavery songsters with 'Words by the Slaves.'"[34] One of the earliest images of black music, an 1835 illustration by the abolitionist publication *Anti-Slavery Record*, made just such an assertion about the aesthetic value of enslaved labor through black sounds (figure 1.4). The public "noise" created by the slave coffle registered the ugliness of bondage but not the inherent brutality of the labor within. The implication was that there ought to be a kind of black labor that was not "distressing" or "unpleasant" to its eavesdropper. It was not just a case of doing away with the whip. A force needed to be imagined that could beautify black labor as the still-necessary surplus product generated from the whip's alleged abolition. Transforming black labor as a form which was not merely coerced from without by the whip but compelled and regulated from within by a nascent black humanity. Out from under the force of the whip, the use value of black music would trickle out, if formed and tamed by the hands of the right kind of artist.

Of the scene and sound of enslaved labor, famed abolitionist John Rankin opined:

> In the Summer of 1822 . . . I witnessed a scene such as this never before witnessed, and such as I hope never to witness again . . . the sound of music (beyond a little rising ground) attracted my attention, I looked forward, and saw the flag of my country waving. Supposing that I was about to see a military parade, I drove hastily to the side of the road; and having gained the top of the ascent I discovered (I suppose) about forty black men all chained together after the following manner: each of them was handcuffed, and they were arranged in rank and file. A chain perhaps 40 feet long . . . was stretched between the two ranks. . . . Behind them were, I supposed, about thirty [black] women in double rank, the couples tied hand to hand. A solemn sadness sat on every countenance, and the dismal silence of this march of despair was interrupted only by the sound of two violins.[35]

The humanizing labor of black music-making arises like a counterposing melody to the silent drudgery of the enslaved procession. Rankin's description of enslaved labor adds an important compliment to Douglass's earlier description of the silence one must sit in first to "analyze the sounds" of the enslaved. Black sounding can thus be made to dialectically work on the black work it emerges from, giving sound to otherwise silent drudgery, and in turn beautifying its own productive capacities as beyond and above such work. This beautification itself thus achieves a new and another kind of work.

The black artist would be the kind of worker to make black work beautiful. The black artist would enact a kind of production to which Marx assigned no material when he argued that out from under the privation of political economy, work would be given its inherent "attractiveness," its innate beautiful character, and would not be realized as the social consequences of its disabling function. Contrary to Marx's assertion, however, that "cause slavery to disappear and you will have wiped America off the map of nations," the liberation of residual and emergent cultural modes of production in the dominion of production expanded the authoritarian power of the slave society, for what polices work into production has an aesthetic character too.³⁶ Black potentiated free labor and incarcerated peonage were the ploy or fulcrum against emerging privileged white, especially white men's, union wage labor in the form of labor rights in ways that Booker T. Washington tried to instrumentalize in his Atlanta Compromise speech or that W. E. B. DuBois, Claudia Jones, Tera W. Hunter, Clyde Woods, Talitha L. LeFlouria, and many others have more thoroughly discussed.³⁷ Out from under the productive capacities of work, the aesthetic character of blackness arted value through and against the waning mode of slave property and production. Again, if the finite and comparatively small community of slaves in the United States had been the extent of the disabling labor that beautified (the culture of) capitalist production, then manumission ought to have roughly disappeared the extractive extrinsic interest in black people and black life. But manumission merely occasioned the legal conversion and accretion in the interest of black people through the legal production of race. The re-formation of black labor was achieved through its arting.

The legalization or naturalization of black personhood was preceded and exceeded by the value of its aesthetic intimation. Marx may have run up against this impasse:

> In order that a man may be able to sell commodities that are other than labor-power, he must of course have the means of production as raw material, implements, &c. No boots can be made without leather. He requires also the means of subsistence. Nobody—not even "a musician of the future"—can live upon future products or upon use-values in an unfinished state; and man always has been, and must still be a consumer, both before and while he is producing.³⁸

Marx can be forgiven for not entirely prophesying what we now take to be the autopoiesis of speculation and financialization predicated on the synthetic future of capital in neoliberalism. But he may be attributed with underestimating the extent to which future music, if not the bondless and boundless speculation of futurity, could precisely arrive from the aesthetic valuation and imagination of something like the legalized nonpersons or nobodies of black music. What kinds of life can be lived as use values in unfinished states is perhaps a better question and is yet another way to stage the even more immediate antagonism that emancipation could have more directly brought about: the needs of black people against the needs of capital. But the extent to which this antagonism is violently discouraged from being waged out in the open is precisely at the heart of the sociability that is the aesthetic character of blackness.[39]

The putatively voluntaristic aesthetic labor of black music speculates on and accumulates the resource of beautified formalized black labor, first by emplotting a (new) will and willingness to work of the humanized character extracted from enslavement and second (and perhaps most obviously or famously) by identifying, in Sylvia Wynter's words, a "raw material" to be worked on as that source of black sociability.[40] The latter quite insidiously and extensively, at its worst, became the working on the proof of a will to work, creating the future in which the future musician could work on creating a future for others. This is a more formal description of the yoke of citizenship and responsibility heaped upon the recently manumitted, for Douglass's "humanizing character" was valued not just for the looking glass into the slave community it created but also for the kind of sociable legal person it could extract from black music. This dynamic is critical, for it would repeat into the twentieth century to similar effect. As I will discuss briefly in chapter 3, which aesthetic ethos would have a profound impact on which black musics got to be black music during the Harlem Renaissance and beyond. The antebellum and postbellum framing of black music was thus critical for crafting the beautified regulation of black life after slavery.

It is the contention of Frederick Douglass and indeed the members of the abolitionist movement that black music would humanize the enslaved as the precondition for or in the service of their journey to legal personhood and civil sociability. However, the extent to which black music would be used to humanize legal personhood and liberate the proprietary aesthetics of mastery that the legal reformation of enslaved labor required has been largely underestimated, if not outright overlooked. Marx's words, "nobody—not even 'a musician of the future'—can live upon future products or upon use-values in an unfinished state," in being so generous to our living, were perhaps too naïve about the parasitic life of capital whose latent presence, by infecting our aesthetic labor, dreams of acquiring our deaths against the necessity of what we might imagine otherwise. Because Marx could apportion the responsibility for revolutionary historical action only to workers, he limited and legislated both the imagination of work and the production to the usefulness circumscribed by the domination of work that legitimated the slave society.

Theodor W. Adorno suggested that Marx ought to have concluded with a "denunciation of useful labor" because its hinge marks the precipice of valuation from which wage labor is extracted:

> The principle of heteronomy, apparently the counterpart of fetishism, is the principle of exchange, and in it, domination is masked. Only what does not submit to that principle acts as the plenipotentiary of what is free from domination; only what is useless can stand in for the stunted use value. Artworks are plenipotentiaries of things that are no longer distorted by exchange, profit, and the false needs of a degraded humanity. In the context of total semblance, art's semblance of being-in-itself is the mask of truth. . . . A liberated society would be beyond the irrationality of its *faux frais* and beyond the ends-means-rationality of utility. This is enciphered in art and is the source of art's social explosiveness. Although the magic fetishes are one of the historical roots of art, a fetishistic element remains admixed in artworks, an element that goes beyond commodity fetishism.[41]

When Marx disappeared art to a mythical origin, a stage in development, he too easily overlooked the original theft that produced the public. The singing of the enslaved coffle in the *Anti-Slavery Record* is indeed regarded as extraneous to black labor itself but valued as a human remainder before and beyond enslavement. Douglass's own oft-cited description of his enslavement and escape—"You have seen how a man was made a slave; you shall see how a slave was made a man"—alludes to the usefulness of enslaved humanity contained in the humanizing character of black music.[42] Black music works on the labor such that black music will be the worked-on of labor, expanding its humanizing utility while itself never appearing as work. The subterfuge of animated black humanity tucked inside yet exceeding the labor of the enslaved in the form of the coffle must be liberated into the use value of legitimating the society that would justify the pseudo-liberation and manumission of the slave. In other words, freedom or the kind of freedom projected as inherent in black music could be dislocated from any autonomy for black life outside the mere humanizing function of black music. What black musical practices and activities—what black life—realized was that black liberation beyond its humanizing ends was merely the *faux frais* of increasingly "official" black musical production.

Perhaps black life lives, in the best way possible, as stunted use values, or use values in unfinished states.

Adorno's own thinking suggests (perhaps against itself) that the plenipotentiary function of art, positively depicted as freedom, can drive exchange to new modes of production by appearing as its glitzy or degraded opposite. Like Marx, this would have required Adorno to consider blackness as that which goes before and beyond the wage, before and beyond exchange, the use value that makes yet exceeds exchange value. The representative capacity or force of blackness eludes such thinking but must be brought back to and appropriated from that which has appropriated and separated it in order to deepen and expand the relevance of the music of any imagined future of any Marxist project. The aesthetic character of blackness attempts to partially think through how black representation, black culture, and black music occasioned the change in the form of value that did not inhere in the intrinsic value of the enslaved commodity form. Further, it is through this aesthetic character that the reimagination and expansion of the world, which required enslaved labor to begin with, will persist and take shape. Because black music often occupied or had projected onto it a nebulous volunteerism, even when inaugurated into more formal coercive labor economies, the modality of its cultural production and formalized beauty reflects a complex sociability and of course, as I will discuss in chapters 3, 4, and 5, an anti-sociability as well. The sociability of black music is thus conscripted to work on, to art, the means of official cultural production that makes black life both a resource and a target to be attacked.

Arting the Means of Cultural Production

It is important to situate Frederick Douglass as the floor rather than the ceiling of what abolishing slavery would involve, although his sound-imagining on the stage of abolitionism was meant to do something like the opposite. I want to situate Douglass's imagining on the stage of abolitionism as not a vivification of the slave's vision of freedom but in fact a constraining of the terms on which the enslaved could realize their freedom. The fantasy that the magic spell of legal writ would liberate the musical life at the heart of commodified slave community was a specific genre of reverie that was waged against the imagination and threats of more violent and total slave revolution. Representation (in all its incantations) would bar the door against the revelation of black humanity that could only be achieved with a forceful termination of the whole colonial order. Douglass was instead meant to establish a new institution, one less offensively "peculiar" (and more profitable to power) and more willfully agreeable to its expanded domination. Aesthetics engendered this regulative function and its productive capacity thrived through delimiting the imaginative end of slavery as mere (and often legal-symbolic) manumission of the enslaved rather than an end of the slave society. The world after slavery would not be the noisy rabble of revolting slaves but the quieter and more amenable frontier of a new aesthetic object: black music, black culture, black representation, and their arbiter, the black artist. Beautifying the world after slavery was of mutual aesthetic interest to hegemonic powers, even if the specific techniques of that beautification varied.

Through the regulative function of the aesthetic character of blackness, black music, and culture as black representation, would be made (increasingly) beautiful to make imagining an end to the slave society impossible and unnecessary. In other words, slavery and slave labor were ugly, but not the wholesale subordination and disposition toward premature death of black folks that would be arted and expanded after emancipation. Douglass's own unimaginative liberalism and assimilationism bounded his sounding on the stage of abolitionism and made audible his call for black humanization through black music's humanizing character. What occasioned Douglass's status as reputedly the most imaged person in the nineteenth century and carved out the space from which he sounded and spoke, as Neil Roberts notes, was significantly "Douglass's expression of assimilationism while he was still a fugitive slave [which] made him an ally of William Lloyd Garrison and American Garrisonians, whose moral suasion denounced racially charged language and abhorred any call to violence, revolutionary slave resistance and privileged rhetorical morality over physical struggle."[43]

Roberts identifies Douglass's belief in moral suasion as conditioned by his investment in Coleridgean romanticism. Douglass was invested in a certain aesthetic capacity that "marginality" could furrow and coax a pathway for itself to live in, by nestling in the imagination of, the mainstream of hegemony and authority.[44] Douglass aspired to occupy, to dwell in (just as the Kantian faculties dwell in), to diligently, but modestly and respectably work and live in (like an artist's live-work space is the compromise in a luxury condo project) the vertical imagination that humanizes domination. As much as Douglass has been largely viewed as a political figure, and while I would not call what Douglass makes art (although what he does puts to work the work of art), I cannot help but see him as a, or even *the* black artist, precisely because of the politics of his imagination or how he arts the world in the wake of the plantation.

That one could learn to read and write under the threat of death, experience and witness the most brutal violence to oneself and one's kin, endure backbreaking labor, realize often and especially one day that it is enough, impersonate a sailor to board a northbound train, jump that train for a Philadelphia steamboat and somehow make it to New York to a sense of reprieve and that from this one would conclude and espouse, much of their life, that voting would save us all, is both an entirely understandable yet wholly unsatisfying failure of imagination. Douglass's advocacy of the abolition of the form of slave property, under which black personhood largely suffocated, is less surprising when it is paired with his advocacy of legalized black personhood as property form—namely citizenship and voting—as the means of breathing life into the expanded artificial personhood and dominance of the state over forms of black life.

The dominant aestheticization of black life and sociality after legal emancipation moved into modes of self-possessed individuation, or what Saidiya Hartman refers to as "burdened individuality."[45] The burdened individuality tethered to the formerly enslaved bound the carrot of self-possession with the stick of criminalization. Between and beyond these structured forces lay the realm of black aesthetic justification that Douglass embodied and through which he created a captive sonic reproduction. Black music emerged at first as a place of imaginative, playful, resistant, and fugitive activity for the slave community, but then also as a site of original accumulation of black sentiments to be speculated upon and extracted from without. Saidiya Hartman notes in referring to Douglass that during slavery, "by encouraging entertainment, the master class sought to cultivate hegemony, harness pleasure as a productive force, and regulate the modes of permitted expression. . . . Slave masters managed amusements as they did labor, with a keen eye towards discipline."[46] The "managed amusements" of black laboring song, as Sylvia Wynter reminds us, contrasted with the outlawed funeral music of black drumming that sometimes "incite[d] slaves to rebellion."[47] Yet Douglass's standing on the stage of abolition stands at the precipice of valuations between the model reared by the plantation and the emerging open space of black cultural labor—and above all its resistances, now implanted within a potentially willful subject who needed to create similar exogenous managerial values through an expanded model of self-discipline and self-policing. Cultural capacity was thus increasingly foisted onto the soon-to-be-manumitted as a liberated form of domination from which new pathways of speculation could occur and from which new forms of productive labor could be realized.

Cultural production entered, and made possible, a mode of increasingly liberated performative social repression and domination as work—not just wage work, but quite importantly the work of art. While the black work of art would not be an explicit term of this period, like all work in capitalism, its original accumulation that established its increasingly official labor would. Frederick Douglass's re-sounding of black song thus made him a crucial artisan and conscript of this new valuation. The humanization of a new frontier is what much of Frederick Douglass's labor was pointing at.[48] W. E. B. Du Bois's early oeuvre of course drew this paradox into stark and violent relief. It was the "souls of black folk" that, animated with black music's humanizing function, were beautiful as they bore forth the aesthetic of a childlike innocence of a civil racial origin. But it was, in brutal irony, the lives and needs of actual black youth that Du Bois depicted in his earlier work, *The Philadelphia Negro: A Social Study*, that needed to be disciplined into sociability through black culture and black labor. Ungainly were the needs and wants of black youth, the very black youth who would grow up to be the blues generation following Reconstruction, populating, sheltering in, and building the urban blues music and blues performance venues, the brothels, clubs, and juke joints of Ma Rainey, Bessie Smith, and so many others. It was these "loafers at Twelfth and Kater streets" and "thugs in the county prison" who lived in a dangerous "atmosphere of rebellion and discontent that [the] unrewarded merit" of work made.[49] Du Bois imagined an internal motivic force, not a whip—perhaps against a whip, a soul to pierce through the "historical excuse" of slavery and Reconstruction that "count for little in the whirl and battle of bread-winning."[50] This soul itself would be beautified into its expressive aesthetic form, or what Du Bois rather famously and controversially referred to as "talent," for negro talents beautify work against the force of their social production of black austerity and misery. Talent speculates on black life through black work—and eventually through the black work of art.

A Musician of the Future

No longer only a site of mythic ridicule anchored to the "repulsive" labor of slavery (although again these exact modes of production persisted), black cultural labor was now granted a beautified relationship to black labor that produced a relatively worthy sociable black character whose participation in the world, however unevenly, would be justified. A new economy opened from the future into which Douglass is pointing. As Saidiya Hartman asserts, "Mastery became defined by self-regulation, indebtedness and responsibility, careful regard for the predilections of the former masters."[51] No longer consigned exclusively to a life of property that could not own or bear the possession of other property, the regulation of the aesthetic character of blackness meant expanding the production of "the self" and the consumption and internalization of "the self" that black life was now coerced into bearing. Adorno illuminates the place of the self and the individual that Douglass's rendering and career articulated: "While the artwork's sensual appeal seemingly brings it closer to the consumer, it is alienated from him by being a commodity that he possesses and the loss of which he must constantly fear. The false relation to art is akin to anxiety over possession. The fetishistic idea of the artwork as property that can be possessed and destroyed by reflection has its exact correlative in the idea of exploitable property within the psychological economy of the self."[52] "The psychological economy of the self" here is part of the economy that black music expands and into which black music escapes. The language of black self-development inaugurates a psychic economic frontier—an emerging market that had up to that point largely been deemed impossible if not useless to the productive powers of the market. Douglass did not point to a specific avenue of escape for the formerly enslaved—indeed, no such route could be so openly announced and represented. Douglass's own work on the Underground Railroad attests to this. Instead he pointed to a new market that would bear "the predilections of the former masters" in the positive character of a regulated black self who was working—as he was—the work of art.

Idealized black self-regulation acquired an insidious materialization that Marx simply called "use-value." Put better, it was that which could be made to work. If, in a very foundational Marxist sense, individuation is the product of capitalist production, then the development of black labor goes hand in hand with the development of a black self. And the problem of how to make use of the more than formal laboring time of the enslaved did not vanish but was dialectically folded into the imagination and aesthetics of emancipation. As the capacity for market wage labor emerged, manumitted black folks needed to be yoked with what we might call market leisure (that makes market labor); that is, a kind of (self-)regulated audible and perceptible time of liberated self-production in which the volunteerism of black art primed the coercion of formal black labor for official market values.

Marx relegated art to an idealized primordial mythology, a perpetual historical childhood characterized by childlike innocence and, most of all, an absented but implicit paternalism that becomes a residual possession and expression of bourgeois society's idealized innocence of its own dependence upon the violent production of capitalist value.[53] This meant that art symbolically occupied the place of the child in the bourgeois Victorian patriarchal family: useless to labor but as its future potentiation and useful to value only as an endless projection of innocence that perpetuates an ongoing if not eternal legacy—a future, almost a kind of property and certainly a possession. The relegation of this "childhood" to art's "uselessness" at once grants art an ambivalent singularity as the sole managerial repository for our imaginations, something like the inherent violence projected in innocence or the abuse of what it often means to be made into the child. Contemporary to Marx, the projections of black folks under slavery and beyond as "the childlike race" and "the musical race" bear out this ambivalent and violent paternalism.

W. E. B. Du Bois invoked this youthful formulation a great deal throughout his early writings, especially in his work that focused on how black spirituals stand in for black folks' souls. Du Bois referred to "the Negro," generationally succeeding Douglass as "the child of Emancipation," who at the dawn of the twentieth century was becoming a "youth with dawning self-consciousness, self-realization, self-respect."[54] Elsewhere Du Bois used another of his neologisms of black civilization at the turn of the twentieth century as a "race-childhood."[55] The violence of contemporary criminalization of black life was justified here under its necessary child-rearing function and the ongoing brutality of black labor was disappeared and resurfaced under an idealization of its aesthetic or beautifying function in marking and decorating black life as corresponding with and heading toward racial civilization.[56] In this view, work beautifies black life by helping black life "grow up."

It is this representative capacity as part of a psychic economic development, a "growing up," and not certain social and material relations that get liberated from bondage. Art too is robbed of its social relationality when its only intimacy is refracted through an increasingly alienated plenipotentiary. Black labor becomes an increasingly representable and increasingly public market, ironically far more public than the troubling coffle trudging through town. The alienation of black music into a productive economy, even when that economy was producing only the potential sociability of its worker, converted the "wild notes" of black being-together into an indifferent aesthetic character for judgment. Productive disinterest or what we might just call aesthetic value would now cohabitate with rather than be solely waged against the enslaved. The coarse desire and abject hatred fused in the consumption of minstrelsy was now supplemented with a universalizable "interest in aesthetic totality"; that is, "an interest in the correct organization of the whole."[57] Black music was no longer hidden from view or a designated quotidian reprieve that drove black people's laboring time—both sites where it often engineered strategic subterfuge and political resistance to enslavement. Now black music would become the burgeoning source for rationalization of black folks and their justification out from and beyond slavery.

Black music as both a closely held secret of a hidden circle and an opaque set of "wild notes" distantly overheard from up north pertained only to a mythology and so needed to be reared with a justification. Thus, for the first time what would become known as black music was subject to the *Gleichgültigkeit* that followed Frederick Douglass. *Gleichgültigkeit* is sometimes translated as "disinterest" or "indifference." However, *Gleichgültigkeit* is more helpfully characterized by Theodor Adorno and Harlem Renaissance aesthete Alain Locke as "aesthetic comportment," a meaning that captures not only the justificatory but also the embodied logic of the regulatory function of the aesthetic. A new value in black music was extracted from this disinterest or "aesthetic comportment" that was being both projected onto and introjected into the soon-to-be-manumitted. Against the (now) purely sentimentalized racism of the minstrel stage, whose dehumanizing mythology could no longer be so easily rationalized and that now needed to be retrospectively inaugurated into a regressive adolescence, a new character heralding a new sociability needed to be animated, for as Adorno intoned of the aesthetic, "there is no liking without a living person who would enjoy it." This aesthetic comportment sought to animate a form of ersatz life beyond the bounds of a living person's mere liking and, by extension, their mere living.[58] Black music would be extracted from black life and used to animate forms of proprietary, consumptive, and domestic life—not unlike the home where the sheet music bearing Douglass's image sits on top of the piano.

This pseudo-living was derived from what aestheticized beauty could capture and bring close and to which it could give justification. The question of whether black music could be likeable was now fused with the question of whether the white world could like black people. Could black music, as black people, be beautiful? Could it ferry this new likeability across from the din of slavery? Mastery needed to be again rationalized through a new objective and objectified order. Distinct from the minstrel stage, this version of mastery did not exclusively hinge on the "customary" purely sentimental rendering of plantation pastoralism.[59] Instead, black music would now be subjected to a deeper aesthetic rationalization, to study, technological capture, regulation, and a kind of legalization. In the next two chapters, I will discuss this means of rationalization, exposure, and representability primarily as it concerns the initial study and phonographic reproduction of black music in the late nineteenth and early twentieth centuries.

Equally important, and this cannot be overlooked, for it is essential to my argument, the humanization of black music would have the even more profound effect of humanizing the litigious eavesdropping and the eavesdropper who ratified it. In other words, it was not just that black music became a kind of cultural labor for producing the beautiful and (in the late nineteenth and early twentieth centuries) a commodity. Because black labor was beautified through black music, the sociability of black life that could be made intelligible, human, and deserving of its domination by the social was beautified and legitimated. This beautifying capacity was not endemic to black music, but it was inherent in the aesthetic character of blackness extracted from without.

In the next chapter I will track a related inscription of the black phonographic voice, whose materialization I am locating in these preceding humanizing gestures of the abolitionist movement. The more explicit technological rationalization I discuss in the following two chapters is thus made possible here by my specific framing of the aesthetic character of blackness and its capacity to make that wilderness more navigable. My analysis does more than locate technological rationalization or technological modernity within the predominant avenues of scientific reason common to sound studies, which tend to see black sounds as epiphenomenal or even extraneous to the instruments and instrumental rationality that captures them. Yet I do not imagine a mythically resistant black music simply takes hold of these technological modes of rationalization. Rather, I see a complex and uneven dialectical cohabitation of these two, if they can even be separated. As Frederick Douglass's standing suggests, this cooptation vests in this black aesthetic character a rented power whose totemic or symbolic realization requires and belies a process of its structuring, its building up, its development, its "growing up." The instituting of this aesthetic character of blackness required the appropriation of our living for its institutions.

By understanding the authority of our audiovisual representation as an always partially rented occupation of power and therefore a partial legitimation of power over us, I hope to bring up its building up as well as the potential for its demolition. This representation and instituting illustrate that the purpose of this rented occupation is to maintain a social order and a life that lives against our own living. Douglass lived in this rented space in the republic he left behind in flight. As we will see, the authority of the rationalization and mediation of this social will make what we leave behind seem and sound even more opaque against its façade of towering glass. The integration of the formerly enslaved (in the next chapter the formerly enslaved and first black recording artist George W. Johnson) will bear out a tenuous need for racism and the slave society to be rethought through the domestic registers of the intimacy of recording. Indeed, through the sounds of the recently manumitted the social order had to imagine and reconfigure its new modes of capture.

To be clear then, there is a complexity to this hollowing out. After all, the horrors of the slave hold attest to something beyond their measured depth. The aesthetic expanded and complicated a power liberated through emancipation that cannot simply be reduced to a recapitulation of formal legal bondage. I interrogate this representative process out of a ruthless critique that centers the possibility of our living in, against, and out from under representation's hold (on us). The recurring figures of empty space, vacuity, hollowed-out holes, and holds that persist throughout this text point out that the perceived nothingness of black personhood is quite often an imaginative space of black social, political, musical, and artistic experimentation. This space is profoundly encroached upon and policed by the instrumentalized imagination and rationalization that thought—and keeps needing to rethink—a property form around the forms of black life.

More Nearly Members of the Family

THE UGLY HISS

2

Sound has no parents.
> Ornette Coleman, quoted in Burke, "The Father of Harmolodics"

Nearness, it seems, cannot be encountered directly. We succeed in reaching it rather by attending to what is near. Near to us are what we usually call things.
> Martin Heidegger, *Poetry, Language, Thought*

The black voice began with(in) a breath of chattel slavery. Born onto a Virginia slave plantation around 1846, George W. Johnson became the first black artist of the phonograph—and one of the first recording artists. At an early age, Johnson became interested in music, allegedly through his proximity to his masters. In an attempt to characterize George W. Johnson's early life, historian Tim Brooks quotes a "local [Virginia] historian" who speculates: "I have a feeling that [slaves] were more servants than slaves in that area of small owners they were more nearly members of the family, as suggested in the case of Sam Moore [the son of Johnson's master] and George [W.] Johnson."[1] In his somewhat apologetic though admittedly expansive account of Johnson's life, Brooks further develops the familial and especially fraternal overtones of Johnson's life under slavery, noting that it was in fact from his master's son Samuel Moore—to whom Johnson was a "bodyservant"—that Johnson became interested in music:

> George Johnson gained more than a long-lasting friendship from this early entrée into the white world. Master Samuel was given instruction on the flute at an early age. As Samuel developed into "an expert flute

player" it was later reported, "the slave learned to imitate the notes. Johnson could soon whistle any tune that he had ever heard." The seeds of Johnson's later musical career were planted.[2]

Apparently, Johnson's imitative capacity, which was the result of and key to his access to the "white world," as much endeared him to his captors, his adoptive "family," as it alienated him from his symbolic kin in the fields. Brooks writes, "[Johnson] was fortunate to be living with a white family who treated him so well. He was envied and no doubt taunted by the field hands whose lives were so much rougher."[3] Johnson's whistling, the means of his sentimental "friendly" endearment and above all recognition in "the white world," was also how his implicitly fractured family lineage under the institution of slavery could be effaced. Johnson's whistling secured his honorary adoptive human status in a familial and social order predicated on the disavowal of the differently brutal and violently inscribed social structure on which it depended.

In Brooks's description, the bonds of affection and even (familial) empathy function as more subtle though still violent modes of possession within the chattel slave system and its aftermath, of which the "white family" was and is a constitutive part.[4] Johnson's prosthetic relation to the white family was fortunate because it achieved an aesthetic value removed from the presumed physical brutality or fight of slavery. Of course, the lives of house slaves were merely differently brutal from the lives of their kin in the fields. But Brooks's projection of Johnson cannot conceive of the brutality of black life after manumission as coercively brought into and sublimated under the white family. Johnson's place as a house slave assigned him a highly proximal coercive intimacy as a "bodyservant," and Brooks's partial celebration of such a position reproduced the same unimaginable violence of fraternity that plagued Frederick Douglass's romantic appeal. The "taunting" that Brooks imagines suggests that he cannot fathom a world in which black liberation means the abolition of the plantation family. The abolition of the white family, whether along with the burning of the plantation that produced it down South or the burning of the factories that built its decadence up north, had to be cast and recast again and against the reproduction of the threat of an allegedly imitative diminished black double that it wished to reinherit and rebuke through manumission. Brooks assumed the necessary and legitimate sublimation of black life into an imitative white family model. The dominion of the white family had to be liberated over the always ongoing and emerging threat of black social relations. The abolition of the human property form required the rethinking of the property form of the family and its interiority that we hold under the intimacy of domesticity or its body service. In this chapter, I raise the question of how nearness is constructed, fabricated, imagined, and contested through the black voice. I analyze this intimacy through and against how originality, origins, and mimesis stalk and engender the canons, communities, purposiveness, and codes of symbolic belonging of the black aesthetic tradition.

In this chapter I will consider the black voice in terms of how it illustrates the variously regulated forms of nearness, proximity, domesticity, and intimacy during legal enslavement and in the Reconstruction Era immediately following emancipation. Thus, I invoke the black voice as a site for considering the aesthetic and especially sonic reformation of social relations after manumission. The humanizing character of Frederick Douglass, rescued from the abjection of slavery and transported to the parlor pianos of white abolitionists' homes, helped carve new aesthetics of social relations for the white domestic, private, and public spheres as well as the spaces of black life from which black voice emanated, including, perhaps most provocatively, the space of the interiority of the formerly enslaved. I thus invoke structures and figures of intimacy and nearness such as family, fraternity, patrilineality, and humanity as further complicated and made possible through aesthetic regulation and characterization of blackness "after slavery." These are all sites that made possible and essential a curiosity, a proximity, and a "love" of black culture while violently regulating the lives of black people. George W. Johnson's life and career illustrate this quite powerfully. Finally, I think about how all these primarily domestic and private spaces of intimacy, accumulation, and knowledge production facilitate a model for navigating the impending world of technological rationalization embodied primarily (sonically) in the phonograph. How did the various "informal" methods of (re)capture or reformed capture of black sounds, black music, and its humanizing character re-create the potentiated masterly eavesdropping on the plantation? And how did this kind of proximity or nearness facilitate technological forms of capture like that of sonic reproduction in the phonograph? Thus, in the black voice I locate overlapping and mutually constitutive crises through manumission to reconcile the social origin of blackness beyond legal enslavement and formal slave labor and the origin of the voice through the phonographic recording's invention. My aim in this chapter is to consider how black representation—here figured as "the black voice"—liberated the world but merely reformed the bondage of black people.

Family Origins, Family Originality

George W. Johnson would never have been adopted by the newly forming canon of the black cultural that Frederick Douglass was arguing for and that white abolitionists and early ethnomusicologists were directly and indirectly helping to construct. In this abolitionist canon, only a putatively original yet imitative complementary sensitive form of beautifully pained black humanity could be located. Johnson stands firmly outside the circle Douglass drew because his mimesis did not require the empathy around which Douglass was building the black musical and cultural. Again we can see an overlapping apathy in Brooks's assumptions about the implicit "safety" of Johnson's symbolic fraternity in the white family. Johnson's presumed mimicry and inclusion fails to adequately occupy and make immersive and inhabitable, to make employable and make more available by making newly plentiful a fruitful black humanity. This partially confesses what I am asserting throughout this work: the humanization of the slave society is a process that requires the capturing, recording, and collecting of its most marginal into a paradigmatic of assimilable sameness through aesthetic regulation. Just as black art and culture would be driven toward a "Negro civilization," so too would black art and culture be refracted through a domesticity that carries the fantasy of the white family. A child does not get to be a child that cannot grow up to reproduce their own (white) family.

This aesthetic predicament of the white family is at the heart of the impending and emerging aesthetic character of blackness. Perhaps ironically for us, the whistling and laughing that defined Johnson's musical career, much like the piano work of Thomas Bethune, a disabled mid-nineteenth-century black musical prodigy, was barred from this kind of black cultural origin of a burgeoning black humanity, precisely because their formal sounding and technical capacities were deemed purely imitative of an a priori white humanity. The bitter irony is worth mentioning that the dependence of Douglass and later prominent "race men" such as Locke and Du Bois on decidedly Victorian prose never called into question their patrilineage or decreased their own paternal authority to construct such canons. Johnson's whistling and laughing, Douglass's black cultural trajectory might argue, both formally and affectively bore no signature of a cultural origin in the pained yet emerging black human, but instead resounded the sealed nature of domination that Douglass identified with the minstrel stage. We might then ask: Does Johnson belong to the regulatory aesthetic of the character of blackness if no human character can be extracted from his alleged imitation? After all, Johnson was, as I will show, a figure whose artistry seemingly affected a naked regression, a "back to slavery" rather than "up from slavery." On the one hand, this lack of originality in Johnson's oeuvre was unforgivable to a black artistry, but in being so condemnable, it raises questions about the limits of the trajectory of the humanizing character of black music and black culture.

Through George W. Johnson, the empty projective space, the frontier to which Douglass is pointing that we might initially assume is north and away from the South, perhaps ironically initiated a new engraving and inscription "down South." Indeed, this contradicts the common contention of a "studied-up" black bourgeois aesthetic tradition that extended from Douglass to DuBois and Alain Locke that would espouse and conflate a progression and development with a northern trajectory as the sociable and civilized fundament for producing an official black art and culture. Alain Locke asserted about black art in the early twentieth century that "the trend of migration has not only been toward the North and the Central Midwest, but city-ward and to the great centers of industry—the problems of adjustment are new, practical, local and not peculiarly racial."[5] Flight from the slave community and the excision of its involuntary racialization became synonymous with the tabula rasa requisite for "Negro civilization" and Alain Locke's famous "New Negro." Of course, we can glean from Brooks's projection onto Johnson's inscription, which took place in 2004 and not 1904, why this excision might be tempting in certain corridors of black thought. A certain aesthetic impulse must fill the projected vacuity, whether it is in Brooks's historiographic fantasy of patrilineage or the Harlem Renaissance's regulation of what is run from in the positive character of a "Negro civilization"; the presumed emptiness of Johnson's ancestry must lead to his eviction. That eviction is only for what cannot be lived in, for, in the ominous contention of Henry Louis Gates Jr., "the only way that you can fight a representation in art that you don't like is to create new art, to create more art, to surround it."[6] The surrounding or "encircling," as Fred Moten and Stefano Harney have called it, must evict people and things that do not adhere to its aesthetic beautification of blackness.

Black music and culture were thus imbued with the desire for both a representable patrilineage and a fraternal functioning, the regulation of a functional home and a sociable brotherly civilizing project as an adjunct to the white world (and not against it). This is sounded in Du Bois's famous words: "Make it possible for a man to be both a Negro and an American, without being cursed and spit upon by his fellows."[7] This fraternity provides the integrity of the black cultural, of the family, of the internalized rationalization and paranoia of the white world's representability, or what Du Bois alludes to as an aesthetic inheritance of black individuation: "For brown were his father's eyes, and his father's father's. And thus in the Land of the Color-line I saw, as it fell across my baby, the shadow of the Veil. Within the Veil was he born, said I; and there within shall he live,—a Negro and a Negro's son."[8] Du Bois embodies in "the veil" what Gates alludes to as bad representations. The responsibility of "surrounding" those with "good representations" is a patrilineal task that reproduces an aspirationally patriarchal structure—a family, a fraternity, a brotherhood, or a fellowship of humanity. This justificatory spirit is implanted in the black artist and in the humanizing aesthetic character of blackness.

George W. Johnson complicates the origination and individuation that the humanizing character of blackness is charged with officiating and regulating. Johnson would certainly not be celebrated by the black aesthetes and cultural theorists of the Harlem Renaissance who came to prominence a generation after him. However, Johnson's individuation, as the first black artist of the phonograph, alludes to and exposes many of the problems with the representability of black music and black art that would become the dominant ethos in the twentieth century. I thus do not seek to add Johnson to the twentieth-century canon of black art and the black artist and by implication expand such a canonizing and categorizing project of patrilineage. Rather I want to listen to Johnson's career precisely for how it disturbs the regulatory humanizing aspirations of later black aesthetics. Johnson's centrality to the phonograph—with which he is far more aligned in historical treatments than anything commonly and canonically rendered as black music—more nearly makes him kin with its modes of reproduction over and against the re/production of the black cultural that Douglass, and certainly later more institutionally minded aestheticians such as Alain Locke or Amiri Baraka would embrace. Namely, Johnson's individuation brought to fruition the symbolic recognition of a human voice; Johnson humanized the human voice, not himself. And this is the dark secret that Douglass could not quite admit. But, interestingly, it was Johnson's rendering by and facilitation of phonographic sounding that points to the limits of "the family of man" through its coerced proximity to that family's most intimate formal registers. This intimacy was repeated in every forcible reproduction of Johnson, including the inscription of him into modes of historical study by scholars such as Brooks.

Brooks wrote, "Nevertheless the 'Peculiar Institution' was a fact of life, one that demeaned and sometimes brutalized its victims. The scars on George's father may bear mute testimony to this."⁹ Brooks's downplaying of the violence of slavery that occasions his speculative and indeed imaginative leap here is intriguing. After an exhaustive and meticulous historiographical project, Brooks could still only speculate about the graphic nature of Johnson's slave genealogy. Johnson's slave ancestry has been all but effaced due to the hegemonic archive, which privileges (however minutely this can even be said of a still relatively obscure figure) the positivism of Johnson's family and fraternity in slavery rather than the symbolic order from which he was perpetually ripped and much later imaginatively and symbolically yoked. With his imaginative leap into Johnson's father's scars, Brooks left the racial pillars of chattel slavery, the slave society, and the white family intact because he could only think to locate Johnson's genealogy within the symbolic order of patrimony and not the alleged disinheritance of the "slave community" whose modes of attachment emerged not from the (self-)possession of inheritance but from getting caught up in practice.¹⁰

It did not seem thinkable for Brooks, as it did not seem thinkable for early scholars of black music in the 1860s, that the "original" proclamations of white intimacy and nearness, from which so much authority over the cultural was produced, were made possible by their refraction through enslaved labor, especially the domestic and emotional labor of house slaves like Johnson. Because the white family's only practice is the (arbitrary) assignation and categorization of its normative domination and authority ("son," "father," etc.) made possible by the subjugation and obliteration of the kinship ties of the enslaved, it must see its own normative cultural registers imitated and reproduced as pure functioning authority. Simply put, what Johnson imitates is not his white family, as Brooks (mirroring Johnson's own phonographic career) reductively frames it. Imitation is the only capacity for having culture, imitation is the only capacity for having. Having, possessing, must come from an origin, it is the childlike foundation, the aesthetic justification for having, for approaching possessing anything like property.

In a complex deconstruction of Lacanian thinking, Hortense Spillers raises such an issue:

> The African-American male has been touched, therefore, by the *mother*, handed by her in ways that he cannot escape, and in ways that the white American male is allowed to temporize by a fatherly reprieve. This human and historic development—the text that has been inscribed

on the benighted heart of the continent—takes us to the center of an inexorable difference in the depths of American women's community: the African-American woman, the mother, the daughter, becomes historically the powerful and shadowy evocation of a cultural synthesis long evaporated—the law of the Mother—only and precisely because legal enslavement removed the African-American male not so much from sight as from mimetic view as a partner in the prevailing social fiction of the Father's name, the Father's law.[11]

For Du Bois, black individuation is the patrilineage and passing down of the veil of racial consciousness, the proper internalization of knowing the white world's judgment and constructing the proper judgment and representations "to create more art, to surround it" as response. Spillers thus alludes to how aesthetic originality itself is a mimetic view that emerges from "the prevailing social function of the Father's name, the Father's law," which excises the kind of shadowy evocation, or what Spillers has elsewhere referred to as "the shadow family" that has no juridical, symbolic, or aesthetic justification or claim to possessing and having. George W. Johnson's alleged disinheritance, which is alluded to only as a disappeared slave community, is thus threateningly insufficient for the rented space of black aesthetic humanization. Johnson's rental application, which he never submitted to begin with, is denied, for no one could vouch for him. He had no credit (which is worse than bad credit), he had refused and had been refused the white humanistic and individuated debt from which the system of lineal credit emerged.

The assignation of the origin as the mourning of the absence of patrilineage is the production of the father's necessary and vital (yet unlived) unfriendly and estranged fullness, the value and authority that accrues through a vacant place. It legitimates the surrogate authority of the father, normalizes the wage-based productive capacity of the family and the rights-bearing subject—which is to say, the authority of the state—as the only capacity to possess and to have, all of which emerges in Brooks's treatment of Johnson. This same justification emerges in certain patriarchal overrepresentative black cultural traditions as the only precondition for saving, keeping, and having, or what amounts to the projective scarring Brooks imagines on Johnson's father. This making present or representation, these representative capacities are very much part of what I am calling the aesthetic character of blackness.[12] This assignation of the origin mistakenly folds the dissension of relation and accountability that the slave community may have practiced and required into the authority of the representation and representability of the family. Origins are how one creates family, not accountability. The mythic origin, which is to say art, arts black life into something like family against its relation, and the rationalization of the black family, "Negro civilization," and later "the black community" runs roughshod over its conditions of accountability.

Nahum Dimitri Chandler sharply expounds such a situation as it pertains to the production of black folk, particularly African Americans, when they are produced as subjects of (patriarchal) discourse:

> Typically, the procedure is something like this: the system in which the subordination occurs, because it exists, is analytically presupposed, and then the subjects are inserted into this preestablished matrix to engage in their functional articulation of the permutations prescribed therein. The general, and salutary, concern has been to formulate, in the most balanced and sustainable manner, an account of the simultaneous production of the position of the subordinated subject as nonoriginary and displaced, and as resistant to subordination and creative practice. Yet in producing such an account, the constitution of the general system or structure in which, and by which, that (African American) subject is gathered or constructed has remained analytically presupposed or unthought, if not simply assumed. Which is to say that the system is not thought, that the system itself is approached within the circuit of analysis as preconstituted, that the system itself is assumed and presupposed.[13]

Drawing on any kind of unitary origin for George W. Johnson would appear to require a fractured social order, an order perhaps as fractured as the supposed purity of the white family and the "white world," whose very name and constitution were continually cut and made possible by Johnson's imaginary and symbolic presence. Angela Davis alerts us to and allows us to think a similar dimension of the unthought inheritance and the felt but unrepresented force of the slave community that remains in black life. In the slave community, Davis suggests, cobbled-together, practiced relations and lineages under forced reproductive labor undergird and exceed its capacity to produce the infinite accrual of the white (plantation) family.[14] For Davis, resistance to structural oppression is the ongoing practice of the slave community's black sociality rather than (merely) the dead relation and the accumulation of symbolic inheritance, of the father, of the father's father and their name. Pulling Davis and Chandler into conversation highlights the slave community and its unknown and unthought origins as more than a total site of loss or nothingness. Quite the contrary, the slave community or "the shadow family" is a robust site against which the aspirational patriarchal authority and its origin of inheritance in the white (plantation) family had to be aesthetically defended.[15] This slave community and this shadow family are that which the positive paranoia of the family as property must be established against.

In thinking of Johnson's phonography, we can think about not just "what binds Johnson to his relatives whether they have claimed him or not" but what remains helpfully unrepresentable in that binding, what must be invented and reinvented against the binding that is the aesthetic character of blackness.[16] My attention to Johnson here also hopes, like the broader argument of the book, to disturb the vaunted idealism and perfectionist development of black culture and black cultural objects as prescriptive sites of resistance in light of their management and regulation of resistance. Johnson's phonography is crucial to a black musical genealogy imagined and created through the phonograph because his work at once allows us to understand the way black musical traditions are and can be "invented" rather than romantically "discovered." This necessarily entails troubling the opposition between black culture and mass culture, particularly the supposed mass culture of technological modernity, which is often figured as the neutral and unremitting captor of black sounds and black lives.[17] From Johnson's narrative we can begin to understand the fabricated nature of technological modernity as one homogenous totality that black music and blackness are seen as mere appendages to, always already romantic vernacular opponents or, equally scurrilously, unthought and presupposed additions.[18] In this regard, Johnson's original narrative provides a provocative conceptual framework through which to understand the phonograph in terms of the aesthetic character of blackness and especially its construction of "the black voice."

Brooks's retelling of Johnson's story implies that from his early life, Johnson's musical expression was reduced to an economy of deficient, even uncanny mimesis. Johnson's voice was a reproduction, but one that was recognizable as such through its differing medium: whistling. Johnson's voice, his whistling—the very means by which he later would attain fame through the phonograph—was deemed a formally different, yet effectively recognizable reproduction of "his master's voice." In whistling, Johnson captured and reproduced the sounds of his master's flute, at once acknowledging the coerced kinship, the proximity, and even the uneven fraternity of their relationship as well as the radical formal dissimilarity of his reproduction. His whistling then also represents the impossibility of the very fraternity that supposedly produced it.

The Mimesis of the Human Voice

The acknowledgment of Johnson's gesture as recognizable only as imitative of "his master's voice" forecloses the possibility of Johnson's equality within the fraternity that supposedly constitutes humanity. Johnson was denied a human voice, or even more insidiously, he was offered one only as a recognizably affective gesture of imitation. Johnson's narrative, however, goes beyond the important though rather obvious point that as a slave he was sentimentally offered and denied his master's fraternal form of humanity.[19] More crucially, Johnson's musical training points to how the human voice and a concept of humanity were never a priori constituted objects within this relation. On the contrary, as the narrative flow of Johnson's training tells us, the human voice always had to be reproduced before it could be present, before it could forge its own recognition. The human voice would always require its imitative, instrumental, and technological other, not as its ontological opposite but rather as its very constitutive possibility.

In his important work *Blues People*, Amiri Baraka highlighted such a condition: "There was no communication between master and slave on any strictly human level, but only the relation one might have to a piece of property—if you twist the knob on your radio you expect it to play."[20] Even in his early years, Johnson was forced to stand in the place of a kind of imitative or reproductive sonic technology, perhaps foreshadowing the waning years of his recording career when he would be replaced by "slot machines."[21] Johnson's capacity for imitation, his technique, which was both the affirmation and disaffirmation of his fraternity within the white world, within his "'family" belied the membranous inscription of his father's scars that made Johnson's reproduction possible and necessary. Like the radio, Johnson was disallowed from having or possessing the music he made, affectively granting the sounds he made a kind of Pythagorean or acousmatic meaning. Johnson's sounds were meant to be more reproductive even than imitative, for they referred to and affirmed his non-origin in the productive capacities of others.

Johnson's imitative whistling then signified a double dislocation in which his genealogical lines were displaced from the symbolic order of slavery and relocated in the novel imitative economy of "the white world." His whistling signified the displacement of phonic material (the black voice) from the commodified (legacy of) graphical inscription of chattel slavery, the very order that made his whistling possible and necessary. Johnson's narrative and, more important, his music in the early days of the phonograph must be understood as central to the genealogy of the phonograph and indeed all sonic technology, particularly because Johnson's work illuminates how the split between the phonic and the graphic was tied to the recognition of the black voice. In this phonographic economy, the human voice was a perpetually offered as a perpetually deferred ideal through the possibility and failure of mechanical reproduction.

This deferment, this mechanical failure of the reproduction of the human voice was supplemented by the ideality and phenomenal presence of the black voice. The black voice was the idealized object in a system of commodification in which the pornographic scars of slavery and the inscription of sound, its very possibility, were at once reduced to what Marx famously called a "social hieroglyphic."[22] The black voice became a force and an object whose capacity to speak, whose animation via its commodification in capitalist exchange, and whose perceived qualitative and quantitative similitude made possible the human voice through sonic reproduction. The black voice engendered the repetition that wrote phonographic modernity precisely when the black voice as a fungible object of plantation reproduction was being gradually dispersed and so had to be reappropriated upon manumission.

We cannot presume that Johnson's work was merely imitative of some prior and now corrupted referent or origin and simply reify the singularity of the reconstruction of the black voice. To take such a position would efface the way his music and his voice engendered the very recognition of such a repetition in the first place.[23] We cannot believe that "his master's voice," the voice of Samuel Johnson, was never whole or never there before Johnson's whistling. Even more, we cannot, as Frantz Fanon has shown us, assume that the body of Johnson's master was present before Johnson's whistling opened and seemingly closed that bodily schema in which the master whistles and the slave copies. To do so would presume a kind of wholeness of the white (plantation) family in which Samuel Johnson was reared, as if it was not violently cut through as it was made possible by the cutting of the black kinship it tried to obliterate as its supplement. The presence of the Negro, as Fanon notes, haunts the white man: "At the extreme, I should say that the Negro, because of his body, impedes the closing of the postural schema of the white man—at the point, naturally, at which the black man makes his entry into the phenomenal world of the white man."[24] If for Fanon this "postural schema" is disallowed closure from its requisite black subjection, then whiteness's project of territorialization is as much constituted by blackness's capacious opening and openness as it is by the requirement of the policing of that open space as its own co-constitutive means of embodiment. Blackness was supposed to be a deeply anticipated emptiness that was available for endless white speculation and projection. Johnson's whistling—through its supplemental mimesis—created not only his master's voice but also its capacity to hear and listen to itself as such.

Johnson's voice was not the origin of the black voice but the focal point through which propriety and property in the voice as such could be reimagined. Thus, we must locate Johnson's music as a central force in the founding of early phonographic technology. I will chart how a conception of the black voice contributed intimately to the forms of imaginative and symbolic embodiment that made phonographic technology possible. Undoubtedly, one of the most pervasive ideals of embodiment that contributed to establishing phonographic technology was the idea of "the human."[25] The structure of the black voice allows us to understand, as Alexander Weheliye has pointed out, that "Blackness ... cannot be defined as primarily empirical nor understood as the non/property of particular subjects, but should be understood as an integral structuring assemblage of the modern human."[26] It is in this sense that we might get at understanding the ear of Johnson's master, the structure of which would be liberated in and as the phonograph. The surrogate mastery made possible by listening would become the supplemented, yet absented means by which Johnson's seemingly mimetic musical practices could be identified and recognized. Even more, we might understand how the supposedly white normative body of phonography is continually cut through and through by the disavowed supplement of the black voice. It is with this in mind that I turn to the blackness of the phonautograph.

Phonographic Inventions

In his "speculative history" of sound, *The Audible Past*, Jonathan Sterne posits the centrality of shifting ideals of the human body in the nineteenth century. Specifically, Sterne considers the attempts to codify something like "the human body" and how they informed key developments in sound technology. Sterne connects the changing conceptions of "the human ear" and the development of Leon Scott's phonautograph and Alexander Graham

Bell's "ear phonautograph."[27] The phonautograph, which French scientist Edouard-Leon Scott de Martinville invented in 1855, was a device that captured acoustical sounds through a "barrel-shaped horn" and recorded them as visualizations in script:

> In this instrument the sound to be examined is concentrated upon a small drum of India-rubber or goldbeater's-skin, to the centre of which is connected a long and light strip of wood having a point at the end. The air-waves [of speech] beat upon the drum and cause it to vibrate in exactly the same manner as the particles of air themselves; the vibrations of the drum are communicated to the strip of wood, causing the pointed end of it to perform the same motions on a larger scale.[28]

The etchings of the vibrations of the air were then committed to a piece of smoke-blackened paper, inscribing the paper with a record of the acoustical source: the human voice.[29] The phonautograph provided a kind of analogy then between the phenomenal and phonological presence of sound and the graphical representation of sound in writing. This acoustical representation of sound looked something like the results of a polygraph or a seismograph; it was often a scribble of lines analogous only to the vibration that caused it, flouting an emerging epistemic idealism by returning the voluminous expectations projected onto the voice into an austere flattened glyph.

The phonautograph's receiving horn or "drum," as Sterne notes, was modeled to mimic the tympanic function of the ear in receiving sound. In Rilke's famous treatment of the inscriptive surface and writing mechanism of the phonograph's stylus, he imagined their impressions to be working something like the opaque capacity of human intellection, memory, and eventually the unconscious.[30] Extending Rilke's ruminations, media theorist Friedrich Kittler wrote, "The markings 'traced on the cylinder' are physiological traces whose strangeness transcends all human voices."[31] The surface of the phonautograph, by merely holding that which exceeded the sound of the voice, threw back at its would-be beholder an uncanny and unsettling—disfiguring even—image of self. The surface onto which the phonautograph wrote engendered a great deal of anxiety about its writtenness as a mode of incommunicability. Not unlike the differentiating force Derrida identified as inherent in quotation, the writing of the phonautograph brought into partial recognition the possibility of death in and against its very offer of what Thomas Edison claimed would be the "immortality" of the phonograph.[32] By "immortality" Edison meant that the phonograph—not the phonautograph—would cement and expand social individuation through the liberation of personal property. This liberation was coincident with and contingent upon the emergence of mass-produced commodities. The precipice the phonograph broached was not the specter of death and the precarity of the corporeality it rationalized. Edison's "immortality" mourned the masterly "body-reasoning" of racialization that was shifting with legal emancipation and that in order to be given greater life had to be liberated and made to deputize more and more.[33] The perpetuity of the phonograph, Thomas Edison ensured, would come from its "captive sounds" or "sounds that were heretofore fugitive," what Edison later called "fugitive sounds," the capture of which would ensure "their reproduction at will."[34] Edison conflated that will over the fugitive with a natural law, the objective reason, that was at the center of the unfolding of the human voice. In Edison's view, the human voice wanted to be captured.

The internal organic logic of the voice was conflated with its disclosure in capture; the rights over the appearance of the voice became isomorphic with its internal properties themselves. This is partially because the aesthetics of the phonautographic glyph failed their mimetic narcissistic function—the glyphs all but looked back like the sound of ripples on the surface of the lake. The phonautographic voice stands obdurate in a long history of the voice as a source of obedience.[35] In the sound-image of the slave coffle of singing slaves in the *Anti-Slavery Record*, the attention to the embodiment of the slaves' music making forecasted the disappearance and disembodied input of the slave master's whip and command. If reproduced music was to help reimagine mastery, its disclosure of "the human voice" had to remain an austere disembodiment that ultimately conveyed the abundance of the black voice, just as the excessive novelty of Johnson's whistling disappeared his master's body but affirmed Johnson's status as bodyservant. This form of mimesis is central to the ontological realization of the force of the plantation, even or perhaps especially in the domestic life that emerged through black music in the waning years of the plantation. What was threatening about the blackness of the phonautographic glyph is that it cast back the claim of and the desire for the automatic or inherent disclosure of the voice. The phonautographic glyph asserted that fidelity—a concept the phonograph and all sound recording since would be painted with—was not a natural or automatic quality of the voice but a prescribed intimacy produced by its coercion through reproduction. The liberation of coercive reproduction of course did not make the phonograph or its succeeding mediatized conception "a slave," as has often been misstated in technological studies.[36] No, this desire for the coerced reproduction of mastery through the reproduction of the black voice was a feature of the slave society's expansion, not of the natural necessity of "the slave."

Edison characterized the impending promises of phonographic reproduction as "the captivation of sounds, with or without the knowledge or consent of the source of their origin." No warrant need be issued because sounds captured retrospectively granted the authority of eternal representation to their listening subject from without. And to the emerging listening subject, Edison added that the phonograph would keep the "Family Record.—For the purpose of preserving the sayings, the voices, and *the last words* of the dying member of the family—as of great men—the phonograph will unquestionably outrank the photograph."[37] The phonograph was supposed to carry on, as uncontestably and faithfully as possible, the patriarchal authority of "great men" over the domain of the domestic long after their disappearance. The domestication of black sounds that Douglass had championed as a liberating force for those in bondage—the circle where those from without would extract the humanizing character of blackness—primed a structure of relation, intimacy, and regulation that would be essential to a new mode of black subordination.

The grooves of the early phonographic cylinder were meant to inscribe and animate the command and authority of patriarchal inheritance that the phonautographic depiction stood up against. Both Mladen Dolar and Theodor Adorno, in referencing the nineteenth-century British record label His Master's Voice, whose records introduced the famously compliant terrier "Nipper," spoke of the phonographic voice as a source of obedience: a transparency to the command that requires an opacity regarding its modes of domination.[38] The patriarchal and masterly command would be made to appear as if it were inherent in the very logic of the voice as a logic of domination. A mimesis that reflected and naturalized domination thus had to be re-created.

As Saidiya Hartman contends, black sentience under slavery was disputed and hence partially fabricated by the white bearer of its capture from outside the circle Frederick Douglass identified. The phonograph extended and automated the disembodied authority that underwrote the realization of black mimesis by enslaved people such as George W. Johnson. Now the authority lay in the making cognizable, the animating, the making live a certain domesticated life that the white family was meant to bear, symbolically and eternally, in as alienating a fashion as possible. The narcissistic function of enslaved mimesis was transferred over to the phonograph.

Because the moral and material authority of the formal slave master was losing its narcissistic justification, its egoism of dominance had to be legitimated elsewhere, not by being demolished but by being liberated in wider, more popular, more domestic, more banal, and more quotidian registers.

David Marriott put this quite succinctly in one of his earlier essays on Fanon, where he asserted essentially what makes narcissism impossible is also what makes it necessary: "The implication is that sociality inscribes itself in the individual, and egoic love is inhabited by the political, and that is why power is both the condition of the subject and the reason why self-love is always a question of mastery. And this certainly seems to be the implication of the stress on narcissism, on what it means to be an alienated, divided subject, a subject unable to represent itself to itself in the racist mirror of culture."[39] Individuation flounders under the failure of the patriarchal and narcissistic reflection of the voice. Indeed, the phonautograph nearly refused this reflective self-affirmation. The boundless inscrutability of the voice's abstraction diminished its authority.

There is always a heretical remainder here of which the perpetual or eternal requirement of voice's obedience and authority is symptomatic. What ontology covers over is a measure "that dispenses with the void, the too full made to avoid the void."[40] The patriarch, the father, the family, the voice of great men and the domestication of black voice(s) as such even as they would be hemmed in by these laws and legalizations must and indeed can break out of and against them because they are but a mere impossible necessity. Aesthetics plays a key role in regulating the blackness of the phonautographic glyph, but beauty would rescue the authority lost in the unfaithful reflection of his master's voice.

The Dis-Credited Structure of Mimesis

Both the pure sensory pleasure of subjective feeling or reflection in positivist aesthetics or its conceptual rationalization within certain tracts of the idealist tradition are failed and made possible by this disfigured glyph that we would increasingly hear as voice and music on the phonograph. The phonautographic glyph was not beautiful. Unlike the space of Douglass's pointing, the phonautographic glyph did not easily reflect the desires and mastery of its receiver or its listener. This failure sent the force of the phonograph to liberate the human voice from its obliteration in the blackness of the glyph. It was representation, through the sublimation of the glyph's refusal, that saved the human voice. Beauty and representation came to the defense of the human voice against a blackened threat that made the human voice possible.

Grappling with this disappearance of the human's "nonorigin" was troubling to its recipients, as nineteenth-century phonologist Shelford Bidwell points out: "No sound, with perhaps the single exception of that of a tuning fork when excited in a particular manner, is a *simple* one. What we are accustomed to regard as simple elementary sounds are in fact more or less complicated chords."[41] Bidwell noted that if all of the "overtones, the high notes of varying pitch and intensity" of the human voice were to be eliminated, it would be impossible to distinguish between musical instruments or for that matter between musical instruments and human beings; it would be impossible to hear human beings as such. Even more important, "all voices would be exactly alike, and no distinction between the various vowel sounds would be cognisable."[42] The tonic messiness of the human voice represented phonautographically could then conceivably be misrecognized as the sounds of an instrument, of an object utterly other than a human being. This glyph carried the potential to efface racial and sexual difference, gender and national accent, speech ability and disability. The nondifferentiation and disfigurement of these differences cut through their embodied propriety as the human voice; they cut through what Edison deemed the providence of the phonograph for bearing forth the authority and propriety of "great men." That is why a law had to be raised up in honor of their violation, but a law, like all laws, that liberates for all the abundant paranoia needed to protect an almost infinite space for the propertied few.

Phonautographic différance would dispute that very phenomenal, experiential difference that Bidwell claimed resided in an inherent logical corporeal difference determined phonologically by the "sounding body"[43] or what Immanuel Kant, in his seminal writing on aesthetics and judgment, simply referred to as "the figure of the human."

> But human beauty (i.e., of a man, a woman, or a child), the beauty of a horse, or a building (be it a church, palace, arsenal, or summer house), presupposes a concept of the purpose which determines what the thing is to be, and consequently a concept of its *perfection*; it is therefore adherent beauty. Now as the combination of the pleasant (in sensation) with beauty, which properly is only concerned with form, is a hindrance to the purity of the judgment of taste, so also is its purity injured by the combination with beauty of the good [i.e., the accordance with its purpose].

> We could adorn a figure with all kinds of spirals and light, but regular lines, as the New Zealanders do with their tattooing, if only it were not the figure of a human being. And again this [ornamentation] could have much finer features and a more pleasing and gentle cast of countenance provided it were not intended to represent a man, much less a warrior.[44]

Departing from an Aristotelian metaphysic, Kant confesses that the human is merely an aesthetic representation that grounds the form of specific being. There is no essential humanness to the human. It inheres in no natural order but is retrospectively used to ground specific figures across aesthetically regulated modes of differentiation. As we see from the phonautograph, there is no such input as the human voice, only what from reproduction can be retrospectively used to cast its reflection. Beauty, specifically its capacity, is to grant purpose to and hence legitimate representation's retrospection.

Kant's anthropological allusions to the Māori can be read on the one hand as suggesting that the ornamental function of *tā mokos* disbar them categorically and hence conceptually from the realm of the human because their glyphic representation presupposes no concept with as much force as the universalizing maxim of "the human," beyond Kant's lack of understanding. Within their own social, the Māori's social inscription of themselves foils the aspirational universal prescription of categorical mimesis conflated with and disguised as an ethical teleology. But a perhaps more meaningful attribution does more than simply reify the corrective authority of judgment, does more than simply rely on Kant being a "bad anthropologist" and by implication invites the even more extensive violence of "good anthropologists" to sharpen his critique.

Kant's early relation of beauty, the judgment to which the ascription of humanity is bound, must itself be humanized by finding fealty, in the form of fraternity or mimesis, in the object to the concept. Rather simply, the concept or category of the human must itself be humanized. Beauty catalyzes this process by propping up, making proper and making of properties in the objects it appropriates to its synthetic modes of proprioception. Perception becomes about properties in a sense that is still bounded by, even as it (allegedly) wishes to depart from, Lockean conceptions of property/properties. Both the extensive dominions of fear that bound the territorial properties of ascription of knowledge, "which all terminate in [necessarily] sensible simple ideas,"[45] and the speculative curiosity that furrows the endless frontier of understanding consolidate in a certain kind of need that must be humanized even if it lives against so many modes of putatively human life. Speculation and paranoid selfish defense collaborate to imagine a beauty they can violently defend, an art market to securitize, a museum to guard.

Both the world-sieging projects of English colonization and the (fantastical innocence) of Prussian expansion after the Thirty Years' War lay at the feet of the need of knowledge for a process for deflecting the dominion over death outward, into, and through orderly relations of exchange, a process we would call humanization.[46] Kant's own language of conceptual deficiency alludes to the (concept of the) need of humans to be fed by life, and in turn black life receives its reduced apportionment under this synthetically produced austerity measure. We ought similarly to note, when moving from Douglass into Johnson, that the manumission of the enslaved was more about feeding the deficiency of the concept of freedom (liberal or otherwise) than about facilitating the felicity or life chances of black folks. We might ask then how black life starves to feed the efficiency of the concept of beauty, including how black life starves to feed the concept of black beauty. This process is what I am calling and thinking around as the aesthetic character of blackness.

A common misstep is to fixate on or reinscribe the alleged purity of humanity without attending to its process of aestheticization. What affirms the transcendental judgment from which the coherent concept of the human is fabricated is precisely the authority, as Sylvia Wynter puts it, of "the specific 'type of non-culture' which enables its self-definition as that specific type of culture," as "the image of man in general."[47] This power (or the authority of) reason must be universalized. Its objects—whatever life the Māori live under and against their aestheticization, in Kant's reading—must be arrested, because its process and practice cannot or will not submit to reason's authority. The spectacular aesthetic production of the Māori as an object of judgment is what constitutes the supposed "nature" of the human (voice). How different the human (voice) might be (or how impossible it would be) if it was the Māori reading books containing descriptions of how Kant looked, dressed, sounded, and lived from 12,000 miles away and not the other way around? This resonates with the space and force of the slave community's knowledge about the slave society, not the desire to expand the slave society's knowledge of the slave community through the humanity extracted from it that would eventually be named black culture. The mastery of reason and its material authority of course rest on

2.1 An original phonautogram (a sound-image produced by a phonautograph) by Leon Scott de Martinville, 1857. The inscriptions were made by a wood-tipped needle on India ink layered on top of goldbeater's skin or lampblacked paper. Source: Académie des sciences de l'Institut de France; Feaster, "Édouard-Léon Scott de Martinville's 1861 Communication," 26, plates 6 and 7.

this political and aesthetic impossibility. I invoke both the material and metaphorical opacity of the phonautographic glyph (see figure 2.1), developed by Leon Scott before the Edisonian phonograph, as a site around which the troubling unintelligibility of black life and sounding revolved. The phonograph's reproduction of the black voice as phenomenal sound sought to resolve this tension. The black voice decorated, marked, and so realized the human voice just as Kant's aesthetic rendering of the Māori realized the human.

Through the phonautograph, the human voice was disclosed as a construction of this suprasensory authority of reason and not a fact of natural recognition. The deficient mimesis of Johnson's whistling and the Māori's *tā moko*—two irreconcilably different practices of the world and asymmetrical relations to maneuvering power—are dialectically resolved into this "vanished authority" of their failure to attain humanity.[48] The ever-violent disputation of enslaved and colonized humanity would expand, not contract with the expansion of the human and the liberation of the aesthetic judgment and categorical understanding over humanity as its authorizing verification. How did the inscriptive or marked surface of the phonographic record provide a new source through which the human (voice) could be redistricted? Black music and the black voice were conscripted to bear the weight of the human's imaginative restrictions. The aesthetic character of blackness repressed this function of the human's dependence on it and internalized and introjected those very imaginative restrictions. Yet what I have picked at through Johnson's recording and the transition to the time "after slavery" it inhabits is the utter precarity and futility of the humanizing character of blackness that Frederick Douglass's sounding drew and that would become even more salient, potent, and ubiquitous in the twentieth century.

Engraving Black Music

As if simultaneously called by the words of Douglass and the impending opaque blackness of the phonautograph, in an 1868 article in *Lippincott's Monthly Magazine*, researcher A. Simpson published dispatches from his extended residency in Rio de Janeiro, Brazil. Simpson set out to dispute the dubious sentimental proximity to pure plantation "negro melodies" proclaimed by the minstrel stage and to verify the widely circulated appeal of Frederick Douglass that black music evinced the verifiable mimetic humanity of the enslaved. Simpson thus sought to establish conclusively whether "the negro is essentially musical in his nature."

> It has been a common idea for many years, accepted without examination or proof, that the negro was essentially musical in nature. We now venture boldly to assert that the claim is unfounded in fact, and that, while the negro possesses a capacity for acquiring a certain degree of

musical knowledge which he gets from his organ of imitativeness, he has in his native state (to which only we must look in examining the question) no idea whatever of music, so far as melody or harmony is an essential ingredient of such a quality.[49]

Simpson reached this deduction through the audiovisual proof he constructed, the recording and reproduction of the enslaved Brazilians' *festa* music, which he simply translated and transcribed as "Ugh, ugh, ugh, ugh or "Eh, eh, eh, eh in every possible scale, and *ad infinitum*." On the one hand, the application of scale to the music of African musicians exposed a colonial ambivalence in the context of Simpson's conclusion that they "have no idea of music, so far as melody or harmony," and on the other hand, it attempted to conceal an authority it disclosed: that the musical concept that verified Simpson's authority was but a contingent ornament that needed to be fed by the sounds the Africans fashioned beyond resemblance.

Although Simpson tried to render the music of African musicians as ornament by wielding the concepts of his understanding in descriptive dismissal, a crack in authority of the human voice burst forth. The dependency and deficiency of the concept of "music" as the condition of possibility for the subordination of these black sounds was further revealed in Simpson's most confident moment of conclusion and disavowal:

> Sometimes they got hold of a name, which they appropriated as a handle of their gruntings. When our distinguished townsman, Condy Raguet, was Charge d'Affaires from the United States to Brazil, the negroes, in some inexplicable manner, got hold of his name, and were frequently heard grunting through the streets:
>
> "Condy Raguet, Condy Raguet."
>
> "Eh! eh! Condy Raguet!"

Simpson concludes after this moment of improvised ensemble and attack, "We do not believe that the negro in his native state, knows what music is." Simpson's statements sound ironic in our postphonographic soundscape, which I document for much of this text, wherein black folks are more commonly framed as inherently knowing music, inherently musical. More immediately telling however, is that his conclusion highlights the hinge of recognition of music, of aesthetic concept as such, which he applies to the very sounds he claims are beyond resemblance to the concept of music.

The very space or "faculty" (a word he uses elsewhere in the text) is constituted by the sublimation of the inscrutable exteriority of the African's sounding, which is nothing more than Simpson's and Condy Raguet's own disfigurement.

There is a clear threat of potential pleasure the African musicians may have grasped when they "got hold" of the official's proper name, both reducing it to a novelty and appropriating it into a story Raguet refused to tell about himself, one he refused to listen to and would not allow to be told.[50] Their potentiated pleasure grates against the potentiation of their human voice and the humanity of music. The knowledges and gnoses the Africans may have been constructing as this grasping and (re)production was taking place at the hinge of sound on their own terms against Simpson's epistemic authority emerged precisely at the hinge of Simpson's rejection.[51]

The African musicians displaced the value of the authority that constituted the later presence of "music" or the human voice. They chewed on and played with these concepts of language and music, which were wielded to authorize their subordination and hence authorize and nourish the concepts. The force of the African musicians' sounds was unreasonable to and even threatening to the concept of music, or even to later culture, because not unlike the force of the phonautograph, it carried the capacity to disfigure the representative authority and not just its representation (which it is of course always bent back toward and consumed by). This is the closest moment in Simpson's brief study when we might imagine the black performers studying the white ethnographers studying them. And it is from this realization that we should glean that even when the yoke of culture and music is being denied to black people, music and culture are in fact the compromise against the forces of far greater fantasies of possession as dispossession.

The phonautograph displaced a particular ideality of the body grounded in a particular (logical) "experience" and aesthetic judgment of the body as inherently racialized, sexualized, and gendered. The problem of the correspondence between the body and the human voice, or more the trouble of the origin of the latter in the former, was called into question by this phonautographic différance precisely when it was the job of a technology to do just the opposite. The possibility of this phonautographic différance was to a degree realized in 2009, when researchers ran the phonautographs through a laser-based computational system to reproduce phonically the sounds written on the paper. The scientists and sound historians were surprised to hear a human voice singing "Au Clair de la Lune," a French folk song, but even more they were shocked to realize that the voice they had extracted from the phonautograph had been played or reproduced at the incorrect speed. The singing voice they had determined the previous year to be recognizably female was actually the voice of Leon Scott singing the French folk song.[52] The human voice in the phonautograph had been written with a glyphic materiality rather than a properly *phono*logical presence. Hence, its translation into or *reproduction* in the phonologisms (or phonologocentric paradigms) of contemporary voice technology made real a troubling notion of difference, one in which the gendered-imaginary of the human voice was recognized as a mere difference of speed.[53]

As if anticipating such phonic and symbolic gender confusion, in 1879, Bidwell critiqued the inability of the phonautograph to carry though the immediacy of the body in the human voice: "The result was that, though the tones of the voice were to a certain extent imitated, articulation was entirely absent."[54] For Bidwell, the origin of the human voice could not be represented in its originary trace, as is the case of the phonautograph. Instead, he argued that there must be a true and direct relation of its origin in what Bidwell referred to as "the cavity of the mouth." Bidwell added, "The great defect in this instrument, as in all others constructed on a similar principle, is its inability to reproduce the qualities of the sounds which it is intended to transmit."[55] The failure of the phonautograph lay in its incapacity to transmit or reproduce the human voice. It only displayed the cutting, the carving of the desire for authority it could never properly narcissistically represent and reflect.

George W. Johnson's Phonography and the Cutting Hands of the Black Voice

Recording the black voice began with the threat and requirement of perfection. Victor H. Emerson "discovered" George W. Johnson whistling at the Hudson River ferryboat terminal, which Emerson passed through on his way to work at the North American Phonograph Company in New Jersey. Emerson commissioned Johnson with a then fairly meager salary, because Emerson realized, like many who recorded on the phonograph, that he needed a musical or sonic source that was "cheap and loud."[56] Cheap because the major companies producing the phonograph—the Edison Phonograph Company, the Columbia Phonograph Company, and the North American Phonograph Company—had all embarked on a scale of overproduction that saw them perpetually on the brink of bankruptcy.[57]

Phonographs were placed on public display on street corners and in town squares, where they were mass marketed chiefly as instruments of entertainment, as "coin-in-the-slot" machines.[58]

Johnson's voice had never been recorded before by phonographic technology—only had the ear of the white passersby on the street achieved anything like capturing his errant notes. In their first recording session, Emerson instructed Johnson, "Sing loudly and clearly and don't make any mistakes. If you do, we have to stop, shave down all the cylinders, and start all over again."[59] Emerson's demands evince the anxiety over the entanglement of technological failure and commodification (reproduction and production) in the phonograph around which the black voice was the fulcrum and in which it became the primary commodity. The black voice was idealized as that which could quell technological failure by enabling the phonograph to provide a true and faithful reproduction of its object. Patriarchal authority demanded fidelity. This was achieved through a disembodied authority that regulated and aestheticized the object of reproduction.

A commenter in *Phonogram*, a turn-of-the-century phonographic trade publication, revealed the fantastical desires imagined in the black voice: "Negroes take [to recording] better than white singers, because their voices have a certain sharpness or harshness about them that a white man's has not. A barking dog, squalling cat, neighing horse, and, in fact almost any beast's or bird's voice is excellent for the good repetition on the phonograph."[60] These comments represent the obverse of phonographic anxiety around the representative limitations of the phonograph regarding "human speech." As sound historian Andre Millard has pointed out about the early phonograph, "The disembodied sounds and squeaks emerging from the tinfoil could be discerned by the listener, but it took practice to recognize [human] speech."[61] The black voice was the ideal object of phonographic reproduction because its entirely knowable excessively embodied phonic difference, categorized above as its animalism, was based in a phonological essentialism: "sharpness and harshness," embodied, excessively so, in modes of hyperembodiment of blackness. The perceived knowability of the black voice deemed it faithfully inscribable in the phonograph while also making it symbolically full enough to supplement its process of mechanical reproduction. The black voice thus became phonographically reproducible, perfecting the deficiency of reproduction as such.[62] The black voice had to sound, excessively so, because the human voice could not.

The ideality and reproducibility of the inherently inscribable capacity of the black voice were predicated upon its weighty instrumentality, its excessive capacity to create a sublime form of almost hyperembodiment that could cross the alienated distance of the voice's haunting reproduction.[63] Gustavus Stadler's research on phonographic lynching cylinders in the late nineteenth century elucidates a particularly ecstatic dimension of the centrality of the black voice in early phonographic technology. Stadler discusses how early lynching cylinders, which simulated the sounds of the lynching of black men for "coin-in-the-slot" phonographs, contributed to this atomization and anatomization of (as it produced) the black body and qualified the ideality of the black voice for phonographic reproduction as an especially excessive ecstatic and hence exotically proximal site of listening: "The recordings surely also drew upon an established and growing white fascination with the sound of black voices and, in particular, with imagining black voices as in some senses excessively embodied and insufficiently linguistic—that is, as less or other than human."[64] Stadler's insights shed light on how the black voice was inextricably tied, affectively even, to the possibility of humanity and the possibility of a human voice via a kind of animalism or inhumanity envisioned in the black body. The human was a perpetually promised and hence perpetually undelivered future precisely through the aesthetic character of blackness.

The black voice supplemented the constant technological failure, the ends of which were to ensure the possibility of the human voice, of true human speech. The black voice sang to feed concept itself, and any black sustenance was incidental. Hence the black voice was an affect not only in the sense of its gestural presence as that which would supplement mechanical failure and hence mechanical reproduction and because it exemplified an affectivity that was prelinguistic and paralinguistic. I mean prelinguistic in a teleological sense that it would provide the "primitive" ground for the possibility of true human speech and language through the phonograph. Yet the black voice was also paralinguistic in that through its fantastical instrumentalization it was instilled with a complex and elusive set of characteristics and operations that undid and went beyond its commodification. The affectivity of the black voice initiated the possibility of both phonographic inscription and reproduction and made possible the promise and deferment of the faithfully reproduced human voice. The black voice established a complex set of imbrications between blackness and technology that George W. Johnson's music so starkly drew to the fore.

George W. Johnson's 1891 recording of "The Whistling Coon" begins with his announcement of himself: "Mr. George W. Johnson will now sing 'The Whistling Coon' at the Edison Phonograph Works." The form of the introduction is characteristic of most early phonographic recordings, which begin with an unidentified voice announcing the recording artist and piece of music that is to follow. Johnson, however, somewhat uncharacteristically, announced himself on his own recordings. George W. Johnson's announcement of himself would not have been unusual in and of itself had it not been musically contrasted and conceptually contradicted by what was to follow. The stilted tone Johnson adopted for his introduction was in some sense a highly common affected voice that required announcers to shout in a strident enunciative fashion to make sure the object of the recording was effectively named. Victor Emerson's command for Johnson to speak loudly then was as much a demand for proper fidelity as it was a kind of violent aesthetic call for Johnson to conform to the phonic and symbolic conventions of early phonography.

Typically, performers shouted unnaturally loudly into the acoustic recording horn, which gave a kind of sprayed or "tiny" quality to their voices that designated them as affectively phonographic.[65] This announcer voice Johnson invoked was—especially in the case of "coon songs"—usually a voice that was recognized as highly exaggerated and for that reason referential in a certain sense only to the phonograph. This aspect of phonography can at one level be attributed to the recording process in which recording artists—as Emerson's earlier demand for perfection implies—performed and re-performed each song continuously all the way through. Due to the limited mechanics of recording and the temporal limitations of the wax cylinder, which could only record about three minutes, it might be said that there was no time or space to cultivate any more dynamic and less standardized form of introduction.[66] Of course, these mechanical limitations do not wholly account for the complexity of the presence of the introduction. I would suggest that Johnson's opening can be accounted for more by the performative function of the announcement made possible by Johnson's formalization of an aesthetic character who was yoked to yet individuated from the minstrelsy to which his performances referred and from which his vocalization was birthed.

The announcement that began early phonographs tried to create the presence of the live stage: the vaudeville stage, the minstrel stage, especially in "coon songs." Yet in so attempting, the phonographic introduction also, often unintentionally, through such a stilted and repetitive form ended up acknowledging the impossibility of the true presence of the minstrel stage in phonographic reproduction. It was the form of announcement itself that called attention to the fact that it and what followed was a phonographic reproduction. One can detect a similar dynamic in the later "coon songs" of Arthur Collins, a white man, whose singing voice sounded comically identical to his own announcing voice, despite his efforts to affect a signature of minstrelized blackness.[67] Bert Williams's brand of "black-on-black minstrelsy" in his recordings of "coon songs" with George Walker—in particular "My Little Zulu Baby" and "Pretty Desdemone"—produced a similar kind of sublimity when Williams adopted an enunciative affect in introducing his songs that trickled perceptibly into his minstrelized "coon" singing.[68]

In Johnson's recordings, the mastery of the minstrel stage is not just preserved; it is reimagined and disseminated. As Eric Lott reminds us about the necessity of the threat of intermixture that characterized the minstrel stage: "Minstrelsy's joking focus on disruptions and infractions of the flesh, its theatrical dream-work, condensed and displaced those [racialized psychic] fears, imaged in the 'black' body, that could be neither forgotten nor fully acknowledged."[69] Lott's point about racialized and sexualized transgression in the minstrel stage is revealing. Johnson's "authenticity" as a black street singer undoubtedly held the potential to fulfill the white private fantasy of black public threat domesticated within the functioning of the recording. After all, Johnson is singing a song that narrates the violent destruction of a black man at the hands of a white mob. Johnson is seemingly recouping the violent symbolics of the minstrel stage in which black performers were made to introject the content and form of their own destruction and desecration.

From George W. Johnson's songs it would be impossible to deny that the phonograph, to a degree, occupied a continual legacy of minstrelsy. Gustavus Stadler points to the centrality of the minstrel stage in Johnson's performance of "The Whistling Coon" and "The Laughing Song."

> These numbers—which were built around refrains in which Johnson whistled and laughed, of course—drew on the same fascination with the black voice as corporeal, inarticulate, prelinguistic, and pushed to the extremes of embodiment as was reflected in the lynching cylinders, and they reaffirmed the sense that these sounds were somehow closest to embodying the process of sound reproduction itself.[70]

The black voice was undoubtedly tied to this corporeal and corporealizing logic through the phonograph. The black voice played a crucial role in displacing the process of inscription from the phonograph—the graphic nature of its writing and the basis of its reproduction—and projecting it instead onto the symbolic scripting of the black body.[71] The black body had been both the mask of nineteenth-century minstrelsy and the monstrously idealized ornament of early twentieth-century lynching. Through these ideological strictures of the black body the black voice acquired a symbolic authority that bolstered its phonic affectivity. Stadler's point is crucial in marking out the affective weight of the black voice in and as phonographic reproduction, which was carried out simultaneously under the figure of the minstrel mask, the minstrel stage, and the scene of lynching. Staking out Johnson's relationship to minstrelsy, the formal context for which "The Whistling Coon" was composed, and the scene of lynching, the violent act that "The Whistling Coon" disturbingly normalizes, is important.

Identifying the place of minstrelsy allows us a kind of cursory listening, one idealized by and through the phonograph. The idealized frontier that Douglass pointed to emerged even beyond the coherent minstrelized embodiment it was meant to capture. The pioneering process of tilling and producing this new auditory frontier of listening was part of what I am calling the aesthetic character of blackness. This is not to say that the black voice is the aesthetic character of blackness so much as it is to assert that it grounds such an aesthetic regulation. I tarry with the intricacies of Johnson's recordings to highlight that no such overdetermination can be made. The authority of the phonograph, especially in its early days, was as contingent as the putatively abject black voice it coercively reproduced. Johnson's career illustrates a mutually uneven precarity between the black voice and the phonograph at the moment of his voice's reproduction. This fracture, which the remainder of sonic technological reproduction, progress, and fidelity would be organized to conceal, both made possible the aesthetic character of blackness and disavowed it through its adherence to representation. As I will discuss in the next two chapters, the precarity and violence of black representation contradicts the necessary assumption of its building up and expansion. Part of why Johnson would not be inaugurated into the canonical imaginary of the humanizing character of blackness has everything to do with the ugly hiss.

The Ugly Hiss of the Shadow Family

The overrepresentative economy that Johnson's voice initiated and was initiated in was constructed as the remedy to the frustratingly unintelligible glyphic economy of the "ugly hiss" that stymied Edison's initial aspirations to commodify phonographic sound.[72] Bryan Wagner makes this point in his book *Disturbing the Peace*:

> At a time when most singers were bellowing or overenunciating into the horn, straining to the point of stilting their words in an attempt to register unambiguously on the needle, Johnson was dropping his closing consonants and slurring between words, sometimes with discernible vibrato, all the while remaining entirely comprehensible to listeners.... When people listened to Johnson's records, they testified that they were hearing a voice that was "exactly like" what they *expected* to hear.[73]

Writing about Johnson's song "The Laughing Coon," which Johnson wrote himself (unlike "The Whistling Coon"), Wagner considers the racial-symbolic legacies of the minstrel stage that contributed to the capacity and incapacity of Johnson to sing or, as he puts it, "to speak." The overdetermining and overdetermined symbolics of the minstrel stage did not end at the phonic and symbolic level of the song but in fact bled into the syntactical and narrative dimensions of "The Laughing Coon." The song tells a story in which the singer/narrator encounters a vigilante mob, possibly a lynch mob, that immediately racially objectifies the narrator for the purpose of doing violence to him. This racial "objectification" occurs through the imaginative production and phonic utterance of the racial epithet the song is named for: coon.[74]

The racial epithets—"darky," "coon," "nigger"—Wagner asserts, continually inaugurate the terms of address between the narrator and his would-be lynchers in the song. Within this context and in the broader context of Reconstruction America, Wagner defines the racial epithet as that which "claims to say everything that needs to be said about somebody. It does not modify or describe its object; rather, it structures the field in which the object is perceived.... [Hence] the object appears within the world, but it does not speak."[75] Wagner invokes Frantz Fanon, from whom a great deal of thought has sprung about the racial logics of the "stereotype," an economy in which the black voice undoubtedly operates, at least partially.[76] It is against this backdrop of historical and ontological referents of police power that Wagner sees early black phonography (and all black popular culture throughout his larger work) as indexically and historically referring to the abjection of the policed black body. Johnson's laughing becomes a point of fixation for its very unintelligibility, for its semantic opacity, which supposedly sheds the referentiality of a black body and any prescribed terms of recognition: that is, the same terms, or even the same body, by which one might be interpolated or called into the racial epithet.

We know from Johnson's earlier history that the epithetic was not purely a function of abject alienation, as Wagner's Fanonian recourse tends to claim (indeed, Fanon's Manicheanism contests the simplicity of this reduction). The epithetic is the hinge of domestic, cohabitative relations and violent intimacies, whose precarity and active constituency the phonograph requires and wishes to reify. Edison's claims about the phonograph's instrumental rationale in fulfilling the ends of "great men" of the domestic property and propriety of the white family complicate and bifurcate Wagner's essential conflation of technological functioning with the appearance of the black voice.

> What encrypted the black voice was not primarily the fact of the groove, not in the sense that record grooves can be "read" or decrypted by a phonograph needle. Rather, blackness was encrypted by the fact that it could only be decrypted by the technology that made the voice appear as if it were already thrown. From this point of reproduction, the black voice's primary effects became indistinguishable from their technological condition of possibility.... Alienating the voice from the body, in this instance, creates rather than disrupts speech's capacity to stand for subjectivity, producing a new opportunity for face-to-face immediacy between collector and informant. The aura is made, not destroyed, by the phonograph.[77]

Here Wagner's goal within his broader project runs aground of its attempt to make blackness verisimilar with the product of its policing in a way that does not help us understand what policing is beyond a kind of contained perpetual ontological reduction. Policing appears almost idiopathic, and blackness purely emblematic, when its historical, aesthetic, and above all processual contingency is disappeared. The "how" of policing is too easily naturalized into fact. How is policing produced and reproduced through black culture?

In Wagner's framing, black culture and music as a product of policing are too romantically held in their alterity, which ironically is the opposite of what Johnson's popularity points to. In Wagner's argument, blackness and its expression in and as black culture is always chased after, always a fugitive from the law. But as we saw with Douglass's fugitivity in the previous chapter, this is never so simple. Moreover, assuming this eternal fugitivity perilously flattens and misapprehends capture's constantly reforming logic through black culture. Policing is denied its (endlessly) aesthetic productive function, which is not just black cultural but endlessly and increasingly multicultural, and which never rests even as it arrests a primary or supremely abject mode of embodiment. If we do not recognize this, we mistake the violence of policing exclusively for its spectacular embodiments and not its increasingly broadening quotidian character. This is much of what I criticized in my treatment of Douglass and the concept of "the slave." Sadly, policing, distinct from the institutional "police power" to which Wagner refers, is far more complex, as I am trying to stake out with the aesthetic character of blackness. I outline something like the opposite of Wagner's project in asserting black culture itself as a policing capacity, the function of which is not a pure outcome or a pure product but at times a coerced or tragically willing agent. This admixture and violent domestic cohabitation are of chief concern throughout this work.

Wagner's critical misstep appears in his rendering of being black itself: "To be black is to exist in exchange without being a party to exchange."[78] I more fully engage this misapprehension in the final chapter of this work when discussing the Black Arts Movement and the inroads of neoliberal beautification campaigns. A common misunderstanding of neoliberal power asserts that blackness and black people are perpetually "outside" the "orderly relations of exchange," so the actual violence of it is our exclusion. However, a more rigorous examination of neoliberalism's powers of expansion and reformation reveal that it is our inclusion and participation within the market and modes of production that are neoliberalism's most innovative structuring violence. Suffice it to say for now that this is not exclusively a neoliberal outlook. Indeed, what would much later be called neoliberalism was developed through the brutal experimentations of black life since the Middle Passage. We have always been subject to violent neoliberal inclusion. In the context of this chapter and the final chapter, this misconception by Wagner disguises the ongoing and expanding legacies of domination that emerged after manumission. These modes of domination of the slave society were refashioned and re-formed through and against black participation through the liberation of contract, "burdened individuality," and the responsibilization we call (black) citizenship and of course the liberated coercive work and consumption of black wage labor, folks including what I focus on in this work: the black work of art.[79]

In and against the continual embodiment engendered by George W. Johnson's voice and intensified most in his whistling and later his laughing, there ebbs and flows the phonographic supplement of another body that perhaps belies the phonic symbolic body of the black voice: the phonographic hiss. In the early days of phonography when Johnson was recording—unlike the successive recordings John and Alan Lomax made of black blues musicians like Lead Belly, Blind Lemon, and many others in prisons in the 1930s, which I discuss in the following chapter—phonographic hiss did not always reify the authenticity of the black voice. Rather, this irregular and intense sound, which for Edison was an impediment to fidelity and hence to the commodification and commercialization of the phonograph, would have gone largely unheard or as something the burgeoning phonograph audience would be trained to unhear.[80]

The phonographic hiss engendered another form of hearing as unhearing, just as it required another form of speaking as not speaking. The phonographic hiss to which I am referring is actually the sound of an arm—likely Victor Emerson's—winding the crank attached to the recording stylus against the cylinder to cut Johnson's voice into the record.[81] At the hinge between Emerson's fast and unevenly winding hands—the threat of perfection they constantly wielded toward Johnson, the way they formed him, formed his voice—and the recording stylus that inscribed the phonic vibrations of Johnson's voice laid the force and energy of blackness. Johnson's voice was the supplement to the surface of the cylinder (record) and indeed the process that bore and was made possible by his voice.

Emerson's arm, embodied in the phonographic hiss, is the trace, the "opaque energy" against which Johnson's voice was defined and which Johnson's voice was supposed to transcend. However, an impasse arose at the surface of the cylinder (record), where both the movements of Johnson's voice and the movement of Emerson's arm were inscribed. Whether in the high tones of Johnson's whistling throughout the song or his whistling of "Dixie" at the end of song or his bellyful chuckles in "The Laughing Coon," Johnson's voice and its (white) mechanical supplement convened irreducibly at the surface of the record. No chain of signification, no sequences of differences, arose in the terms of recognition because it was the inscriptive convergence of the surface that Johnson's voice was supposed to obscure. Johnson's voice and, both following it and preceding it, his body, became the terms of recognition, they became presence and constituted the basis for phonographic experience. Even more, they became our listening. In other words, the always-already-arrivedness of Johnson's body and voice within the symbolic economy of minstrelsy and the "racial epithet" precluded or obscured the always-already-thereness of phonographic inscription and hence partially blocked another kind of listening, another kind of time, and another world perhaps moored to other modes of embodiment.[82]

The aesthetic character of blackness sublimates the phonographic hiss into the fullness of the black voice. If the grooves of the record are merely consignable to and cognizable of facticity, as Wagner would have it, then blackness becomes the flatness of the surface whose penetration into the groove realizes an impenetrable sound. This impenetrable sonic representation is reproduced as an impenetrable domestic mastery that the phonograph would like to promise but that it can never deliver. The incapacity of mastery must be raised against its wishes for totality. In Johnson's work, it is the dissonant and discordant hiss of the mechanical inscription of his voice embodied in Victor Emerson's threatening and reeling arm that directly sounds the precarity of the impenetrable domination it wishes to inscribe in the black voice.

The problem for us then is that the ugly hiss, as it realizes the nearness of black representation, is disappeared into an ever and progressively beautifying object: fidelity, clarity, the lossless of the digital. Black culture became more pathological precisely as the mediums and media become more lossless, more faithful, and more authoritative. This initiated a kind of mastery over the cultural that is not exclusively the provenance of a white outsider. The dominating authority of the technological rationalization of black culture led to complex emergent responses that black representation would have to chase after, corral, wrestle to submission, and in the process negate to produce its official fullness. This pressure over and against black life is the aesthetic character of blackness, whose processes of austerity make a representational volume of increasingly carved-out and speculated-upon black life. Under threat of eviction, black life must squat in the spaces of the intentional vacuity of value, taking up and living life that is actively being taken from us and ransomed back as us.

Ma Rainey's Phonograph

3

> They say lust is a sin, *concupiscence of the flesh.*
> Flesh of formidable volume. Listens attentively.
> Dawn Lundy Martin, "The Symbolic Nature of Chaos"

> The bourgeois want art voluptuous and life
> ascetic; the reverse would be better.
> Theodor W. Adorno, *Aesthetic Theory*

Setting the Stage of Black Sounding

A huge "old Victrola" phonograph is wheeled onto the stage. A stagehand places an oversized record on it, and when the stylus is lowered, the Georgia Jazz Band strikes up a rendition of Ma Rainey's "Moonshine Blues." Following the band's usual eight-bar introduction, Ma Rainey's "gravelly" voice begins emanating from the phonograph, singing as if it were there, as if it were present. Rainey's voice continues to fill the crowded venue, yet she remains unseen to the expectant audience. Finally—likely at the peak of the audience's confusion or anticipation—the "huge cabinet doors swing open" and Rainey steps forth from the Victrola in a shimmering dress to reveal that she had always been there, inside the machine, making it sound all along.[1]

    This description, compiled from small newspaper clippings and twice-passed-down testimonies, details a performance routine invented by the queer black blues artist Gertrude "Ma" Rainey that graced black musical venues in the North and South from roughly 1923 to 1925. The beginning of this routine and the tour of northern cities in particular, coincided with Ma Rainey's first phonographic recordings, which were made in 1923. Yet despite Rainey's nuanced production of black sonic-visual spectacle, no photographic or phonographic record of these routines remains. It is perhaps ironic, then, considering the sparse material documentation of these performances, that this tour was launched partially at the behest of Paramount Records as a promotion for Rainey's first officially captured blues recordings. What remains so deeply intriguing about these performances is that they seem to have formally drawn upon and anticipated the modes of sonic capture and embodiment that blackness has attained in modernity. Rainey understood that the sonic legacies of black embodiment were central to the form and function of the phonograph, precisely at the moment of formal emergence of a regime of the commodification of black sound.

These performances by Rainey engaged and thought through how sonic modernity was founded through black music as an embodied documentary object that facilitated the (aspirationally) disembodied functioning of sonic technologies such as the phonograph. Through a provocative theorization of performance and listening, Rainey's dramaturgy subtly troubled the expectation of the dialectical functioning of the phonograph as reliant upon the expectation of the functioning of blackness to facilitate the phonograph's functioning. By acknowledging the technological history of the genre of blackness, or the functioning of blackness for a particular genre of the subject and the human, Rainey also imagined blackness as exceeding the generic aesthetic means of phonographic capture. Here what Sylvia Wynter refers to as the "auto-institution" of the genre of the human—the listening subject of the phonograph—and what Theodor Adorno frequently identified as the reification of musical genre that occurred through the phonograph and reproduced music are shown to be contingent on the functional commodification of blackness.[2] The captivity of representation that Douglass and Johnson distinctly presaged was thus expanded during Rainey's time through both the exogenous (technological) rationalization of black music from without as well as the rationalization of black life from within black culture. Yet Rainey's routines highlighted how black performances carry the capacity to interrupt and dissemble the functional essence of blackness as enshrined in a certain musical genre of the subject. I will partially stake out the form of this subject in this chapter through Ma Rainey's antagonists in the Harlem Renaissance such as Alain Locke, but I will also more extensively theorize this subject's genrefication in the treatment of jazz in and through Toni Morrison's novel *Jazz* in the next chapter. For now I want to emphasize how Rainey's performance picks up on and reimagines a mode of black performativity and black music that enlists blackness as an opaque mode of objecthood that refuses to function, refuses to report, and refuses to sit still as a (sonic) document.[3]

Ma Rainey's phonographic performance series played within, complicated, and undid several legacies of black aesthetic regulation. First and quite overtly, her undressing of the phonograph—rather than its revealing of her—alluded to the previous history of rationalizing the black voice as the possibility for the recognition of the human voice. In conjuring the immediate context of the mass production of and ascension of the phonograph in the 1920s, Rainey also drew on a split that was occurring at the time around the authority of conflicting media as sites of authorization and the consumption of difference. Quite famously, early twentieth-century film and music studies discuss the ascension of the cinema and the phonograph as precipitating the decline and downfall of the vaudeville stage. According to Walter Benjamin, the expansion of mechanical reproduction presaged the photograph. Ma Rainey's performances emerged from black burlesque traditions of "Babylon girls," young black women who performed in vaudeville, cabaret, and theater venues, the likes of which Josephine Baker trained with, and the comedic ventriloquism gags of the vaudeville stage and tent shows. In these registers, the formalization of skin and embodiment as poetic surfaces and substances, even when they spectacularly bore violent inscriptions of race and gender, disclosed a precarity that automated technological mediums like the phonograph would attempt to dispel with their documentary capacities.

The technological and instrumental rationalization of blackness vis-à-vis audiovisual reproduction systems imbued their forms with more rigid truth content and more regulatory functions waged against the communities they claimed to document and disclose. Frederick Douglass's description of himself as "a brand new fact" not only indicated an expanded interest in black music through manumission but expanded what would by the 1920s and 1930s become a more rationalized form of technologically capturing black life and black people as embodied documents. Ironically, this made the putative fact of blackness more rigid and more authoritative than it had been even in previous regimes such as minstrelsy whose currency was always understood to be slightly counterfeit, absurd, and irrational in its capacity of cultural production.

In this chapter I establish this documentary capacity, or what I term documentary embodiment, as an essential part of the aesthetic character of blackness. This newly formed capacity, which instrumentalized and was instrumentalized through black embodiments, attempted to expand

and formalize the scientific investment in blackness I highlighted with George W. Johnson and the African musicians in Brazil in the previous chapter. In contrast to late-nineteenth-century claims I discussed in the introduction by writers like Nietzsche, I argue that the aesthetic and the scientific were not opposed to each other but rather the aesthetic arted the reason and authority of the scientific as George W. Johnson's capture illustrates. I will also argue in this chapter that the black aesthetic achieved its own borrowed or rented authority as a response to its technological rationalization. The willful justificatory power Nietzsche wished for art colluded with the scientific rationalization it arose as a response to, and this synthesis attempted to snuff out the black life in whose name it was raised as justification. Although George W. Johnson's tenure in the phonograph represents a troubling ratio in which the rationalization of racism suffocated the capacity of black cultural production, an official black art, black culture, and black representation was waged as the positive character that could internalize and balance out the values of this juridical equation.

The budding formalization of black representation in the Harlem Renaissance, especially under the stewardship of Alain Locke, internalized (and to a degree accepted) the drive to create a rationalized usefulness out of black life by injecting it with a formal sociable law-bound way of aesthetically comporting itself. Simply put, black representation, or what Alain Locke termed the "New Negro," was a kind of shield against racialization from without and a dagger against "bad" black culture from within. In fact, the authority of the former was increasingly attributed to the responsibility of the latter. Informed heavily by Angela Davis's and K. Hammer's trans/queer black blues scholarship, I locate the aesthetic politics of black representation in the Harlem Renaissance as a litigious and regulatory response to an earlier black queer gender-transgressive and poetic "concupiscence of the flesh," in Dawn Lundy Martin's words.[4] I will extend this treatment of gendered black sexual regulation in the next chapter through the seminal black feminist scholarship of M. Jacqui Alexander when I discuss Toni Morrison's protagonist Dorcas Manfred in the novel *Jazz*.

This chapter is not organized with a progressive logic toward more atomization, precision, disclosure, or fidelity like the technological rationale it discusses. Instead, I adopt an approach of constant return to Rainey's performative repertoire as a disturbance and critique of the progressive technorationalist logic it undoes. Rainey's embodied performative practices, which were rooted in black queer social life, antagonized the instrumentalized embodiment enacted through George W. Johnson's recordings as well as the embodiment of "aesthetic comportment" that would be raised by Harlem Renaissance aesthete Alain Locke's "New Negro" as a response to Rainey's wayward sartorial presentation. If the mastery of the minstrel stage, funneled into and liberated further through George W. Johnson's voice, helped build the domestic world of the slave society, then I attempt to think through Rainey the undersides of black intimacy that evaded or undercut that domestic building up.

Stripped significantly of the nearly totalizing legal demand wherein black skin bore an aspirationally absolute reproduction of its slavability, whether it was the symbolic skin of the minstrel stage or the symbolic blackness of the phonographic black voice, black queer deviant practices like that of Rainey reimagined a more intimate, perverse, and fleshy social arrangement. I will chart this trajectory of black queer women's performances as it informs Ma Rainey's routines and career. I will end this chapter by theorizing how the formal and official aesthetics and edicts of the Harlem Renaissance, especially in the writing of Alain Locke, sought to regulate and excise black queer blues in order to produce a positive and beautifying character of blackness. Ma Rainey's performative repertoire thus suggests a refusal to show up in the court of black judgment that was enlisted to encircle, surround, and regulate black life through its own sound-images.

The regulatory power of domination became encoded quite explicitly within a black beautifying character in the aesthetic. Black lives became black art. Both become documents, evidence to beautify us to the world and beautify the domination of the world over us. Ma Rainey and a history of black women and black queer blues performance have a complicated, confrontational, elusive, and poetic relationship to the regulatory function of aesthetics. By playfully referencing and refuting the demands for a sociable, representable, and intelligible rendering of blackness, Rainey introduced a black sociality that although deeply aware of the forces waged against it, did not feel the need to be accountable to those forces. Rainey was not interested ultimately in being accountable to the sound-image the phonograph reproduced of her or the world the phonograph built from her sound-image. Moving against Douglass's expectations Ma Rainey refused to appear in court. Her performances, even or perhaps especially in their ephemerality—we only really have twice- or thrice-passed-down tales—refused to accrue and amount to the kind of evidence that would characterize black representation.

Poetic Embodiments

The poetics of Rainey's performance hinged on creating multiple embodiments of blackness that made it a lyrical dissemblance at its very moment of concealment and captivity. I am interested in Rainey's performance for how, in sound and movement, it imagined blackness as a formal, sonic, and embodied aesthetic practice that both facilitated and ultimately disrupted technological forms of sonic capture. Rainey's knowledge illustrates a history of blackness as a sonically and visually mediated symbol in voice, body, and movement, a symbolization whose constitution is not eternal or absolute but processual and contingent. She further theorized how that history of blackness enabled the functioning of sonic technologies like the phonograph. The genealogical line of the sonic and visual captivity of blackness for the subject's sensorial consumption and proprioception goes back to the very production and circulation of blackness within the reproducible storage medium of the transatlantic slave ship and the audiovisual regime of the slave plantation. As Hortense Spillers and Riley Snorton have asserted, the gendered legacy of black captivity is central to the production of a "living laboratory" in which a technology like the phonograph can emerge. The desire of Paramount to set Rainey on this tour to extricate, commodify, and infinitely reproduce Rainey's voice beyond the life of her performances—a desire Rainey thoroughly and continually challenged—attests to the legacy of captive black flesh in the phonograph that Rainey contested. Spillers asserts,

> The profitable "atomizing" of the captive body provides another angle on the divided flesh: we lose any hint or suggestion of a dimension of ethics, of relatedness between human personality and its anatomical features, between one human personality and its anatomical features, between one human personality and another, between human personality and cultural institutions. To that extent, the procedures adopted for the captive flesh demarcate a total objectification, as the entire captive community becomes a living laboratory.[5]

Rainey was by no means remitted to living bondage. Quite the contrary, her autonomy as a performer was an undeniably important dimension of her performance. However, her autonomy was a product of her rigorous yet playful performative capacity that clashed with waning and emerging networks of documenting and capturing blackness.

The legacy of blackface minstrelsy's symbolic trade in atomized black body parts—the fleshiness, skin, voice, face, lips, and variously fantasized black physiognomy—was liberated but not done away with by the demise of the formal minstrel stage. The ongoing mythological fantasies that conditioned the prurience of minstrelsy were expanded through their formalization into deepening modes of mediation and genrefication. The vaudeville stage, the phonograph, the cinema screen, photography, and lynching portraiture all comingled as influences and points of contestation for Rainey's revelation. All these emerging media attained their eventual dominance or popularity at least partially through the semblance character of minstrelsy, which undergirded and authorized their increasingly entrenched modes of alienating rationalization. All these media and technology achieved their ingratiation to and production of an audience through granting a masterful expectation to the uses of blackness like that which evolved in the minstrel stage. Yet what earlier forms of minstrelized stagecraft consigned to the ritual of public spectacle, newer media would make more rational and rigid.

The versions of blackness reproduced by the phonograph or the cinema screen were functionally more rationalized, and perhaps most dangerous of all, their truth-contents were harder to refute, more factual and especially more instrumental as their mass production and abundance effectively made them accrete far more rapidly and more densely, making them even more hegemonic. Black performances were thus even more regulatory, more automated, and more legalistic. Even if more black representations could be enlisted to refute specific truth-contents, they always did so in partial affirmation of the very judgment they wished to refute. For black performers like Rainey, this created something like a wanted poster or a mug shot (forms that perpetually criminalized black queer performers were all too familiar with) that positively authorized their character beyond the autonomy of their performances and living.

Rainey began performing as a youth in small tent-show minstrel numbers before she found and developed her signature singing prowess. She certainly would have been increasingly aware of the mass-produced cultural and phonographic experiments and their attendant production of sentiment that were beginning to take place through her own iconicity and sound-image.[6] In the idiom of "Babylon girls," which had been traveling the world since roughly the 1890s—during the nascence of the adolescent Rainey's performances on the vaudeville stage—black dancers performed a wide variety of racialized-gendered caricature in which they were at once conscripted to evince black women's compliance to an increasing voyeurism of the black cultural but through which they also created spaces of black gendered deviation and autonomy. The ecstatic practices of black women's minstrelized performances—playing dress-up and modifying corporeal presentations into more spectacular and "absorptive" forms—certainly overlapped with Rainey's rearing in vaudeville in which she carved a complex and humorous space of performative agency.[7] Having come from this tradition of minstrelized blackface performance and vaudeville, Rainey embodied a rich and complicated articulation of aesthetic capture.

As K. Allison Hammer notes, "Vaudeville allowed more cross-gender performance in the name of theater," which, not unlike the juke joint or the brothel, included the more "sinful" black musical forms that passed into ephemera, in contrast to more official black cultural accounts.[8] The fleetingness of the record of these forms, including Rainey's performance described here, was a strategic aesthetic restriction, because these transgressive repertoires balked at and refused the codes of black patriarchal Christian respectability deemed worthy of preservation by both white ethnomusicologists and the increasingly institutionalized black bourgeoisie that would establish the Harlem Renaissance and sculpt much of the "presentable" black music from this point on. In fact, these sinful and queer black forms precipitated a deeply conservative religious gendered and sexual reaction from the enduring patriarchy of black culture and the arbiters of the New Negro in the Harlem Renaissance that Rainey would have to perform through and against. Indeed, sartorial and sumptuary restrictions during the Harlem Renaissance preserved a patriarchal, hypergamous, classist, and monogamous moralizing respectable black feminization as a space through and out from which Rainey had to perform, an aggressive mode of social production she had to steal away from and against.

In this regard, we may think of her black vaudevillian performances for the Theater Owner's Booking Association (TOBA, known colloquially among black performers as Tough on Black Asses for its stingy and demanding labor practices) as the double to and in the "laboratory" of captive flesh that Spillers evokes. This is not to conflate Rainey's performance, career, or life with the captivity of the slave plantation or the contemporaneous prison into which she was occasionally and reputedly interned, but to argue more rigorously that the logics and desires of captivity were formalized, warped, sublated, and expanded through new and prevailing modes of mediation and aestheticization that cohered and structured the aesthetic character chasing after her. In this chapter and even more extensively in the next, I will argue that the putatively social and technological aesthetic registers of petty black patriarchy from within and technological modernity from without were co-constitutive forces whose coherence Rainey had to disassemble.

The "laboratory of flesh" Hortense Spillers and Riley Snorton invoked is a provocative and helpful framework for illuminating the potentialities of the transgressive historical and genealogical moment during which Rainey performed, a moment when the rational aesthetic of skin's semblance character was both a body's sensual performance on the stage and the more deeply inscribable and authoritative rationalization of the body's ordering in and as the world. From the tangled lineage of Babylon girls, artists such as Ma Rainey and, as Anne Cheng's work has astutely pointed out, Josephine Baker, adopted skin, surface, and other means of membranous forms of performance not just as medium but also as media that disfigured their embodiment and created momentary spaces of play within larger racial-gendered orders of inscription.[9] The playful perversity of these embodiments subtly created cracks in the surface of the inscriptions of domination. I don't want to overstate the ambivalent complexity of the performances of many of these artists, who, like George W. Johnson, in many ways trafficked in the pervasive symbolics of minstrelsy. However, the alleged "backward-looking" nature (in a double sense of Rainey's transgressive appearances) of the blues performances of black women positioned their history, not unlike the surface of Johnson's record, at a point of antagonism with respect to the canonized black aesthetic tradition from which they would be evicted. The aesthetic character of blackness arose as a response to an unwieldiness of black life, even as it appropriated the guises and postures of black life. Rainey embodied a critical refusal of the regulation of black life into austerity.

The Opacity of Skin and the Transparency of Phonography

Rainey was enmeshed in a "fleshy" tradition of black women's performance that trafficked self-consciously in what Daphne A. Brooks refers to as a nineteenth-century black performance tradition of "smoke and mirrors." Brooks identified a genealogy of "secondary anecdotes and forgotten tales" that characterize a richly risky tradition of black performance that through its subterfuge and ephemerality earned the ire of both the "white supremacist legal system" and the progressive "race men and women" of the black elite.[10] In the late nineteenth and early twentieth centuries, much of black musical performance dwelled in and nurtured "shadow" social relations with the normative establishments of an increasingly official black culture that would excise itself from the structural effects of racism by imagining the aesthetic as a sociable contestation of or a formal amendment to it. One pervasive node of the coalescence of oppression was the skin that would form the "semblance character" of so much late-nineteenth-century black performance that moved out of the specter of the minstrel stage.[11]

Rainey's performative history, along with that of Josephine Baker and their fellow Babylon girls, illustrates an era or ethos of the precarity of skin during the moment of its most extreme rationalization. It was not so much that skin did not become violently phenotypically encoded; quite the opposite occurred as a response to this period when colorism expanded and comingled with the celebration of black class division. The aestheticization of skin expanded with its rationalization, not just its encoding on bodies but its building of worlds, its precipitating of effects, and its overall regulation of black life. We can see the early inklings of this venture in the romantic aesthetics I have cited in the writings of Kant and Schiller, and such an implementation is more overt and more fully rationalized in Alain Locke's aesthetics, which I will examine toward the end of this chapter. This expanded speculation in the surface of the skin, again most prominently figured through the minstrel stage, paralleled and intersected with the speculative drives of the phonograph. Ma Rainey's performance was not merely an event in the dialectical history of the unfolding of the phonograph as an emerging or predominant technology. On the contrary, Rainey's performance in some consonance with that of Josephine Baker was a milestone in the failure of the phonographic to imprint its forms and authority of desire. In many ways, Rainey's performance was a refusal or failure to perform. The performances and the lyrics of "Moonshine Blues" that operated in her performances must be understood within the genealogy of the phonograph as relying on the coherent and seamless functioning of blackness.

In part this is to acknowledge the sonic stasis of blackness, the way it became an extracted singular social relation for others only through the ethnomusicological field-recording work of almost exclusively white folklorists such as Dorothy Scarborough, Howard Odum, and Natalie Curtis Burlin, and the infamous black prison excursions of John and Alan Lomax. As Roshanak Kheshti has pointed out, scholarly and informal field-recording projects such as these have always been tacitly involved in colonial projects of producing documentary knowledge about an aurally consumable

Other.[12] John and Alan Lomax in particular gained popular and academic recognition for their "discovery" of the "authentic" instrumental blues artistry of Huddie Williams Ledbetter, aka Lead Belly, a discovery that came from their penetration of the putatively unknown and supposedly misunderstood segregated black prisons of the American South in the 1930s and beyond. After decades of sonic field trips to the black segregated prisons of the South, Alan Lomax gave the reason for his sojourns with his father: "I do not believe that the pattern of Southern life can be fundamentally reshaped until what lies behind these roaring, ironic choruses is understood."[13]

I raise the presumed functioning of blackness to contextualize its increasingly generic representation through recorded and reproduced sound. The humanizing character extracted from black life did not grant a reprieve from the machinic functioning of blackness as a source of labor and above all value. Rather, this aesthetic character deepened the speculation in, investment in, and extraction from black life and expanded the valuation and the value-making and value-producing capacities of it. Black cultural production was both value-making and regulating, even criminalizing, further expanding its value-making capacities as and through black representation. Benjamin Filene has extensively charted how the white liberalism of the Lomaxes led them to produce knowledge of supposedly abject black life as proof of and justification of the need for a desegregated South instead of for a liberated black community. The document and documentary form that the Lomaxes wielded attained their epistemological and formal (aesthetic) authority from what Heidegger might call the technologically reflective capacity of (scientific) reason to offer up a functioning symbolic essence. There is a parallel here between what the phonograph wanted and what Alain Locke would later demand in the New Negro. The tautological, automated, and technological nature of this purported essence is what Sylvia Wynter has so extensively theorized as the "infrasensorily ontologized" that allowed the colonially prescriptive human/man in general to discursively subsist. Wynter discusses the authority of this infrasensory essence as reliant on "domesticating representations of the Other" in which "the representation of the Other must function in a rule-governed manner."[14] Here the generic symbolic essence of blackness as abjection, its violently genre-gender-specific functioning, made possible and cohered with documentary's epistemological and formal production of a detainable essence.

I tarry more with Lomax's configuration of black choruses as ontologically opaque and in need of epistemic penetration and exposition through his field-recording trips because I am attempting to engage the centrality of the phonograph to the sensorial, affective, and epistemological valuation of blackness. This sonic primitive accumulation of blackness was not only about the further translation of blackness into emerging networks of exchangeability and valuation. Rather, I would suggest that the sonic and aural valuation of blackness—its use value that makes its exchange value—has been its fantastical infrasensorial power as dark, inscrutable, and impenetrable to sensing and knowing yet highly penetrable to being sensed and known. Such a fantastical materiality was essential to the sensorial precarity of the new and emerging genre of the subject in and as the new and emerging technological and mediated regimes of the phonograph.[15] The simultaneous projected opacity and penetrability of blackness within the transatlantic slave trade and its formal afterlives thus secured a fantastical dialectic of recognition between the subject and its technology. I am calling this emergent and still largely predominant genre of the subject documentary and, as I will discuss shortly, I will further theorize both black objecthood and its inherent excess in the concept of documentary embodiment.

In Rainey's performances of "Moonshine Blues," the evidentiary and documentary assertion of the lyrics regarding the endless policing of queer black life is volatilized. Rainey's artistic phonographic capture and escape enacted black music as a perpetually fugitive process—a refusal to remain in the fugitive captivity that constituted (phonographic) representation. The lyrical embodiments that Rainey conjured through her performance traveled through what Peggy Phelan has identified as the place of the unmarked. Rainey's phonographic performance resists the representative economy of black sounding that writes the prescriptive invaginative (w)hole of sonic modernity. Phelan tellingly alludes to (sonic) modernity's consumptive and digestive motivations of representation:

> Hunger for the same—including the sexual same—*demands* a difference, if only to elicit the pleasure of resemblance. If there is no perceived effort to "convert" or "transform" the apparently different into the Same then there is no "production" at work. And in looking there is always (re)production. The conversion of the abject other (the racially marked, the sexually unmarked) into the Same is an integral part of artistic production.[16]

Rainey literally sits within the belly of modernity's hunger for sonic representation in that phonographic cabinet. Her emergence from the phonograph reveals her parodic embodiment of phonographic abjection, of what the phonographic commonly spits out, the fungible sonic double or what is always the redoubling of blackness into the ears, eyes, and mouths of its listeners and consumers.

Rainey's performance does not end in mere parody; on the contrary, it disfigures the terms of representation against which something like parody's "original" object might be recognized through its abject double. She both emerges and retreats into what the invaginative totality of the phonographic record—precisely through its inscription and, by extension, symbolic capture of black voice—has left unmarked. That carved-out and unmarked phonographic cabinet, that garreted space of unmeasured and unrepresented interiority, is a lived and sounding inside before and beyond the symbolization of the voice. The conscious withholding of the structure of meaning of the sound-image is a refusal that is also always excessively lived inside. Rainey's performances remind us that listening in modernity, as modernity, has always been indifferent to the sounding poetics of the commodity that speaks.[17]

Rainey's performance was not so much a formal revision of the blues as a radical black queer formal critique of the official black culture with which the radical spirit of the blues would be increasingly conflated. Instead, Rainey's lyrical emergence from the phonograph enacted an idiomatic, rather than a generic, realization of her voice and her body; that is, the lived experimental materiality of her listened, danced, and lived voice, something like what George Lewis understood when he theorizes listening (and living) as improvisation.[18] That is the difference between the "placing-at-hand" that the phonograph promises and the "readiness-to-hand" of the force of Rainey's body and voice.

This is not just to speak of an alternate meaning-context for Rainey's voice beyond the content of the lyric and genre, but rather to understand Rainey's voice as a practice of lyrical embodiment, the practice of being a sonic thing in an eminently musical sense. The phonograph was meant to produce a normatively consumptive body for representation—a record, that opaque inscribable surface, that black body as fungible pantomimic nature that when struck produces its master's sounds. Rainey's performance disfigures this normative consumable and consumptive body; it troubles the world of sonic representation that inscription builds. It is that danced body, those swooned hips, that hand that placed the stylus on the record that with every turn unknows the hands that tried to draw it.[19]

The space to play in, to feel in, seems so different than the sentimentally filled in yet practically evacuated space of the words on the stage that

Douglass already arrived in or the expedited speculated spaces into which George W. Johnson was coerced to whistle and laugh. The unspoken unrepresented time of inside the machine, the time between Ma Rainey and the inside of the machine, between Ma Rainey and her audience, is a kind of nearness that goes unmeasured, an immeasurable intimacy that evades the symbolic. What does life feel like being lived under the symbolization of blackness? What kinds of intimacies sing out to each other across that white void and what kind of world can they make against the world that only wants to regulate us as art?

For the pontiffs of the Harlem Renaissance Alain Locke and W. E. B. Du Bois, like the mid-nineteenth-century ancestors of "race men and women," the specter of blackface minstrelsy imbued "the skin" or its symbolic representation with the exogenous and dehumanizing character of antiblack racism. Black art was thus a positive regulation of that putative negation. Indeed, this is the structure and sign of denigration under which George W. Johnson's career remains excisable from the aesthetic character of blackness or is included only as that which the aesthetic character ought to be raised against. The site of blackened skin is also the source of the internalization of antiblack racism expressed in colorism, which quite infamously expanded during the Harlem Renaissance through both its avowed classism and through aspirations of "class division" in Alain Locke's words. For Rainey, however, skin was not just an exogenous production, not just something on the outside forced upon black life. Ultimately, Rainey centered a black world in which skin was also a source of intimacy and poetry.

Documentary Embodiment

The blues as an automated confessional unfolding of blackness as fact always denied the performativity of music even as it relied on it to produce a simultaneously abject and celebratory myopic black essence in representation. Albert Murray quite famously identified this problematic of the theatricality and lyricism of the blues being reduced to a form of semantic realist reportage, a diminution that has largely functioned as a denial of the technical virtuosity and artistry of blues musicians.[20] While Rainey's performances overtly referenced the ideality of phonographic recording and reproduction, they require a critique of the presumptive embodiments of black liveness to work as performance. Therefore, the cleavage exposed by Rainey's dramatic stagecraft centers not just on the supposed opposition between live and recorded sounds, but also on the founding condition of their distinction. To further this tension raised by Rainey, I use the concept of documentary embodiment.

With the term "documentary embodiment" I am thinking of a distinctly modern conception of technology that is broadly theorized in the work of Martin Heidegger. Heidegger's work remains prescient, along with the writings of Sylvia Wynter, as a way to think the "wilderness of technological rationalization" as constituted by and from the position of the instrument and the object of capture, or, as Fred Moten has repurposed it, the seemingly impossible "commodity that speaks."[21] In some sense, documentary embodiment is a way of engaging Heidegger's concept of *Gestell*, or framing. My invocation of *Gestell* within the context of Rainey's performance offers a way to consider how the documentary forms and technologies that came about in the nineteenth century—phonography, photography, film, and the modern museum—were made possible by and bear the formal mark of the objects they sought to capture.[22] In some accord with Heidegger's *Gestell*, I am trying to understand documentary technology, mediation, and, by extension, a kind of blackness as the aesthetic formalization, narration, and poetic fabrication of placing objects at hand. The very gesture of fabricating the nearness of the object not only creates the object on some level but also imbues it with a kind of facticity or evidentiary quality for the beholder. This is the "dominance of the distanceless," the fabricated distance and traversal of that distance, the prescribed nearness, that Heidegger attributes to modern technology and that I would locate in modernity's colonial production and traversal of the New World as the aesthetic character of blackness.[23]

The phonograph, much like the specific filmic or photographic genre of documentary, was heralded for its capacity to symbolically and narratively traverse time and distance, to bring remote, obscure, or lost sounds near. The mechanical ideal of phonographic capture explicitly promised the ability to place at hand any "fugitive sounds," as Thomas Edison called them.[24] This notion of fugitive sounds, which Edison used in his first article discussing the invention of the phonograph, suggests that the sonic capabilities of the phonograph and indeed its very invention were founded upon objects that narratively and symbolically resisted this invented traversal of distance. In Edison's legalistic designation of sound, we glean how phonographic capture is imbued with a disembodied authorization that emplots, narrates, and embodies the object of capture as a condition of its functioning: Sounds become fugitive by virtue of their capture in the phonograph.

William Stott speaks of the emergence of the production of the human document in the 1930s culture of photography and field recordings, which he defines as that which speaks sensibly to an audience through the perceived facticity of its sense of perception and mediation in sound and image. For Stotts, the human document achieves its facticity as document through its inherently empathic similitude with the audience.[25] By the 1930s, the pejorative proslavery assignation of mimicry to black musicians of the mid-nineteenth century had joined the liberal humanizing fraternal mimicry of the abolitionist movement. Yet this drawing close of black culture precipitated a need for the abjection or spitting out of black life as a remote frontier of human discovery and documentation that was yet to be fully speculated upon by knowledge and capital. The ability of the document to symbolically traverse its mediated distance constituted its affective attainment of recognition. In the ambivalent lineage of Josiah Wedgwood's famous eighteenth-century lithograph *Am I Not a Man and a Brother*, affective similarity must be raised to traverse and facilitate a synthetic aesthetic distance, adding perhaps an antecedent and variation to Gregory Bateson's technologizing of "the human" in the mid-twentieth century as "a difference that makes a difference."[26] The recognition of this empathic similitude or affective parity is what Sylvia Wynter might simply identify as the formal bedrock of the "genre of the human."

An eminently Kantian aesthetic of judgment emerges here wherein the nature of what is emotive, sensible, and beautiful, and for that matter human, is obtained through its conceptual and above all teleological submission to a kind of knowing or judgment, what in the Kantian system of thought amounts to the transcendental structure of the understanding.[27] What the Kantian dialectic always overlooked, of course, was how the consumptive drives of the understanding were fundamentally (if at times secretly) written by the animistic reproduction of commodities that could speak. Something like a human document, as it emerged in the 1930s, was always already being written within the violent aesthetic trajectories of the transatlantic slave trade in which human cargo lined the holds of ships docking into port and the plantation songs of human chattel resounded in the ears and covered the sheet music pages of white interlopers.[28] In order for something like humans as documents to be a thing (by the 1930s at least), something like a document needed to put to work, in one way or another, the idea of a human in the first place.

This production of sonic interiority we call the human and its sensuous object—music—has been realized through a kind of sonically embodied black exteriority that often takes the form of a retrospectively projected black interiority. This is the impasse that arises between the recognized exteriority of Ma Rainey's singing—the phonic presence of her voice—and the inscrutable interiority of her life lived in the phonographic cabinet. The nothingness of her phonographic concealment can only always be heard as her phonographic presence, as an exposition, whether that consists of the disclosure of her voice or the (eventual) disclosure of her body, as an object for sensual consumption.[29]

My emphasis on documentary embodiment is also a way to reframe my prior treatment of the invention of the phonograph in the mid-nineteenth century and its precedent in Frederick Douglass and in what Jon Cruz identifies as the coincident pathos of "ethnosympathy" that arose with the newfound study of black music in the middle of the nineteenth century. Cruz notes that Frederick Douglass's call to hear and study slave spirituals as a reflection of the inner world of the slaves inspired a functional interpretive response that inaugurated black music into new webs of scientific and documentary meaning.[30] What was becoming embedded in the technology of writing in the mid-nineteenth century had by Rainey's time been liberated and homed in the technology of the writing of the phonograph.

The excessive sensuality of black sonic bodies that was produced in the nineteenth century capture of black music partially accounted for the phonograph's claim to technological neutrality. The phonograph had no drive, no extension, because it achieved disembodiment at the expense of the fugitive embodiment of the sounding object—the "fugitive sounds" Edison sought to capture. Like the supposed neutrality of the law, the regulative function of reproductive technology was artfully disguised in the abundant aesthetics of the object it reproduced. The history of field recordings of Other cultures, especially the recording of incarcerated black blues musicians, emerged from this Romantic fantasy. This fantastical understanding of a technology as extractive and exteriorizing of an inner essence yet somehow wholly epistemically disembodied and neutral allowed for the documentary to emerge. Thus, I consider documentary not just a genre or exclusively as a drive, as Fred Moten has importantly discussed it, but as a distinct form of fantastical material embodiment to which certain subjects/objects are routinely exposed and through and against which certain bodies are lived and realized.[31] This is yet another tenet of the aesthetic character of blackness.

The Minstrel Stage, Now a World

By the early twentieth century, the scandal of minstrelsy, largely framed as an attack on black dignity by the emerging black cultural elite, had to be assiduously managed and quelled. The minstrel stage was now a world, and everyone was listening and watching. The mechanical reproduction for which George W. Johnson had been an early test pilot was fast becoming ubiquitous with the advent and expansion of sound recording, film, and mass-media journalism. An expanding black representation had to fortify and justify its reasoned valuations. Only beauty should arise, against the gatherings of black life below its surface. The incidence of black musical performance would need to be rendered into a phonic, cultural, and aesthetic essence as black representation composed of a regulative internal logic that would authorize the extrinsic valuation of its imaging. Architects of the Harlem Renaissance such as Alain Locke would conclude that only value could be waged against value: Henry Louis Gates's "art we don't like" waged "against art we do like." This expanded art and its value, and by implication it expanded the misguided presumption that we share in the expansion of value or its trickled-down apportionment.

Arguably the first and certainly one of the most solidified early attempts to build up and institutionalize black culture in the United States was carried out in the Harlem Renaissance. A black cultural, artistic, and musical resurgence stoked by the Great Migration of black folks from the South to northern cities, especially Harlem, New York. While the raison d'être of the Harlem Renaissance is often framed as the black sigh of relief and shout of excitement that came from fleeing the regulation of Jim Crow laws down South and the later the trauma of World War I, I want to highlight how these excretions of desire, liberation, and need came up against different aesthetic, sartorial, and sexual regulations in the pontiffs of the Harlem Renaissance. The cursory and precarious sketches of black music and life illustrated in nineteenth-century writings and early recordings (and the even more wayward livings happening in and underneath them), from Frederick Douglass's soundings to George W. Johnson's singing, were being cast off for their exogenous racist character. The restrictive nature of these earlier reproductions would be refracted through and wedded to much more authoritative valuations within a black culture that increasingly created its own protocols. As black art and culture became increasingly solidified concepts, they also became a regulative force engineering much more officious smoothed, reflective surfaces against an increasingly uninhabitable inside. The aesthetic character of blackness emerged more clearly. The expanding representational outside of black art, constructed through and against its inside, in which less and less black life could live, was increasingly made to present a respectable and austere posture of contestation. Dignity, representation, and value were primed and wielded against the exogenous values of "the white world."

Rainey's performances troubled multiple emerging and ongoing regimes in which plenipotentiaries of blackness were rationalizing black life. The scientific rationalization of "the black voice" engendered in George W. Johnson's phonography expanded through both the emerging mass production of the fledgling recording industry and the technological innovation of stereo and electrified sound that would expand the isomorphic pathology of "body-reasoning" between a body, a culture, and the reproduced voice, intimating modern parasocial relationships with the celebrity that was emerging and affirming the kind of propertied domesticity that was increasing through managerial class expansion.[32] The emphasis of the blues on the black work song such as "Washer Woman's Blues" attests to the black underside of the latter, as has been thoroughly explicated in the writings of W. E. B. Du Bois, Claudia Jones, Hazel Carby, Angela Davis, and Tera W. Hunter.[33] Rainey's music spoke to the most denigrated black women and gender-marginalized people, against whom emerging regimes of official black culture and dignity were being built.

Black women's invisibilized domestic labor as maids, nannies, and caretakers increasingly propped up white domestic class division and the gendered social normalization of the white patriarchal family. The belittling of the lives and labor of poor and working black women, which many blues work songs sought to highlight and bemoan, was carried out double fold. In the white homes that exploited them as essential domestic and care labor, black women were stigmatized as a contagion, and in the homes on the black side of town, the time black women spent laboring on the white side of town was branded a pathological hindrance to black patriarchal domestication. This double jeopardy was the two-sided cudgel of impending black class division that was being championed by the conservative aesthetes and vanguards of the Harlem Renaissance.[34] The latter is what I will spend the remainder of the book discussing, as the aestheticization of black life—its internalized and internal judgments—increasingly became the liberated property of our aesthetic justification and cultural labor. In myriad ways, the idea that black freedom centers on and is evidenced by our endogenous representative capacity would become the contention of many luminary purveyors of black art and culture. Our ability and capacity to make sounds and images like us would increasingly be conflated with the lushness and capaciousness of our living.

We could now trod the infrasensory field upon whose precipice Frederick Douglass stood. Our making, and our need to prove, to be seen and to be heard completely and progressively, mistakenly fused with our need to live, our dignity, our aesthetic justification, would leech our living for the triumph of an emerging and ongoing black aesthetic character. In keeping with my previous critique of Wagner, it is not just the idea that "white people are watching and listening, so we'd better show them we're good," it was as much if not equally the self-motivated self-regulating attitude of "white people, look at me, look at us, see, we're real good" that coalesced as an emerging and expansive black aesthetic propriety and propped up a world-building proprioception that follows us today. This protected paranoia, this wishfully guaranteed expectation, was the vanguardist frequency to which the Harlem Renaissance tuned its own rationalist projects of black representation.

The New Negro, the New Law

In 1925, a couple of years after Ma Rainey began her performance routines and black women blues artists like Bessie Smith, Clara Smith (no relation), Trixie Smith (also no relation), Ida Cox, and Sodarisa Miller were touring poor and working-class black communities, Harlem Renaissance aesthete and philosopher Alain Locke, with just such an internalized investment in representation, wrote: "And finally, with the Negro rapidly in process of class differentiation, if it ever was warrantable to regard and treat the Negro en masse, it is becoming with every day less possible, more unjust and more ridiculous. . . . The Negro, too, for his part, has idols of the tribe to smash."[35] Locke's revelry in increasing black class stratification came from the developmental logic steeped in Du Bois's framing of black folk's "race-childhood" as a domestic moment of maturation in which first black class division and then black patriarchal domestication could take root. Locke makes plainer even than Du Bois how aesthetically rooted and realized this limited imagining of black life would be. Black aestheticization was key to structuring the valuations of the projects and strictures that Rainey and many of her fellow queer black women blues artists preformed in and against.

Poor and working-class black life was pushed against the yoke of its rationalization during enslavement and its immediate aftermath. As

Rainey's life and performances attest, new sexual, gender, and social needs and desires arose out from under the surveyorship and eavesdropping of the slave master or its alleged savior in the paternalism of the state. Rainey's poetic performance symbolized the break that was taking place imaginatively and in practice across the various spaces of black music making and living in the generations born after manumission. Yet in a burgeoning conception of black representation brandished by the black elite of the Harlem Renaissance such as Locke, these transgressors and their failure to internalize "the veil" were categorized with the regressive threat of minstrelsy, or what Locke called a "tribal idol." For Locke, the internalization of and response to this "tribal idol," this totemic rendering of blackness, would disappear and disguise the austerity of racist demand as the surplus of black art and representation. Certain kinds of black affinities were constrained under the writ of the new order of black representation. For Rainey, Locke's New Negro formed both the grave and the engraving functions of her symbolic phonograph. The New Negro was a complementary form of containment that tried to contain her and bring about the prescriptive partial disappearance of her performance from the dominant historical record.

In "Enter the New Negro," Locke expanded on the "tribal idol" that he wished to displace with the New Negro:

> The Old Negro, we must remember, was a creature of moral debate and historical controversy. His has been a stock figure perpetuated as an historical fiction partly in innocent sentimentalism, partly in deliberate reactionism. The Negro himself has contributed his share to this through a sort of protective social mimicry forced upon him by the adverse circumstances of dependence. So for generations in the mind of America, the Negro has been more of a formula than a human being—a something to be argued about, condemned or defended, to be "kept down," or "in his place," or "helped up," to be worried with or worried over, harassed or patronized, a social bogey or a social burden. The thinking Negro even has been induced to share this same general attitude, to focus his attention on controversial issues, to see himself in the distorted perspective of a social problem. His shadow, so to speak, has been more real to him than his personality. Through having had to appeal from the unjust stereotypes of his oppressors and traducers to those of his liberators, friends and benefactors he has subscribed to the traditional positions from which his case has

been viewed. Little true social or self-understanding has or could come from such a situation.[36]

For Locke, the "true social understanding" or "personality" of the Negro was painted over by the "brush of discourse." This social character suffocated under the violent empathic sentimentalism that bound Douglass to the stage of his alleged "liberators, friends and benefactors," as it was profitably atomized in "formulas" of prescriptive and proto-technological scientism that rendered intelligible the black voice in the phonograph. But in some sense Locke rehearsed the mourning for the loss of the "true man" in the conversion of captivity (and liberation) that Douglass famously imagined and expounded ("You have seen how a man was made a slave; you shall see how a slave was made a man").[37] It was this man who Locke and Du Bois often identified as lost under the social calculus of the "Negro problem."[38]

> By shedding the old chrysalis of the Negro problem we are achieving something like a spiritual emancipation. Until recently, lacking self-understanding, we have been almost as much of a problem to ourselves as we still are to others. But the decade that found us with a problem has left us with only a task. The multitude perhaps feels as yet only a strange relief and a new vague urge, but the thinking few know that in the reaction the vital inner grip of prejudice has been broken. With this renewed self-respect and self-dependence, the life of the Negro community is bound to enter a new dynamic phase, the buoyancy from within compensating for whatever pressure there may be of conditions from without.

The "buoyancy" Locke spoke of was not merely a personalized or even a communal sense of esteem, but a robust purposive black culture unearthed by the black vanguard, of which Locke was of course a part, that would establish the increasingly institutional black persona against the "shadow" of blackness. For Locke, black art, namely the curation of black art with which Locke was vested, was the buoyant truth: "We ought and must have a school of Negro art, a local and a racially representative tradition" that "must discover and reveal the beauty which prejudice and caricature overlaid. And all vital art discovers beauty and opens our eyes to that which previously we could not see." Long out of sight was the fight Schiller had alluded to just over a century earlier. There was in Locke's building up of the aesthetic a clear movement away from the racialized fight of the last century, which was still raging and intensifying: "But the decade that found us with a problem has left us with only a task."[39]

On the one hand, the institution of the New Negro opened a fascinating and varying international relationality of "detours," however vanguardist, as Brent Hayes Edwards has characterized it.[40] Yet the formal foreclosures the New Negro asserted were raised around the specific inheritance of value that Locke deemed essential to black art. For Locke, ancestral "buoyance" of black art was formalized and institutionally conflated with a kind of legalistic right of accretion or juridical conception of inheritance. Is buoyancy drafted aboard the decks of a sinking ship or is it a sublime experience cultivated from the shore? With buoyancy Locke seemed to privilege a prescriptive and evidentiary—and increasingly anthropological—facticity of black life. Locke quite powerfully spoke to the threatening properties of black art that resonate with disruptiveness of Rainey's performances. But Locke did not allow for such difference as an inheritance of an ongoing practice, something that might increasingly unmake the world that made the phonograph. Rather, Locke's conception of inheritance, or what he often called "legacy," was aspirationally proprietary, increasingly institutional, and wrapped up in a propriety toward (infinite) accumulation within representation that would itself never be undone. Black representation was to be scientifically fortified, added to, built up, and legalistically expanded by the verifiable social character or value of the black work of art.

For Locke, the emerging conception of artistic legacy meant the potential to make verisimilar the speculation of imagination with the representable speculation of value, or what Marx simply called "labor," that would increasingly be understood as the black work of art.[41] That is, Locke assumed and required, and indeed the New Negro unambiguously invested in the production of a system of value and valuation around which the (artistic) imagination might retrospectively be trained to conform and hence verify and represent. Even though Locke's emergent broader conception of black artistry might at first appear to be incompatible with the dominant trends of documentary and documentation, it too was caught up in and required a related form of self-possessive and self-possessed documentary embodiment.

Black music, art, and culture for Locke were tied to a rather exuberant expansion of the capacities of black folk in the deeply instrumentalized rational sense that black music and art would anchor. Locke was essentially rationalizing the sentimental humanity and "heart" of the slave that Frederick Douglas claimed black music would explicate. Here we can glean not only the earlier nineteenth-century informal ethnomusicological studies of black music but the increasing number of phonographic and ethnomusicological recordings and studies that emphasized a proto-proprietary differentiation of black musics through the "nature of black culture." Du Bois and Locke's oft-repeated emphasis on a Negro civilization as that which sends and is sent by the delineation of a verifiably documented and scientific Negro "personality" was bound up in this propriety and proprietary endeavor: "For this [the New Negro] must know himself and be known for precisely what he is, and for that reason he welcomes the new scientific rather than the old sentimental interest." Locke advocated for an explication of black life that, although it was superficially rid of overt white involvement such as the Lomaxes', internalized their mode of representative and verifiable humanity. It created the good representations to fight the bad representations; it made the good law to fight the bad law.

Locke formally named what is so sentimentally unknown: "The Negro of today [must] be seen through other than the dusty spectacles of past controversy. The day of 'aunties,' 'uncles' and 'mammies' is equally gone. Uncle Tom and Sambo have passed on, and even the 'Colonel' and 'George' play barnstorm roles from which they escape with relief when the public spotlight is off. The popular melodrama has about played itself out, and it is time to scrap the fictions, *garret the bogeys and settle down to a realistic facing of facts.*"[42] Already we can see how an artistic personality or institutionality of self-knowing might be complicated by an artist like Rainey who was equally interested in being unknown to (phonographic) representation, in being differently known, in playing with being known and unknown to and by her audience, and in subjecting the self to a certain kind of dispossession that it relied on in its possession of the individual as black artist. Against the melodramatic and performative trajectory, a path disproportionately forged by black women and black queer folks, Locke offered facticity that corresponded to the same reductive rationalization of life that documentary embodiment entombs. The challenge for Locke was not a matter of reducing black life to the evidentiary but to deposit within the black imagination a kind of detective or judge—a sense of self and a force—who would marshal black life into evidence, into proof, and into justification for those from without. Because he refused the fight, because the fight was not even within earshot of the shore for him, Locke merely proposed a new value to replace the old value of a life lived as facts.

The New Negro, the New Value

The breakdown of the propriety of the New Negro took place along the lines of what Lindon Barrett theorizes as the relation between blackness and value to which the disavowal of black queerness and gender transgression are essential as an explicit site of disinheritance, an anti-estate. I would encourage us to think of this lived disinheritance more critically as the failure of proprietary inheritance, of property, to inscribe its violent seal of (fictive) protection. Barrett, referencing Walter Ong's work, discusses the hegemony of the technologizing literacy over the black voice in a manner that bears stark resemblance to the hegemony of the technologizing of black culture and art. Barrett discusses literacy as coercing the consensus from which value can be disclosed. In Locke, and in the broader Harlem Renaissance, this disclosure of value was related to a certain kind of hierarchical "race pride"—not to be conflated with a shared esteem of black life—that was explicitly echoed in Locke's demand to "scrap the fictions, *garret the bogeys and settle down to a realistic facing of facts.*" The fact and facticity of black art was meant to write and rewrite the fact of blackness. Black art was vested with an implicit capacity to document black life and even more with a proprietary potential, a market-rationalized character in form, content, and (institutional) framing, a rational aesthetic conduct (curation, canonization, saleable rights) that was implicitly and explicitly yoked to improvement and beautification, cleaning up the streets, and pulling up our pants: the garreting of bogeys and the settling down to facts.

It is no wonder, in line with Kay Hammer's contention, that the New Negro's aesthetic moralism so unsubtly adopted the language of closeting monsters to disclose beauty and in so doing relegated to obscurity the largely feminized, queer, and gender-expansive space of variety stages, vaudeville venues, and minstrel stages on which some of the biggest and most talented queer black women and gender-transgressive folks performed. It is not a formal opposition between the supposed ephemerality of performance and the timelessness of painting that occasioned this disavowal, but the conflation of disinheritance with nonrelationality and the conflation of life with speculation. As Locke pontificated, "Culture . . . is a matter not of consumption but of production. It is not a matter of degrees and diplomas, or even of ability to follow and appreciate. It is the capacity to discover and to create."[43]

The speculative capacity to discover, create, and accumulate culture aspired to an emergent black capitalist ethos. This spirit emerged from but was beyond the self-possessed individual's mere possession of "the right to work and the right to consume." It aspired to a token authority, a petty-capitalist power, a proto-sovereignty to be enshrined in what Locke referred to as the personality and the personal, extending into "personal relations." Thus the "buoyancy" of Locke's New Negro yoked cultural production to "an important sign of newly negotiated and exorbitant subjectivity passing for essential human subjectivity."[44] Locke institutionalized the constraint of this subject position in the Negro "personality," or with more grandiosity as Du Bois's "Negro civilization," the site from which (Kantian) judgment and appreciation supposedly lose their absolute idealist tendency and acquire the cultural pluralist and pragmatist vision for which Locke was famous.

As Brent Hayes Edwards, Hazel Carby, Houston Baker, and many scholars of the Harlem Renaissance and the Negritude movement have pointed out, brushing off of the authority of universalist judgment involved characterizing blackness as "uncivilized," "barbaric," "backward" or "without culture" by identifying "a culture that projected onto the world (with the aim of dominating it) and a language that was presented as universal (with the aim of providing legitimacy to the attempt at domination)."[45] For Édouard Glissant, one of Negritude's most seminal thinkers, the critique and undoing of domination required a poetic expanse against the world where any traversal with each other would only be framed in terms of our possessive self-interest, what Glissant simply calls "relation." Glissant challenged the buoyance of Locke that aspired to mere traversal of the dominant order. What if we all swam ashore together? What if there are enough of us that we put the ocean out to sea? What if we sea so much that we are the ocean? Glissant writes, "For though this experience made you, original victim floating toward the sea's abysses, an exception, it became something shared and made us, the descendants, one people among others. Peoples do not live on exception. Relation is not made up of things that are foreign but of shared knowledge. This experience of the abyss can now be said to be the best element of exchange." Édouard Glissant's privileging of the shared experience of the abyss (of antiblack racism) as the basis for relation to navigate black life collectively challenges Locke's espousal of class division to create proper black culture to navigate the world or world of black representation.[46] In Locke's prevailing formula, the ship of black representation, in order to stay buoyant and shore-bound, must jettison black life to the sea. Black art, black culture, and even black music will create a shore, a riverbank, from which to bear proper witness to black life's swirling toward the abyss.

Against this expansive and potentially contaminant and messy commingling and flirtatious oceanic imaginary that Ma Rainey and indeed the black queer blues invoked and relied on, Locke proposed value. Specifically, Locke proposed black cultural value as self-imposed moral comportment. Indeed, for Locke the supposed monoculture of (enlightenment) domination, what Locke might view as the blackness of blackness, would only fall away (it was not contested or confronted for Locke, who despised and aimed to decrease the politics of conflict) through the buoyancy of culture as moral comportment—this is, the volume of black culture, its collection, accumulation, and self-verification against what would render it aberrant. Comportment for Locke was the heart of his philosophical concern of the valuation of value or was simply how to produce value "by understanding how and why, to find principles of control from mechanisms of valuation themselves."[47]

If the prescription of domination over black life made it this empty, voided, vacant, garreted space (what Locke once referred to as "Saharas of culture") that Rainey performed in and out of, then for Locke it was an emptiness that needed to be responsibly and respectably but vigorously filled. Black culture for Locke was a regulatory function to fill the ruptured space of black carryings on with the endless emptiness of valuation, of the value-making process of the New Negro. Indeed, Locke's thinking was integral to the marriage of document with comportment, of fact with value, of (internalized) authority with capture and collection. Locke was foundational in making the black document a self-regulative functioning, a technology in Lindon Barrett's sense. Unleashed upon the world this technology would make possible pluralist white imaginations "outside" black culture as much as it would build and embolden the black class-divided expropriation and representation of black culture "inside" black culture. What is "truly representative" about black culture, even in its varied formal registers that are assimilated to its whole, became the supra-value of it or the comported compulsion to represent (for representation).[48]

The reappraisal of the blackness of the New Negro, its "newness," was its ability and imperative to comport, because this was the bearing of its institutionality and hence its moral right to the representative function of inheritance: its recording, capture, collection, documentation, its arrest with a hearing, a trial, legal representation, the juridical legal accretion as fact, as legacy as inheritance. As Locke said, "The ideal culture is representative of the entire personality even in the slightest detail. . . . Culture likewise is representative of the whole personality when it is truly perfected."[49] For

Locke, black culture beautified value, and this beautification—its essential function—is what created its inheritance. Disinheritance for Locke was conflated with a lack of institutionalized authority that we might call the inability of deviance to reproduce (the fantasy) of itself as the authority that produces it, a deviation from the production of the state, the family, the self-possessed individual. These aspirations for curatorial accumulation as black culture are anchored with a decidedly patriarchal mode of (gender) policing and possession. Locke intoned: "As Goethe says, 'What thou hast inherited from the fathers, labor for, in order to possess it.' Thus, culture is inbred—but we ourselves are its parents."[50]

For Locke, Glissant's oceanic poetics of relation were subsumed under a territorializing gesture through which Locke and countless black musicians in his wake would try to make black music American music and so anchor the paternalism of the state from which their pluralist patriarchal and petty-capitalist authority could accrue as value for value's sake. Locke's domestication and domestic fantasy of black culture, its surrogate authority, enshrined in its capacity to produce value, carried no capacity beyond value to make the world more ethical, only to produce a dignified "ethical culture" for an unethical world (where the world is made more and more "the world picture" of representation). What deviates from value, even if it is an original opposition to value and valuation, cannot properly convey the engendering force of the cultural. Only some of black life can be let onto the buoyant vessel of black culture; a ship that sails increasingly toward value and away from black people.

Black culture will lock the doors against black life too. Austerity measures must be meted out if value is to be produced. For Locke, the domestication of black culture upholds the integrity of its engendering modes of patriarchal comportment. This fatherly stature is the internal whip that makes black culture productive for value. For Locke, granting black culture "a place of licensed heresy" within the dominant engines of facticity also granted comportment and integrity to the institutionalization of black culture.[51] Locke imagined the institutionalization and domestication of black culture (under patriarchal supervision), its dwelling within, as the capacity to bear the infrasensory capacity of audiovisual technologies in a way that more playful regimes of mediation, especially the mediation of transgressive embodiments of black genders, simply could not or refused to attain.

The vaudevillian and theatrical skills and skins that Rainey and other black queer blues performers were honing were a threat to the legislation of the technologizing of black art precisely because they were doubly barred from its fantasies of surrogate authority via its facticity (of blackness). Josephine Baker's skin was a medium, not just an art, but one that by virtue of its absolute practiced precarity refused to or could not bear the authority of facticity that would be all but guaranteed with emerging media like the phonograph, film, radio, and, later, television. As Anne Cheng writes, "At the moment *La Baker* was invented on stage we see not the affirmation or the denial of Modernist Primitivism but the failure of its terms to inscribe its own passions."[52] The precarity of Baker's media was as much reflective of the desire of its beholders to see and to know as it was of its own objectification as something to be inherited and known. If, as Hortense Spillers contends, the media and medium of captive flesh (perhaps overlapping with but not reducible to the flesh of the captive) bore the aspirations of variegated projects of social, geographical, and aesthetic domination, then this medium of captive flesh both presaged and was conscripted to reconfigure the authoritative capacities of the phonograph. Locke would not have approved of Ma Rainey wearing the phonograph in a historical but all-too-ongoing sartorial condemnation precisely because it limits and undermines (if not abolishes) its authority to bear facts and produce values that it had been enlisted to inherit and further accumulate in and as the aesthetic character of blackness.

Music Against the Subject

4

Certain blacks, certain blacks, do what they
  wanna, do what they wanna
Certain blacks, certain blacks, go wild yeah,
  go wild yeah
Certain blacks, certain blacks, groove on love,
  groove on love
Certain blacks, certain blacks, dig they freedom,
  dig they freedom
Whoaaaaaaaaa, Bwahhhhh, Haaaaaaa!!!

> The Art Ensemble of Chicago, "Certain Blacks 'Do What They Wanna,'" on the album *Certain Blacks*

The whole history of suffering cries out for vengeance and calls for narrative.

> Paul Ricoeur, *Time and Narrative, Volume 1*

Dorcas Manfred does not care that people talk about her, gossip about her, narrate her life and its consequences, and pathologize her desires. The elliptical, almost excised, protagonist of Toni Morrison's *Jazz* embodies the wayward spirit of the novel's titular music against the prescriptive and limited subjectivity black life is granted in the social. What we get of Dorcas Manfred is only partial. Fragments of her wayward life are largely made present for us as the reader only through the self-negating of her desire. Dorcas is a funeral procession of the people she has spurned, fucked, pissed off, titillated, ultimately those whose desire she has marked and from which she has evaded total capture. Dorcas is a young black woman who flirts with Joe Trace—her eventual murderer—to the scorn of Violet Trace, the wife Joe abused. Dorcas has moved through the house and against the values of her deeply religious and strict aunt Alice, whose kinship with Violet centers substantially on the aunt's generational ageism, allegiance to reinforcing patriarchy, and prudish disapproval of Dorcas's capricious lifestyle. Even Dorcas's perhaps sole advocate and friend Felice, who tries to "solve" Dorcas's murder, which begins the novel, is an odd and unsatisfying complement who serves mostly to further fracture the total picture or frame that we as readers would love to hang around Dorcas Manfred's posthumous portrait.

Toni Morrison's inspiration for Dorcas came from *The Harlem Book of the Dead*, a collection of performative funeral portraits by the Harlem Renaissance photographer James Van Der Zee. Although the images in the book were originally taken in the 1920s, the photographs were collected and supplemented by black filmmaker and artist Camille Billops's interview of James Van Der Zee and scored with contemporary poetry by the black queer poet Owen Dodson and released as a volume in 1978. Morrison wrote the preface for Van Der Zee's collection. Like her later novel *Jazz*, *The Harlem Book of the Dead* was a more experimental approach to relating black life. In Van Der Zee's book, the narration and reportage of black death are elevated yet shown to be incapable of encapsulating the poesis of black life. Both Morrison's and Van Der Zee's works deal with explicitly macabre subjects and confront the political contexts that condition black death, and, in some consonance with Ma Rainey's phonographic refusal, they do so against the documentary capture and pathology that chases after black life.

In this chapter, I invoke Dorcas Manfred as a figment—for she does not quite appear as a character—to trip up the way narrative and pathology create a legalistic and juridical form of capture of black life. Just as Alain Locke tried to lay down the New Negro as a new law, the narrator of Toni Morrison's novel attempts to encircle and surround the black life embodied in Dorcas's ungovernable and never quite intelligible movements. The narrator of *Jazz* extends the legalistic logic of Alain Locke's aesthetic comportment and the demand that black art narrate a sociable black cultural subject in order to contest the abject authority of racial pathology. The formal question I ask, via Morrison and Frantz Fanon, is What does it mean to insist that "our stories" ought to counter pathology? This is a crucial and long-running demand for black art and the black artist dating at least as far back as Frederick Douglass. Such a narrative demand, often couched outside the form of configuration or emplotment that is characteristic of narratives, is a form that forms form. Both Morrison and Van Der Zee contest this form and all its attendant authority. In the spirit of Dorcas and Van Der Zee's funeral portraiture, I insist on the unintelligibility of black life and its deviance from the dominant social that pathologizes us. Inspired by Morrison's wonderfully wayward protagonist, I do not engage in a totalizing explanation of Morrison's *Jazz*, although I convey basic plot, structure, and character information where necessary. Ultimately, I engage Dorcas and the funeral portraiture of James Van Der Zee as forms that trip up and negate the kind of juridical and regulatory conscription of black life as a dignified character narrated before and for the law. Narrative, or the dignity of "our stories," does not counter the gossip, the slander, and the slights of racial pathology but instead gives rationality to their effects. The object of my analysis in this chapter is less Dorcas Manfred and more the social she exposes as simply not good enough for our living.

The Dignity of the Subject Before the Law

An enduring and essential consequence of the aesthetic character of blackness, which is part of its broader regulative function I have theorized, is the linking of pathology and narratology that enables the conflation of voice with being heard, being understood, being represented, and subjectivity itself. If being black is having always already arrived in the world through myth, gossip, and pathology, as Fanon famously expounds, then producing a more precise, accurate, or truthful account of being black has, since at least the days of Frederick Douglass, been championed as a solution to our supposed misrecognition. Such a paradigmatic (black) liberal assertion runs exactly counter to Fanon's argument that it is (black) representation that regulates our misrecognition. Fanon famously identified the cinematic screen as the site where the Other's *imago* of the Negro is "faithfully" reproduced.[1] Slightly later in *Black Skin, White Masks*, Fanon suggests that this split is formal: "The Negro is aiming for the universal, but on the screen his Negro essence, his Negro 'nature,' is kept intact."[2] In resonance with Fanon, Frank Wilderson refers to this predicament as "the unbridgeable gap between Black being and Human life."[3] The bridging of the racist *imago* with black folks' persona (an increasing condition of shared mass mediatization) splinters black esteem, not just for the racist material forces visited upon black life but also for the black incapacity to comfortably gain a foothold on the racist bridge. In Alain Locke's New Negro and Du Bois's conception of "the Negro artist," aesthetic judgment and aesthetic comportment are tasked with producing an equivalency, starting a dialogue, and creating a shared language of justification for the ineffable experience of racist terror.

In this equation, pathology and the violent forces and effects it visits upon black folks is met with and bridges narrative and narratology. This is precisely the bridging that Ma Rainey's performance refused.

As the past three decades of scholarship on the slave narrative suggest, the humanizing character of black music is extracted from the supposed need to narratively bridge racist pathology.[4] Narrative is vested with a symbolic legal function that is aspirationally totemic but that is more accurately understood before or underneath that symbolism as aspiring to a legal process and logic of accretion. Narrative thus adopts a reforming logic, entering, amending, and expanding the law against us. This stacking up, this legal accretion builds an official black culture, a "New Negro" and his authorizing judgment; it builds a black social against the already abundant black social life that Fred Moten refers to as "a language lab, which fact does not lessen but rather intensifies the ship's and the shipper's brutality."[5] Fact and narrative aim to accumulate as black representation. Conspiring against "the language lab," they plead their case and make their pledge in reaction to racial pathology in an ever-expanding court of law, whether this be the cinematic screen, the photographic frame, or the phonographic record. What I am tracking in the aesthetic character of blackness is not just black representation, but how the process of these media, especially the sonic, acquire this evidentiary and legalistic function through blackness.

By giving us a proper hearing in the social and before the law, black representation as black music and black culture is often championed as a panacea to this already-having-been-spoken for, to this waiting that Fanon alludes to. This is our aesthetic justification, the positive assertion of our regulation against what is misconstrued as our totalizing negation, a plea, or for Fanon, a shout amid a sea of seemingly ubiquitous gossip. The arbiter of racial pathology, as much as the albatross of official black culture, has already plotted our footsteps, however formally or sentimentally varied they may be. As Alain Locke's demand for aesthetic comportment suggests, our movements are burdened by this weight of caring endlessly about how we sound and how we appear.

This representational and representative anxiety is created by the law, which can never remedy it. Our only aesthetically justified responses are bound to the act of creating more law, creating more representations, an act that is increasingly conflated with creating more life, more care, and more sociality for us when the effect is actually the opposite. This demand is echoed in Henry Louis Gates Jr.'s statement in Charles Burnett's brilliantly experimental documentary of Nat Turner that "the only way that you can fight a representation in art that you don't like is to create new art, to create more art, to surround it."⁶ Our aesthetic justification adopts an accretive logic that is wedded to aesthetic judgment. Our art is not just evidence in court; worse, it is the regulation of our living by an aestheticized evidentiary standard. How does a law like existence chase after us even as it feels like that which we perpetually arrive at? In this chapter, I think through and against the formal underpinnings of the aesthetic character of blackness around the relationship between narrative and pathology.

The commonplace notion, implied in Gates's language and indeed in earlier exponents of the black bourgeoisie such as Locke and to a lesser extent Du Bois, especially during the Harlem Renaissance, is that black cultural narrative can counter racial and racist pathology. The institutionalization, genrefication, and officialization of black art all speak to this legalistic edict: that good law can fight bad law, that good representation can counter bad representation, that beauty can properly, wholly, or even ethically speak our truth to our oppression and our oppressors. The overt critique of racial pathology in *Jazz* is inextricably bound to its critique and disturbance of narrative. Morrison's *Jazz* critiques the aesthetic integrity, the beauty of testimony of black music precisely as an agent of pathology. The conflation of social pathology with the social, even at its most challenging point of affirmation in black death, is antagonized as a regulative formal project. The world view of James Van Der Zee's portraiture weaves through Morrison's novel, which asks if black life and music live beyond the aesthetic character of blackness, live beyond the violence of mere narration or pathology.

Frantz Fanon famously identified both the logic and the effect of this aesthetic concern of our narrative reportage: "And so it is not I who make a meaning for myself, but it is the meaning that was already there, preexisting, waiting for me."⁷ For Fanon, the unfolding of narrative subjectivity or the narrative subjection of blackness in "the social" is bounded by a capacious space that elsewhere he generalizes as the pathology (as well as the function of the cinematic screen) that is endemic to a modern sociegeny, against which black life must be a lived austerity. In Algeria, from which Fanon wrote, the luxurious social life of the pieds-noirs section of the city where he lived was built entirely on the austerity forced upon the social world of the native (Algerian, Arab, and before them, Berbers). The Manichean world of the colony fostered the decadent life of the colonizer against the exploitation of the colonized. Fanon coined his scientific term "sociegeny" to describe this "creative mode of invention: that of a subject whose destiny is marked by something other than itself."⁸ Much like, though perhaps a bit less than, his progenitor Freud and his Caribbean contemporary Sylvia Wynter, Fanon temporalized the rationalization of racial domination that produces modern subjects. Both racial pathology from without and "our stories," or narrative from within (that extractive circle Douglass drew), reify this subject against the ways we do and might imaginatively live otherwise.

Racial domination is temporalized and rationalized narratively and aesthetically as the subject who also disappears its dependence. This recalls the "specific type of non-culture" that depends on us to be overly and officially culture.[9] Virginia Woolf's (in)famous "room of one's own" (of the subject) grants the positive language of property to the lonely life of (literary) freedom, a freedom that formally prized because it is built on the backs of the coerced collectivity of oppressed black life. This domestic interior also functions as that which black life is collectively barred from, a set of laws, of moral codes of comportment, rights, responsibility, and respectability against which black life is constantly measured—even and especially when it lives collectively outside these. Black life may live outside, in varying proximities, but as Fanon asserts that just as the threat of the Negro haunts the psychic space of the subject, so too does the symbolic rendering of blackness stalk and penetrate every corner of the projective space of the cinematic screen, the exotic African "tom-toms" floating on the radio waves and emanating from phonographic grooves.

There are even within Fanon's world voluminous rooms decorated and sounded by black voices and black music, lined by black portraits that build a world from which black life is increasingly evicted. In this calculus, little more than waiting lives outside the abundance of the narrative pathology of black subjection. Very little black life is deemed livable outside the storehouse of representation presented as proof against that narrative-pathology. Fanon's arguments of course stoked the predominant consideration within fields of black study that there is nothing outside (black) representation that relegates blackness to a "zone of non-being." Yet Fanon himself acknowledged that it is precisely this "zone of nonbeing, an extraordinarily sterile and arid region, an utterly naked declivity where an authentic upheaval can be born."[10] The extent to which the subject's living allows any life, the extent to which those vacant rooms live or let live anything other than the life of racial capital, of property, ought to itself be called into question because in this room, in this world, the subject and the self become the barest form of possession, a constant site of endless defense whose esteem or standing is realized only from without, through the exogenous and tenuous dignity of property, of work, of culture—of the work of art.

I want to engage Morrison's brilliant provocations in *Jazz* to suggest that there is a form, and by extension a limit, to this hegemonic empty room of self-possession that is the black work of art and the black artist's strained-toward. Fanon's thinking of the formalization of the subject in *Black Skin, White Masks* provides an important grounding for this problem space:

> In its immediacy, consciousness of self is simple being-for-itself. In order to win the certainty of oneself, the incorporation of the concept of recognition is essential. Similarly, the other is waiting for recognition by us, in order to burgeon into the universal consciousness of self. Each consciousness of self is in quest of absoluteness. It wants to be recognized as a primal value without reference to life, as a transformation of subjective certainty (*Gewissheit*) into objective truth (*Wahrheit*). When it encounters resistance from the other, self-consciousness undergoes the experience of *desire*—the first milestone on the road that leads to the dignity of the spirit.[11]

For Fanon, the formalization of subjectification, which is to say its aesthetic regulation, ultimately lies in, as it requires, dignity, the standing and standing up in recognition or a valence of the "aesthetic comportment" to which Alain Locke referred. Suffice it to say that god has no internalized need for dignity, no extensive accountability, only imagined (narrative) authority. It is this power of reportage, of history, of pathology, of gossip, of retrospection, of "I-told-you-so's" that, for Fanon, black subjectivity must dispel in order to achieve a "primal value," in order to "win." Black dignity, as black subjectivity, would be a disjoining of the constant conflation of narrative subjectivity with racial pathology that makes possible social and civic life as such. Fanon forecasts or calls for a black dignity against which no gossip and certainly no pathology about us could stand or prosper. For Fanon, gossip, narrative, and pathology ascend to the danger to the aesthetic character of blackness that builds the neurotic or phobic life of blackness against a habitability for black life.

This dignity is the impossibility of doing anything but waiting, a propertyless state defending itself against the expectations of others. Waiting is perhaps deceptive, because dignity is another form of work that hides its domination in the accrual of its standing, of its building up, and the liberation of its cultural production and representation. Dignity is labor that we are lured into assuming is for us, or, even more, is us. However, to evoke

Fanon's famous revision of Hegel, the labor of dignity is merely for the colonizer. The humanizing character of blackness pulled from the songs and narratives of enslaved black life as a prize becomes a new internal whip to drive black folks to work, especially to the work of art.

The constant paranoia of dignity, its (aspirational) property, is exhausted by the voluminous weight of its abundant (self-)image, for dignity is the integrous "social" that takes precedence over its practiced and careful social relations. The fixation on how we are gossiped about comes to displace and distract from how we are with each other. Morrison's novel *Jazz*, in conjunction with its photographic inspiration in James Van Der Zee's intimate black funeral portraiture, troubles and challenges these paranoid desires for civic life, for narrative (authority), for (authoritative) gossip from which black life is displaced, made moribund, or litigiously celebrated. Somewhere beyond social death and we-can-become-the-police-too as life, black life wades and waits but is also probably doing something else too. Morrison and Van Der Zee accomplish this something else, or "otherwise" in Ashon Crawley's phrasing, from different angles that converge in their animation of black life beyond civic life (perhaps ironically) through depictions of the intimacies centered on black death.[12]

Paul Ricoeur's provocative statement that "the whole history of suffering cries out for vengeance and calls for narrative" resonates with and formalizes Fanon's subject, where a certain kind of heroism must rise up (or its impossibility must be mourned) from the everyday into and as the representative totem from which a new world is founded.[13] Piercing through the surface of quotidian racial terror, something ought to be sent, to be represented, representation must be an ought to be—a just, an aesthetic justification. Out from (made from looking into) the idealization of our suffering, we are waiting for a hero, and for Fanon this presents or formalizes a narrative solution or teleology, whereas for Morrison this is part of the narrative problem. It is not just the hero—Fanon is not saying anything that simple—but it is the heroic function of narrative that strains toward enacting a reasoned and just reprisal, a right/a property, an aesthetic justification, a representation. It is not even so much that Morrison and Fanon disagree, because they both acknowledge the logical and rational authority of narration, but for Fanon, narrative is a realization of imaginative subjectivity, and for Morrison, narrative and narration are the restriction of the most poetically and above all musically imaginative elsewhere that thumps against the surface of narrative. Because the logical coherence of narrative grants the lie of self-governance to our lives, it can and will be mistaken for how we (want to need to) live, how we might want to self-govern, and this is the problem Morrison raises for the grounding of narrative as the grounding of the social. Morrison's and Van Der Zee's works reorient the music of black life away from the allure of its being narrated or even being represented.

A Story Less than Half the Story

The incessant talking of the narrator in *Jazz* filters out the unwieldy sounds of black life bumping up against the novel's frame. On the same side of Harlem, James Van Der Zee's carefully framed black funeral portraits in *The Harlem Book of the Dead* partially allude to affective imaginative black social relations beyond its framed representations of black death. The objecthood of these black images does not seem to be mournfully invested in a subjective reclaiming, as if their supposed voicelessness demands that we speak up for them. Yet speaking for is the very being and miscue of the narrator in *Jazz*. The entangled imaginary of black sounding and living that is so often silenced by the subject is uniquely theorized in Toni Morrison's and James Van Der Zee's works. Black life is often at imaginative odds with the world as a practice of symbolic naming and narration, and the genres of subjection for which black life is understood as a lack, as propertyless, rightless, as pure functioning as already-arrivedness, as only waiting (for). Dorcas Manfred, Morrison's posthumous protagonist, illustrates how the lack of the lack lives as a realization of its appropriated plentitude that defines the social against which it is measured and maligned. Black life in Morrison's novel and Van Der Zee's intimate funeral portraiture, which I will discuss at the end of this chapter, is an irreducible music against the subject that performatively draws the limits of the subject's modes of inscription, conscription, and liberated dominion over black life.

Not unlike Rainey's outing of the phonograph's attempt to symbolically render her body and voice in a manner that it had done with George W. Johnson, Morrison situates jazz and the music of black life as a mode of outing the narrator of her novel and of outing narration itself. The seemingly omniscient narrator in *Jazz* has not been subjected to the same fate or shared the same future as Dorcas, or indeed any of the characters it narrates, gossips about, and describes. But the narrator's own lack of precarity does not grant it a totalizing narrative authority. The narrator's regulative desirous legislation of the characters is ultimately made uncomfortable by the black living of the novel's characters. *Jazz* repeatedly attempts to conjure the music of black social life in the wake of Dorcas Manfred's murder at the hands of her predacious lover Joe Trace and the attempted desecration of Dorcas's corpse at her funeral by Joe's jilted wife Violet. Initially Dorcas's murder and the narrator's fixation with it as the organizing explanatory force of *Jazz* and its characters would appear to confirm what discourses of black abjection have so frequently maintained: that the symbolic lack of normative kinship and subjectivity of blackness inherently forecloses the possibility of a black social.

The lens of black positionality would argue that Dorcas's death is totemic, almost sacrificial, as the novel's social and the narrator's presumed omniscience and even sovereignty are actualized. To restate Wilderson's point about unbridgeability, Dorcas's positionality remains abject. She forcibly bears the presumptive bridge between the narrative of her life and death, and the pathology projected onto her founds the novel's social.[14] Dorcas's positional precarity within the novel is the symbolic pivot. The social of the novel is represented as the engine of its narration. Everyone talks and gossips about Dorcas, and that holds the novel's social together, drives it forward and gives it meaning. It is especially what grants the invisible narrator its authority over the black life in the novel, which it often describes through pathology. However, the narrator eventually confesses to the impotency of its mode of hearing and understanding all the black living that brushes past its production of the social. The narrator concedes that its legalistic and authorial demand for fidelity from Dorcas's symbolic objecthood—her pathologized desire, her presumed ignorance and naïveté—is not so much a listening in the music of black life as it is a speaking for and speaking over. At the end of the novel, the unnamed narrator opines:

> I thought I knew them and wasn't worried that they didn't really know about me. Now it's clear why they contradicted me at every turn: they knew me all along. Out of the corners of their eyes they watched me. And when I was feeling most invisible, being tight-lipped, silent and unobservable, they were whispering about me to each other. They knew how little I could be counted on; how poorly, how shabbily my know-it-all self covered helplessness.[15]

This narrator, it is suggested, is none other than jazz, the musical genre and the nominal and symbolic container of sound that now discursively centers *Jazz* (the novel) on Dorcas's death. This narrative authority of the novel laments its own discursive mastery, wrought by the epistemological obscurity of the black social relations in the novel that come to light under its structure of interpretation and narration. The opacity of the characters' actions emerges because they refuse to conform to the narrator's prescribed pathologies, behavioral assumptions, and projective rationalizations of their social life and they similarly refuse to share any stories that justify their actions.

In plain sight, these lives operate in jazz's misrecognition, illustrating the failure of what Lauren Berlant calls "the performatively sovereign" subject who willfully acts as some discernible articulation of the performatively sovereign structure.[16] Sovereignty is realized not just through force, but also as a kind of reflective belief (from force) of those it tries to characterize. Morrison suggests that this characterization, and the character that emerges from it, are far more tenuous than it might be initially felt. To invoke Fanon, the death of the other is sovereignty's most mythic characterization of its own mastery, of its sociegeny. As we saw with Edison's phonograph, "the words of the dead" and especially "the words of great" men more readily provide a totemic and litigious precedence for mastery's always imaginatively limited ventriloquism. Specifically, the power to "make live and let die," or let succumb to pathologically failed responsibility and animate though consumable arted life, articulates sovereignty's fantasy of power.[17] Jazz is the inscriptive power of the law, the law of the phonographic capture that faithfully reanimates or restores for the subject the words of the dead.[18] Morrison's narrator, like Edison's "words of the dead," highlights quite importantly that the very hinge of justification and rationalization of the authority of mastery, its positive character, its narration, its regulation—for it cannot all be pure naked abject force in order to live against our living—is both insidious but also quite interestingly open to exposure. This process of aesthetic regulation is what I am calling the aesthetic character of blackness, and its identification and contestation is made possible at the very site of (symbolic) black death and abjection from which it gains its supposed saving power.

The retrospective designation of an abject black essence as either the absolute cause or context for Dorcas's murder is also always the limit of the interpretive symbolic structure of the law. The designation of a legal reality has, as much black feminist jurisprudence would argue, always involved the violent submission of a reality to the symbolic authority of the law.[19] The music of the characters in *Jazz* is pulled into the symbolic overvaluation of the narrator's generic interpretation; it is pulled into the sentimental recognition of the genre of blackness as abjection that the narrator wishes to produce. Yet, as the narrator's confession also reveals, this misrecognition is also precisely the moment when the characters begin to live in the nothingness and the excess of jazz's "genre flail," that is, jazz's inherently and often explicitly violent call that they recognize a greater hegemonic social.[20] Only the narrator stages the dialectical battle for social recognition in *Jazz*. Dorcas's death becomes the stage of subjectivity the characters are coerced to perform on. But the affective flattening out of Dorcas into a loose coherence of sentiments only seems to out the narrator's drives rather than offer any totalizing or indexical explanation of black social life in the novel. Dorcas's death formally indexes the failure of the attempts to prescribe and inscribe the black social as mimetic of the sovereign prescriptive that named it as marginal, nonsocial, or perhaps even socially dead.

The narrator's generic failure to narratively capture black life formally imagines the objective inscriptive power of the law as an always more embodied and embedded practice. The symbolic voice of the law aspires to be both exegetic and diegetic in *Jazz*, as if its perspective could be totalizing. The narrator tries to sing what the characters consume, what they have listened to as well as the insides of what the characters have spit out, what song falls out of their lips, yet this is the limitation of the law's genre-specific autopoiesis, as Sylvia Wynter might put it.[21] In hearing the voice of jazz, we, as readers, are being pulled into an elaborate formal process of subjectification predicated on the symbolics of black death. The voice of the reader, like the voice of the narrator, tries to speak into a space of the object as a relation of possession and apprehension, a property, a protected expectation, to what is an evacuated interiority. The narrator and the reader invest in the abjection and symbolism of Dorcas's death as an absence to be spoken into, to give a trial, to investigate, to give a hearing to her death as a mode of only symbolic life.

The claims for an absolute black abject always run the risk of reifying what Gayatri Spivak called the "transparency of the subject," which gives an object a hearing by granting it symbolic and discursive life at the expense of other more inscrutable (ontological) deaths.[22] This transparency operates in the reductive assumption that the subject translates and gives a hearing to the object or grants "voice to the voiceless." Such a voice-granting endeavor was of course central to the Lomaxes' appropriation of the blues. Morrison formalizes this desire for subjective transparency through the voice of the narrator of *Jazz*, who arrogantly presumes their own hearing as that which the objects it narrates and describes must completely and utterly lack and what it must be, in its prescribed silence, saying. Morrison thus formally draws a distinction between the authority of hearing (and narrating) and the precarity of listening. Morrison also opens a profound dislocation from the hearing genre is given and by extension the subject to whom it gives genre: jazz, and the more unwieldy musical worlds of black life that lead to this retrospective and generic naming.

The formative yet evasive and anti-foundational "anoriginal" characters of black music, to again poach from Moten, gives way to its misrecognition in symbolic death. That is the irreverent, violatory, or what Moten aptly refers to as "juris generative" nature of black life in Morrison's novel that is chased after and retrospectively and pathologically rendered by the narrator of *Jazz*. The narrator attempts to reduce and capture sound, the messy improvisatory relations of black life in the novel and especially Dorcas, make them testify before the law, regulate them as these characters. The discursive authority of the narrator, the law of narration, of Dorcas's life and actions as conforming to social pathology are the regulative inner workings of the aesthetic character of blackness, of the law that attempts to make sociable and in so doing attempts to destroy black life. Dorcas represents this precarious detachment from and fragile impasse in representation that strains against representation, that strains against the synonymity of representation with being given a hearing. The narrator's voice, however, is the anxiety that cannot leave a moment of silence unspoken (as if silence might not always contain a speaking and sounding otherwise).

The narrator observes: "Dorcas, at least, was enchanted by the frail melty tendency of the flesh." The narrator digests Dorcas's precarity or investment in a frailty, which is also a disinvestment in a willful sovereignty, into the deterministic and allegedly death-driven fates of black music: "They believe they know before the music does what their hands, their feet are to do, but this illusion is the music's secret drive: the control it tricks them into believing is theirs; their anticipation it anticipates."[23] For the narrator, black music contains a threateningly motivic power that the narrator can only mock as a way to bolster its own pathological projections. This is an admission by the narrator that is amplified by its concession that it could not completely predict, pathologize, or prescribe the movements of the characters that it concedes almost as if by exhaustion of its own reason and authority only at the end of the novel. Dorcas's movements and the asymmetrical movements through and around her, the black living of the characters in the novel, evade the narrator's prescriptive sounding. The characters dance brilliantly, sweat covered, and awkwardly out of sync with what time tries to tell.

The Death of Individuated Agency, Not Dorcas

Dorcas's character is not a romantic and conventional reassertion of individual agency or proper black possessive individuation in death or as death. Instead, Dorcas represents a perhaps more inscrutable embrace of the violently necessary affective fragility of the world, of the melty flesh of its falling away. Dorcas is something the law attempts to sublimate and disavow in its symbolic mark and marking of power as and over blackness. For the narrator, Dorcas's "frailty" and her death become emblematic of a failure to act willfully and responsibly—an articulation of her waywardness. Here the paternalism of the law emerges in the terror of this precarity and transfers Dorcas's bad fulfillment of subjectification to Joe Trace, the novel's most coherent and overt patriarch. Joe must counter, reinforce, and ultimately police Dorcas's failure to submit or aspire to subjection. His actions throughout the novel are thus granted a relatively opaque veneer of willfulness. The voice of *Jazz*'s narrator repeatedly tries to track and explain Joe in terms of his desire to reproduce normative heteropatriarchy vis-à-vis his acquisition of both Violet and the much younger Dorcas and summarily Dorcas's desire to acquiesce to such normative desires to become a possession for Joe.

Joe's willfulness is deputized by the aspirational "grand patriarchy" of the narrator, to use Sanyika Shakur's phrasing.[24] Grand patriarchy is the hegemonic and generic social world of antiblack cisheteropatriarchy embodied in Morrison's narrator; the haunting specter of the Moynihan report's racial pathologizing of "the Negro problem" of the dysfunctional "Negro family" and its obstructionist "domineering black woman," as has been explicated so expansively by Angela Davis and Hortense Spillers.[25] The narrator in *Jazz* is the law of this racial pathology, which dispatches its most legible deputy, Joe, to chase after Dorcas. Joe is an articulation of "minor patriarchy," another of Shakur's pillars that prop up "grand patriarchy." The concept of minor patriarchy is best explicated in the pathbreaking work of Nsámbu Za Suékama: "There are non-hegemonic nexuses that the Grand Patriarchy has decimated, with detrimental consequences for the internal relations of the colonized, which incentivizes the growth of a Minor Patriarchy to fill the vacuum."[26] Indeed, we can see Joe as fulfilling, or filling, the "vacuum" of a merely borrowed sense of propriety and comportment, of patriarchy from the narrator who describes his actions as willful and intelligible in contrast to those of Dorcas.

The derivative economy of black patriarchy to which Joe subscribes is perhaps the most obvious deposition of the derivative investment of black cisheteropatriarchy in the reproduction of black death in *Jazz*. But Morrison does not loosen the yoke of black patriarchy by pathologically tying it to just Joe's willful or compulsive behavior or actions. Morrison diagnoses the narrator's investment in and perspective of grand patriarchy to the desire for symbolic authority as symptomatic of a shared penetrative black heteropatriarchal drive that constitutes "the social" and of which the novel is a dogged critique. In other words, the symptomatic nature of black patriarchy is not merely the deputized pathology of the narrator's perspective. Black patriarchy, because it also props up, fills, or gives suction to the power of grand patriarchy, is a contingency that Dorcas can antagonize and undo.

The narrator's grand patriarchal public policing of Dorcas supplements the domestic minor patriarchal policing enacted by Joe. The narrator's condescension toward the black social of *Jazz* encircles and surrounds it in the very way it hopes (minor) black patriarchy will subsequently encircle it. The narrator boasts: "I like the way the City makes people think they can do what they want and get away with it."[27] In the narrator's condescension we can glean Bryan Wagner's assertion of the jurisprudential force of US law, in which "what looks like conceptual disorganization becomes, from the policing perspective, rigorous adherence to principle."[28] To corral the merely feigned and nonsovereign disorganization of black life, the narrator must send a case: Dorcas's death. A "case" or "the case of blackness" in Fred Moten's sense, is enlisted to forcibly bridge the variegated goings-on of black life in the novel with the facticity or fact of blackness (as pathology, as regulative character) through a synthetic categorical judgment. Moten, in contrast to Wagner, characterizes this case as a "broken bridge," partially because it is not the neat and tidy containment of a disorganization by a proper judgment or principle but embodies warring disorganizations.[29] The organizing principles of police power, the law, are, as Moten and Morrison suggest, not purely synthetic judgments but desperate responses to an anoriginal violation.

In making both Dorcas and the narrator a character, Morrison outs the formalization of police power, criminalization, and the pathology of the "rigorous adherence to principle" that Wagner describes. Morrison does not let *Jazz* and specifically Dorcas's death reinscribe the criminology and pathology in "the logic of the case" that the narrator brandishes and that serves ultimately to exonerate the organizing logics of the law that gives Dorcas's death a hearing. In her seminal essay "The Case," Lauren Berlant discusses how "the case" "organizes publics" and socials, for "the case represents a problem-event that has animated some kind of judgment. Any enigma could do—a symptom, a crime, a causal variable, a situation, a stranger, or any irritating obstacle to clarity. What matters is the idiom of the judgment."[30] This idiom I will translate here more in Derrida's sense of law, which is to say genre. Quite simply, this is the genre of the narrator of the novel: jazz. The aesthetic judgment that drives Joe's decision to kill Dorcas is coeval with the narrator's aesthetic judgment to speak on behalf of Dorcas in death and render her a singular objectified signification, an aesthetic character. The regulative function of jazz narrates the black social as a character against the black life that made it sound.

Jazz Is My Gov'ment Name

The etymologies of "jazz" or "jass" are vaguely rooted in the regulation and misrecognition of desirous black waywardness, of fucking, of promiscuity, of gender, of sexual and social nonconformity. A slang term suggesting raucous, perverse, or unwieldy movement and behavior, "jass" or "jazz" would later be consolidated into a musical genre with increasingly formalized musical standards, rules, and prescribed ways of playing and listening to a discrete set of instruments, performance practices, and sonic figures.[31] As Nathanial Mackey has critically pointed out, the term "jass," which has been so extensively configured as a noun, actually began as a verb that described a rather open way of operating musically before it was rigidified into its nominal property form as a genre, as a law. That is, "jass" represented both the identification of excessive behavior as well as its symbolic container.[32] Jass put to language a set of musical, sexual, and social libidinal desires that had to be deemed ornamental and extraneous to the normative social world that wished to limit and legislate black life. The unwieldy desires and libidinal energies of "jass" were understood as black, and not just because of the putative symbolics of the people and peopling in its moves and movements. But what also coded "jass" as black inhered in the nature of these movements, energies, and soundings as refusing a certain normative proximity to whiteness as the intimacy to being black together, to dancing, to (queer) fucking, to improvisational composition and practice, which all operated at an immanent and immediate evasion of the sensory apprehension of the normative subject. The need to regulate and ensnare these musical relations undoubtedly emerged as a palliative way of dealing with the musical blackness of black music, precisely as Morrison's narrator in *Jazz* is struggling to do.

For many white authors, from Sartre to Norman Mailer, jazz symbolized a moral, sexual, racial aberration from their own presumptively dominant social. Sartre's violent and fetishistic occupation of the "Negress" in his novel *Nausea* and Norman Mailer's exotic displacement and consumption of the Negro in *The White Negro* enabled them to symbolically escape the supposed hegemony of the social while maintaining access to its literal modes of inscription, writing, and recognition as a singular signification. White sojourns through the alleyways forged by the perversions of jazz adopted the symbolic skin of blackness endemic to white appropriation. This prurience Morrison broadly theorized as a form of "playing in the dark," an undertaking of white authors in which blackness becomes the illuminating shroud of their own complex interiority and subjection. Morrison focuses on the long literary history of formalized black subservience through which white characters acquire a heroic subjectivity. The function of black formalization that is tracked in Sartre, Mailer, and Kerouac navigates the perversity of jazz to heroic formalizations that are virtually identical with prior instantiations of the white literary imagination in Edgar Allan Poe, William Faulkner, and Flannery O'Connor.

Morrison opens her pithy work *Playing in the Dark* with a similar recognition in Marie Cardinal's *The Word's to Say It*, where almost identical to Sartre's *Nausea*, Cardinal's moment of psychic break and assertion takes place through listening to Louis Armstrong. Morrison, eyeing this well-worn trope, asserts that these "narrative gearshifts—metaphors; summonings; rhetorical gestures of triumph, despair and closure [are] dependent on the acceptance of an associative language of dread and love that accompanies blackness."[33] As I have argued earlier, aspects of Morrison's position in *Jazz* are in close agreement with Fanon's rendering, that the force of representation, through all of its world-making associative logics, installs against black life a form of suspended animation, a form we stand before as a law against which we are also perpetually waiting for our hearing. Yet with Morrison and especially her rendering of Dorcas, there is a strong suggestion or imagination or inkling that no matter how sealed within the law and aesthetic regulation our hearing may be, it is always threatened by the possibility that we are just not listening.

Morrison makes an important point in *Jazz*, which she alluded to in *Playing in the Dark*, that underneath the stultification of jazz as genre and representation there is an ongoing anarchy against which the law is raised and after which the law is interminably chasing. Our hearing is not a hearing, Morrison suggests; it is merely the law of genre talking over us, trying to drown us out.

> It is precisely a principle of contamination, a law of impurity, a parasitical economy. In the code of set theories, if I may use it at least

figuratively, I would speak of a sort of participation without belonging—a taking part in without being part of, without having membership in a set. With the inevitable dividing of the trait that marks membership, the boundary of the set comes to form, by invagination, an internal pocket larger than the whole; and the outcome of this division and of this abounding remains as singular as it is limitless.[34]

Genre, or the law of genre, seeks to memorialize a form of life by eradicating it, not killing it, as with death, but sterilizing that life of the messiness and ugliness of its practices. Jazz—black art and the black artist—evokes an arrested form of participation against our participation with one another. Jazz—genre in memorializing Dorcas's death—in memorializing our deaths seeks to separate them from our lives. What arises thus in *Jazz* as a point of critique is not just whiteness but also the container of subjectivity itself, against which black life is measured, merely made ornament, and violently sifted through narration.

If we take seriously Toni Morrison's claims about writing *Jazz* that "I didn't want simply a musical background or decorative reference to it. I wanted the work to be a manifestation of the music's intellect, sensuality, anarchy; its history, its rage and its modernity,"[35] then something of the immanent improvisatory operations of black music must found the law of genre that Morrison is writing against even as she is writing the law and voice of jazz (the narrator). Some originary violation must found the ceremony of mourning, something must establish the hermeneutical ring of limitations that reads *Jazz*, even if its origins get understood as an after the fact, as an "*anoriginal* displacement" of the law's ontology.[36]

Speaking especially of the early twentieth century, Saidiya Hartman describes such a living violation as "the gender non-conformity of the black community, its supple and extended modes of kinship, its queer domesticity, promiscuous sociality and loose intimacy, and its serial and fluid conjugal relations."[37] The failure of black desire to materialize an essential black object (Dorcas) represents not only the impossibility of black desire vis-à-vis conventional dominant object relations but perhaps more profoundly the incongruity of black desire with the violence of the (legal) subject as an aspirational container of and extension for desire. M. Jacqui Alexander empirically traces what could be called the obverse of the volatility of black desire, which includes, but is extraneous to, its inherent violation in the law. Alexander's work theorizes how black desires are rendered with a certain generic essence in (colonial) law that belies (even as it tries to regulate as deviant) their performative, and above all practiced, excesses.[38] The incongruity of black music with its abject essence in the law is not just the failed moral trajectories that the narrator of *Jazz* tries to lay out. The disavowal of black music's otherwise nature is precisely what is written into the law of jazz as a symbolic and pathological myopic black essence that it tries desperately to capture.

Dorcas refuses to invest in the overinflated patriarchal masculinist fantasy of disciplinary self-making that the narrator's twin discourses of black abjection and respectability require as the preconditions of the proper subject. The discourses that cordon off and retrieve the absolute abject are largely symptomatic of the kinds of contingent fantasies of a proper subject. The narrator proclaims Dorcas the kind of abject wayward youth who "made no pretense of listening" and who "was always running the street."[39] Dorcas embodies the gossip that lives as failed responsibility, failed (aesthetic) comportment and proper individuation. As Saidiya Hartman writes, "Responsibility essentially denoted the duty of self-making and the virtue of individual accountability" to such a degree as to prevent a full accounting of the vestiges of chattel slavery. The accoutrement or mere adornment of black rights and duties never amounted to anything like liberation and certainly never to black needs getting met. Instead, manumission was folded into a domination by dignity and comportment fleshed in the ornamentation of a (new) civil skin and its attendant legal individuation. We have been made responsible to our genrefication, to our representation. Emphases on black self-making and sovereign subject construction in the afterlife of slavery often adopted symbolic autonomy through aspirations of rights, choice, and free will that "instantiated only the want of equal rights rather than their enjoyment."[40] Within these discourses of black autonomy and responsibility, black subjects were often "free" to work within the symbolically similar yet materially worse labor conditions than those of whites. And they were often disallowed kinds of responsibility and obligation to and between each other in ways that could not yield universally productive values.

Max Roach famously highlighted how jazz has been an act of symbolic naming and valuation, a legal economic way of (re)producing blackness as the propertied, the proprietary proprioception of listening: "Let us first eliminate the term 'jazz,'" Roach writes. "What 'jazz' means to me is the worst kind of working conditions, the worst in cultural prejudice.... The term 'jazz' has come to mean the abuse and exploitation of black musicians; it has come to mean cultural prejudice and condescension."[41] Jazz becomes a way of putting to work the dialectic of black abjection and subjection; it becomes the means through which black music can be violently inaugurated into the modern legal and symbolic sameness of the human subject who domestically houses black labor. A reading that would attribute the characters' symbolic misrecognition to either their evasive lives as objects or their active resistance as subjects would still reify the authority of jazz, precisely within the sovereign dominance of the labor economy Max Roach is criticizing, the very economy in which choice is always a ploy of recognition.

The submission of the practiced reality of black music (and black life) to a dialectic of legal recognition of jazz rehearses a fantasy that much black music and black life refuses to listen to. The improvisation Max Roach wants to privilege is still happening under the veil of jazz. This is why he contests jazz's sonic shadow. Max Roach's critique of the limits of jazz also implicitly emphasizes the misrecognition of improvisation against genre, precisely because for black music, improvisation is so powerfully generic and powerfully idiomatic. Living and working under the yoke of blackness has often involved seeding affective relations in profoundly unwieldy ways, creating noisy, unrecognizable sounds created from overlooked practices of listening. While these practices are not always inherently politically efficacious, as I explore in the following chapter, they may offer material trajectories for forming efficacious black politics that operate beyond the reified and prescribed politics of coercive sovereign recognition and its Bantustani registers.

Black Listening and the Impersonality of the Ensemble

For Dorcas Manfred, death is always also a staging and a framing. Dorcas's enchantment with the "frail melty tendency of the flesh" leads her to a fixation with what Morrison, in her characteristic pastiche of novelistic technique and historical research, alludes to as *The Harlem Book of the Dead*. Distinct from Van Der Zee's catalogue of iconic black celebrity portraiture or his documentary photography of Marcus Garvey's Universal Negro Improvement Association, *The Harlem Book of the Dead* approaches a more quotidian but also more ornamentally rich and processed technique of photographic production that includes double exposures and superimposition. Van Der Zee's photographs produce a self-consciously prosthetic effect that is rooted in an unmistakable investment in the sentimental and personal sense of black death—these are, after all, photos of loved ones for loved ones—and that ostensibly (re)produce black documentary objects (dead black subjects of the photograph).

In Van Der Zee's funeral portraiture, black life, much like Rainey's brilliant subterfuge, is not characterized by its fidelity to the normative genre of the social raised against it, either its negation as racial pathology or its positive assertion as a coherent narrative as "our stories." Black life does not need to assert a positive character in narration as a refutation or defense against the rationalization of racial pathology—a variation of what I characterized earlier as the coercion of "documentary embodiment." Complementing the negative space of character—character as dissemblance of narration—that Morrison gives us in *Jazz*, James Van Der Zee's intimate funeral portraiture tentatively attempts to theorize a playful illusive positive space of esteem that does not reinscribe normative value. Van Der Zee's photographs are not a narrative appeal in court trying to dispel the antiblack law by expanding its rationalizing authority and force. In Van Der Zee's portraiture, the perforated and ungainly waywardness of black life is allowed to live with black death. Not unlike the elided presence of Dorcas Manfred's life and desires, James Van Der Zee's poetic funeral portraits attempt to challenge the standpoint of pathology precisely at its precipice of valuation at numerous sites of black death. Refusing to simply be documents, stories, or symptoms of abject racial pathology, Van Der Zee's portraits bump up against any attempt at their subjectification.

In *The Harlem Book of the Dead*, Van Der Zee's experimental documentary photographs directly confront the legal-symbolic grounding of the social against which black life is measured. Black life's ongoingness is not verisimilar with the endurance of its pathologization. Whereas Locke's prescription of the New Negro demanded that black be a regulated austerity so that black representation and "Negro civilization" could be luxurious—a restriction on the productive imagination that is the aesthetic—Van Der Zee's photography creates a space where black imagination and black need cohabitate through a messy process of mourning in life, as life, not in exogenous representation, but in an intimate interrelationality that bumps up against the frame.

> At least
> I got me a new dress
> An' a hair ribbon
> Like a bluebird.[42]

Van Der Zee's work and his photographic subjects must traverse the same "documentary embodiment" that stalked, and was ultimately contested in,

Ma Rainey's performances. Specifically, the documentary specter of contemporary lynching portraits, replete with what Erin Gray calls their "nephrological" function, not just of ominous symbolic threat but of violent consumptive incorporation into the body of the beholder.[43] All abound at the moment when Van Der Zee clicks his shutter or places his images in the photographic fix and wash. Yet the affective force of these images as unapologetically imaginative, even fantastical, is achieved primarily using photographic superimposition, multiple exposures, and prosthetic religious iconography and text, processes that acknowledge the formal and poetic fabrication undergirding the threat of both their wholly consumptive or (reductively) empathic sentiment. If Dorcas Manfred was a negation or an affront to the logic and force of black pathology, of the logic of the case and the sterility of genre, then Van Der Zee's funeral portraiture offers a positivist attempt to reimagine black intimacy from beyond the yoke of the law, beyond the evidentiary character of black life as human document.

Van Der Zee's fantastical imagery moves away from the kind of documentary embodiment that I discussed in the previous chapter and that was perhaps most prominently established in the photographic medium of the time. As David Marriott's writing on 1930s lynching photography suggests, it was precisely through the stark "drive to document" that the most pervasive, prurient, and spectatorial fantasies of defense were achieved.[44] The racist white captors of mutilated black lynching victims often looked at the camera in a desire to collapse the formal distance between the imagined and the real, ironically with the desire to make manifest an extreme racist fantasy that Marriott entombs in Richard Wright's words that "you don't have to see a lynching to live with its effects."[45] Erin Gray refers to this broad fantasy of US lynching culture as engendering a "necrophagy" that preceded and rivaled the imaginative spectacle of cinematic screen but with perhaps even more deeply embodied and consumptive incorporation.[46] The photographic violence of lynching thus relied on an adamant facticity to produce a mass prurient fantasy. Black death became a kind of genre of photography through lynching portraiture and its fixed meanings. The symbolic circulation of these photographs was meant to install black death as law in the black imagination.

As a complementary imaging of black death, lynching portraiture bears a unique contemporary contrast to Van Der Zee's images in *The Harlem Book of the Dead* in which the facticity of death is tripped up with self-consciously fantastical visual language. Even though Van Der Zee's photography is an overlapping though admittedly less spectacular visualizing of black death, he relies on the fantastical to remove these images

4.1 *Baby Girl in Coffin*, photograph by James Van Der Zee with text by Owen Dodson. Source: *The Harlem Book of the Dead*.

from the realm of public fantasy commonly reserved for black facts. As Leigh Raiford notes, lynching facts entombed in the photographic were central to evidentiary legal claims for black civil rights and the justificatory imaginary of black legal defense most famously proposed in the Dyer Anti-Lynching Bill.[47] But no such evidentiary publication quite arises in Van Der Zee's portraiture. The juxtapositional aesthetic of Van Der Zee's work is not cynically ironic or perhaps even fully ironic because it refuses to sentimentally let go of the original referent to such a degree as to allow for ironic (or parodic) distance. The deceased black folks of Van Der Zee's images and Dodson's poetry are killed by the antiblack forms of social precarity affecting many of Morrison's characters in *Jazz* (see figure 4.1). Yet unlike the narrator in *Jazz*, Van Der Zee and Dodson do not invoke black death totemically or pathologically to discipline black life, but to realize a kind of black life, a social relation, in black death.

Ironic distance prevails in these images, instead of collapsing the black lives lived into their deaths, to create an intelligible narrative or a resistance

4.2 (*this page*) *Couple Holding Baby*, photo by James Van Der Zee. Source: *The Harlem Book of the Dead*.

4.3 (*opposite*) *Rachel Van Der Zee*, photo by James Van Der Zee (photographer/father), 1927. Source: *The Harlem Book of the Dead*.

to pathology through facticity. The images of some of Van Der Zee's subjects were made out of the coffin, photos in which Van Der Zee instructed living parents to hold their dead infant amid the mise-en-scène of a funeral parlor made to look like the couple's home (see figure 4.2). In these instances, no formal double exposure is used, but the superimposition is revealed to be affective as well as formal. Premature death caused by antiblack racism drives the economy of black infant and youth mortality that Van Der Zee images. The parents of pneumonia-stricken children whose deaths are birthed by undeniable institutionally produced mortality are brought from the loss of symbolic kinship into a prosthetic sentimental relation to their loss, an unreadable and perhaps unfathomable interiority that is only gestured at but is gestured at beyond the frame in their staging and imaging.

A language of relationality around loss emerges in which death is not the unspeakable, inscrutable absolute but a performative engagement with what is recognized imaginatively and symbolically as the absolute loss. Blackness becomes a tenuous but intense affective yoke of misrecognition that the camera can only gesture at with sentiment. The generic totality of the aesthetic character of blackness is muted for an unwieldy and overwhelming personalization that evades the kind of vertical, regulative,

and universalizing value of the aesthetic. The fragile real of the traumatic world lived through black life is not rendered inscrutable but is formally built with a force of intimacy, a readiness-to-hand of black life that moves beyond its objectified sentimental prescription.⁴⁸

One of Van Der Zee's most powerful images, a portrait of his teenage daughter Rachel Van Der Zee (figure 4.3), who died at age sixteen of appendicitis, removes any sense that the photos are intended to, or achieve, anything broaching a comedic irony or indeed a fully cynical detachment steeped in a rejection of the object of black death or (symbolic) removal from the prescribed social order. Aesthetic comportment is at best shaky as the line between the production of a generic beauty is suspended or regresses into a castigation of the impersonal look.

The distance Van Der Zee's images produce is formal but also affective. They make a bifurcated demand or plaintively split request of their observer: let in but let go. Mourn, but not as the passive consumption of self-affirmation, but, indeed as the whole book bespeaks, look at and feel the very force of a world against the world. These images are not case files or "cases," but even in death are the force of black life bumping up against the surface of the image. The superimposed clipping of Alfred

Lord Tennyson's melancholic poem "Crossing the Bar" seems to mournfully drive this home. These are not images of shock, because a certain quotidian stillness removes them sentimentally from an iconic and spectacular economy of black death as shocking and abject, and yet their self-consciously ornamental, prosthetic, and overtly personal nature instantly removes them from a legalistic fantasy of pure documentary realism and facticity. Neither resolvable within the violently abstract taxonomy of the autopsy photo nor the romantic pseudo-individuality and respectability of conventional portraiture, Van Der Zee's aesthetic invokes blackness as a fantastical poetic impasse, never fully reducible to a formal generic resolution or living aesthetic regulation in which the objects are a consumable possession of the subject.

The fantastical and spiritual imagery imbues these images of black loss and life with a powerfully imaginative quality, an ethereal worlding that just brushes by the putatively cathartic desires of the subject to personally hang on to loss or, conversely, to the traumatic bearing of abstract loss as merely the machinations of an abstracted historical determinacy that overdetermines them. Without completely conforming to genre, this black loss manifests a world. The photo *Rachel Van Der Zee* centers on the loss of a deeply personal (object) relation for James Van Der Zee; the looming melancholy is overwhelming in an image depicting someone Van Der Zee reveals is a relatively estranged daughter and so perhaps a double loss (once to the relation of symbolic kinship and again to the relation of symbolic life). Van Der Zee's partial detachment from symbolic kinship and move into an elusive formal relationality may at first appear completely cold, antisentimental, and even deeply repressed or naively forbearing, a purely disinterested aesthetic posture. But in an interview with black artist and filmmaker Camille Billops, Van Der Zee's contemplative yet taciturn words leave us to wonder:

> Billops Didn't you find it hard to photograph Rachel in the coffin?
>
> Van Der Zee Not as I recall because she hadn't been with me at the time. Her mother had taken her up to Maine during the summers. She had just graduated from school when she was stricken with appendicitis. I have some very nice watercolor pictures that Rachel painted for me before she died.[49]

Rachel Van Der Zee's (unseen) watercolor paintings send her father's representation of her death. An imaginative relationship is proposed beyond that of symbolic kinship, outside the inscription of patrilineage. Rachel Van Der Zee is not merely the unmarked succession of patrilineal inheritance; her paintings inscrutably mark her father and his imaging of her. Unquestionably somewhat nostalgic and reverential, these watercolor paintings exist only beyond the frame as dissembled belongings that make formally possible a letting go—a frame bespeaking (further) severed symbolic kinship or a symbolic kinship that James Van Der Zee seems to (re)kindle only in her death, in the wake of her death, as an intimate form of aesthetic detachment in the loss of the image. The prescriptive bond of patrilineal parentage does not bear the eternal marker of the father's voice as Edison envisioned. Instead, an ensemble takes shape in the silence of the parlor, where the piano re-sounds Douglass's song or Johnson's record, breaking the silence where Dorcas Manfred's photo hangs, a daughter and a father finally re-sound.

The doubly exposed superimposed image of an open-eyed teenage Rachel in profile looking upon her own body in the casket holds both the unrepresentable loss and the formal and affectively impersonal relationality produced through Van Der Zee's practice. The kinship the photo produces, its sociality, is not the normative prescribed relation of a father to a daughter but a poetic filiation produced formally in a relation beyond the frame into the intimate and imitative circulation of the image, of the inherent excess of the prescribed non/relationality of blackness. This is a kind of convening, a kind of love not of the eternal symbolic domain and dominance of the patriarchal family, of the patriarch, but of an actively fashioned relationality and an infinite implication of one in the other beyond representation.[50]

Through his superimpositional technique and Owen Dodson's accompanying poetic scoring, the absolute personal sentimentality the subject might desire is interrupted because death opens up into a redoubled life. It is an anti-cathartic opening, a "performative contradiction" that abounds in an affectively powerful yet inscrutable social relation.[51] It is within this impassive and opaque misrecognition that Van Der Zee's aesthetic undeniably invokes a potentiated practice of black relationality. A kinship emerges in shared perpetual misrecognition, shared mourning that is a refusal to understand the loss of symbolic kinship as the only social kinship. This relationality evinces the inheritance of listening and its attendant formal precedent and antecedent in improvisation: the inter-animated grappling with the affective weight of being in tangled nonsovereign relationality, the sound of being in relation to loss. Van Der Zee's careful editorial composition and the circulation of the photographs offer up the formal and aesthetic "daily caretaking" that Omi Osun Joni L. Jones identifies as endemic to the jazz ensemble.[52] These images subtly impersonalize personal loss and trauma in order to make possible a complicated black lifeworld, a detached consolatory black sociality where the complexity of black living as a formal and performative fabrication commingles with the misrecognition of blackness as absolute loss.[53]

The desire to seek esteem for the dead as "comfort" for the living does not mislocate the reality of black life in a naïveté regarding the structural violence of social death or its alleged counterposing in the world-destroying memorialization of murals with which I opened this book. On the contrary, this "comfort" far more subtly opens up an affective relation as an aesthetic and poetic relation across time, one that complicates a reduction of black life to social death in the first place.[54] This speaks of the objective formal bearing down of history as the aesthetic, what Theodor W. Adorno found simultaneously impossible in both the mass-produced sentimentality of phonographic music at the turn of the century and the excessively authoritarian institutional art musics in the same period, most notably the emergence of total serialism.[55] For Adorno, how art resists eternity, how it "endures" life, is how it becomes or practices becoming human.[56] For "if the idea of artworks is eternal life, they can attain this only by annihilating everything living within their domain."[57] Yet rebuking patrilineal authority does not simply reinscribe a reactionary transience. The contestation of eternity of the work of art necessitates an actively practiced temporality, neither the aspirationally sovereign property of the family and its patrilineage nor a romantic ephemerality that is often assimilated into the former, illustrated in the temporary murals with which this book began. Between Rachel and James Van Der Zee two warring lonely freedoms of the artist are challenged and the messiness of being together and its temporality must be practiced. These photos do not programmatically presume the flat temporality of relationality across the black bereaved—though it does not seem out of the question that such a relationality could have taken place if only between Van Der Zee and his customers as his own flesh and blood is carefully inaugurated into this aesthetic and affective economy.

In Van Der Zee's images and their context of production and circulation there is not the regulatory and interpellative demand to homogenously commune black subjects/objects around one prescribed symbolic order or object of attachment or (negated) structure of relationality. Nor do these photos necessarily reify the assumption that blackness, as the predisposition toward death, is merely an a priori position to be arrived at, an always already "waiting" social skin wholly enveloping black life. The assertion of the surfaces of the photos is also always a new and contested materiality, a new skin, or shroud in which its beholders might walk, always at odd angles. Even the religious iconography, by virtue of both its fragmented and cut-up prosthetic nature, as well as its personally tokenized and miniscule standing in the images substitutes a hard ideological interpellation for a tenuous affective reparation. Instantly acknowledging the shared symbolic economy of death as a loose and tangled relation—even if they are all dead, even if we are all dead, we are not so in the same exact way by the same exact hand, for we still talk, image, look, sing, and desire in a way that the social's foretelling of our death cannot recognize but that will misrecognize death in its evasive utterances and calls.

Van Der Zee's photographs are not pictures of dead objects but processes that are subtly doing away with and disturbing the legalistic aesthetics of social death, a poetic relationship to a nonrelation that changes the relationship, the improvisation of the ensemble given over to an only partially discernible listening. The affectively tangled irony of this aesthetic evinces something undeniably black in being in the world as being in worlds. If, as Saidiya Hartman suggests, "the language of the slave ship" was about the violence of (language as) recognition such that the economy of black sound could only be (condescendingly) given a hearing by the dominant sovereign of the ship's deck, then Van Der Zee's portraits are not only a "grammar of blackness" in the positivist sense but more subtly and importantly they are a negative poetics of black listening that make possible and emerge from an improvisatory relation as a refusal of the given.[58] As Toni Morrison exclaims in her brief foreword to *The Harlem Book of the Dead*, "How living are his portraits of the dead." The moment jazz symbolically falls away and is given away in the early Association for the Advancement of Creative Musicians improvisations is also often the moment when formally and practically a kind of jazz becomes possible precisely beyond its symbolization in sound. This at times inscrutable looking away of sound involves a listening.

The Voice that Stares Back

Toni Morrison directly invokes the massive weight of Van Der Zee's oeuvre and all its effects in her novel *Jazz*. By giving Dorcas a fixation with *The Harlem Book of the Dead*, Morrison suggests a complex misrecognition of the seriousness of death as contingent upon its performance and staging. Black death is not apart from or opposed to black life, and it is only through a performative stance, a performative staging, or an "aesthetic comportment" that they can be separated or differentiated as opposites. Black life and black death are linked through their haunting superimpositional or palimpsestic layering. Like the weight of Van Der Zee's images, Dorcas's death is deposited into an affective economy that does not yoke black death to a symbolic exercise of the sovereign will to which black life is opposed. Joe and Dorcas do not get to be the conventional patriarchal opposites the narrator would like. This does not imply meaninglessness to black death as socially produced and co-constitutive. For Dorcas, it is not as if black death signifies nothing in the social, the purely totemic, the purely legislative, or the nothing and everything that it is in the law as the case, but rather it suggests the recognition of the frame, of framing, in the misrecognition of blackness as a potentiated relationship with an unwieldy black life beyond the frame.[59] Dorcas's fixation with the staging and framing of black death ironically foretells the posthumous framing of her image over Joe and Violet Trace's fireplace mantel.

Violet hanging Dorcas's picture above their mantel is both an obvious punishment for Joe that converts the force of resentment into a (selfish) reaction of guilt: Joe Trace "cried all day."[60] But more profoundly, Violet's active gesture invests in a performative reclamation and re-creation of relations of black death rooted in the creation of a now in the context of the everyday. Violet does not publicize the traumatic and violent implications of Dorcas's death into the void of a disinterested psychic totem. Nor does she personalize Dorcas's murder through a form of violently empathic overidentification in which she would structurally reposition herself in Dorcas's coffin. The public history and private force of black women's responses to violent black misogyny and black patriarchy are complicated in a space resonant with Violet's performative gesture of filiation with Dorcas. The narrator announces "A paper laid bare the bones of some broken woman. Man kills wife" and then cautions "Read carefully the news accounts revealed that most of these women, subdued and broken, had not been defenseless. Or, like Dorcas, easy prey. All over the country, black women were armed."[61] The narrator makes a final stab at proscribing Dorcas. She is no longer consigned to a pure victimology, something she always refused, but is part of a long-overlooked and disregarded genealogy of black women's self-defense. Dorcas, and indeed the black women conjured in the narrator's words, powerfully bind precarity with self-defense.

Dorcas's vulnerability is a reality and not an imaginary absolute because her precarity operates in relation to complex affective responses and resistances to violent objectification and abjection. Yet Morrison is not telling us only that "the resistant" are redeemed; she injects the care of Violet for Dorcas (even in death) as complication to a potentially fetishized symbolic strength and even militancy of black women. The formal responses to violence invoke a relation between Dorcas and Violet as much as their structural predisposition to be the likely recipients of black patriarchal harm. And this relation cannot be reduced to a notion of absolute a priori symbolic death, especially once Violet hangs up Dorcas's picture. In some kinship with Van Der Zee's imaging, Violet's performative framing of Dorcas's death interrupts the coherence of the casket and the violence of the symbolic that stabs the real of sound "with the signifying dagger" that "does away with [sound's] living presence, with its flesh and blood."[62]

Van Der Zee's decision to publish and circulate personal performative funeral portraits accompanied by poetic and visual prosthesis enacts a sonic, visual, and affective relation of blackness across an impersonal intimacy. Unlike the contemporary representative economy of lynching photography, in Van Der Zee's portraiture, blackness does not become the index of abjection—simultaneously the bearer of altruistic liberal politics and the wretched totem of black public life (as wrought by white sexual fantasies).[63] Nor does it become a depersonalized dignity with either begging appeal or sanitization of any political grievance. Additionally, because *The Harlem Book of the Dead* does not rely on the aesthetics of blackness as a spectacular shock rooted in a bare symbolic documentary facticity of black death, the book does not reinstitute a politics of subjective appeal or guilt for its beholders; it does not submit to and hence reauthorize a hearing. Listening thus becomes the formal improvisatory social relation through which the poetic obscurity of *The Harlem Book of the Dead* must be traversed.

The Harlem Book of the Dead carries the symbolic figure of black death that initiates the social as it carries in and beyond the frame the playful and musical aesthetics of black living, a detached openness it encourages through its improvisatory demand of circulation and relation. The partial introjection, the intimate and domestic holding close of Dorcas's death as an image, "a dead girl's face has become a necessary thing for their nights," invites both a self-effacing yet also self-refashioning through listening. Violet's gesture reconfigures an affective relationship to nonsovereignty as an unmistakably improvisatory and potentiated listening as a black social, a simultaneously contested placing and being placed.

The practice of black life potentially troubles the legalistic notion of testimonial hearing that is a reificatory gesture of the social's narrative and inscriptive authority because it is this fantastical emplotment of authority that we make complementary to sovereignty and tautologically (retrospectively) identify as an expression of the sovereign will as a will over time and death. However, *The Harlem Book of the Dead* does not so much document the fact of death because it is already in that precarity. Rather, it imagines the poetic staging available and realizable in the face of supposedly absolute authority. Genre's hearing relies on a consumptive drive of expectation, a fixation with melodic resolution, traditional conventions of agreeable harmonization, and structurally individuated musical expression and soloistic turn-taking as discrete bearers of an identity's totality in the structure of the nominal—jazz, blackness. The negative poetics of listening sent in Morrison's and Van Der Zee's creations demands (as it produces) more complex filiations beyond the prescription of an abject anteriority, beyond a testimonial, evidentiary integrity of genre. Van Der Zee's work, rather than lingering in the evidentiary, "giving a hearing to" black loss before the singularity of the law, manages to create a complex site of mourning and above all relation beyond the law.

This black relationality is the shattering of the fantastical monolingualism of blackness in another; the supposed monolingualism of the slave ship that never quite existed beyond the fantasy of the hegemon.[64] The awkward discordance of the slave ship's hold, never rescued from the tumult of the sea or the fight for escape soon to occur on deck, always exceeded the monolithic character of blackness. This bickering, this gossip, this need for more than the reprieve of token authority we have only in scraps like what Dorcas formalizes as her elusive living, like Ma Rainey's unwieldy performances, black relationality through and across loss. It is a knocking, a loud constant bickering, a blaring, an irreducible music against the subject. The pressure to produce a coherent representative subject who can produce representations, who can sublimate the bickering into a clarion voice, dominates Alain Locke's black aesthetics. Indeed, Dorcas's elusive living is a casualty of the narrator's representative desires. For the capaciousness of black representation to live, it must evict black life from the winding intimate corridors it walks. We shelter so that alienated empty regulation can luxuriate in our stead, so aesthetics can produce a façade that is never enough of a fortress for us, so the beauty can feign our protection while imagining its life without us.

This imagined life without us is a form of beautifying the world picture against us. Throughout this work, I have touched on the various forms and modes of re-formed capture that constitute the aesthetic character of blackness, and beauty has been among those I have referred to most often. In the following chapter I will consider what re-formations of capture emerged through the expansion of "black beauty" in the 1960s in and around the Black Arts Movement. The blues and the improvisatory musics captured as "jazz" were massive influences for that movement, particularly as they were made during and in many senses politically and sentimentally countered to the avowed black bourgeois politics of the Harlem Renaissance. Yet the specific (albeit quite partial) genealogy of blues and jazz I have offered in this text complicates and even antagonizes the aesthetic regulation commonly understood to be beauty.

How Ma Rainey hides in the phonograph or Dorcas Manfred walks through the novel and the genre of jazz exposes the facility and subterfuge of beauty's population and living of our lives. The alleged benefits of what I will define more rigorously in the following chapter as black beauty do not necessarily accrue to these figures and they do not quite work with George W. Johnson's voice and its cohabitative hiss. The sonic bickering, the infinite demands, sounds, and ethics of being together, often grate against our regulated being together. In the preface, I opposed our black being together as a practice of blackness's beautification of the world against us. In the next chapter, I will discuss how the Black Arts Movement, which is among my biggest intellectual influences throughout this entire work, complicates and extends my concerns. Can the ethics of sharing and meeting the needs of black life be reconciled with the lofty value of black beauty and what is gained through such a potential marriage?

Sounds Like Us

ON BEAUTIFICATION

5

> To worship
> At the altar of Beauty
> Is a pleasure divine,
> Not given to the many many
> But to fools
>
> Langston Hughes, "To Beauty"

> What has been said of moral experience is even more true of the phenomenon we call beauty. Its entire magic rests upon its secret, and by dissolving the necessary bonds between its elements its very being melts away.
>
> Friedrich Schiller, *Letter upon the Aesthetic Education of Man*

Aestheticizing Black Attachment

When Langston Hughes warned in 1926 against building beauty its intoxicating altars of worship, he did so with the suspicion that beauty could build worlds against us and could eventually build worlds without us too.[1] Despite the cautionary tone of Hughes's words, in the last century of black art and representation they have resounded more as a challenge not to abolish beauty but to liberate its dominion over and against more and more black life. This is the fear with which I opened this book: that more and more of us will be made black art. In this long process, through which the aesthetic character of blackness is revivified, beauty is made verisimilar with our life and the liberation of beauty is conflated with our liberation. This chapter attempts to understand the contours of this structuring moment: the nascence and pinnacle of black beautification that is partially what this book has been leading up to, but also from where it departed. What is involved in blackness making things beautiful and for whom? What bonds does black beauty necessarily hold together? What relations does it secretly attempt to destroy?

My primary occupation in this book has been to understand black music, black art, black representation, black beauty, and the black capacity to make beautiful that ascends without the black life and peopling that take flight through and against it. There was a long moment in the 1960s and 1970s when all these trajectories become more densely entangled and conflated. I begin with and weave throughout the words of Langston Hughes, who during the Harlem Renaissance was an early skeptic and critic of the concept of "black beauty" that would become rather predominant in the 1960s and beyond. I spend time putting the spirit of Hughes's warnings about beauty into conversation with several theorists and architects of the Black Arts Movement in the United States who similarly grappled with the form and function of black beauty. My aim here is to loosely bridge the questions and anxieties between black life and black representation that I raised around the Harlem Renaissance with similar tensions that arose during and after the Black Arts Movement in the United States in the 1960s. Finally, I hope this genealogy or prehistory sheds some light on why I began and end this book with the predicament of black representations used to protect luxury real estate from the needs of black life.

This chapter attempts to take an admittedly partial account of how the aesthetic character of blackness ascends in and through the ethos of the Black Arts Movement. I take this point of departure to conceptually link the distinct eras, moments, and strands of black music and art I have referred to thus far at the turn of the twentieth century and into the Harlem Renaissance, as well as to, however incompletely, theorize our contemporary black aesthetic moment, which has been marked by the various strands of neoliberal institutionalization of black art. Simply, I broach in this chapter what it means that we now have even more sounds and images of black culture—even more sound-images of Frederick Douglass, if you will—lining the walls of private and public spaces yet have even more violent and intensified attacks on black life from and for the benefit of those very spaces. To think through this predicament, I re-stage and expand a bifurcation that was profoundly staked out in the Black Arts Movement between the ethical imagination for our togetherness that operates against our transcendent and prevailing codes of beauty.

The negated legacy of the Black Arts Movement that I partially explicate here is located in some of the movement's totemic idealizations of black beauty that emerged through and moved against the equally powerful ethical pillars and practices it theorized. What did it mean to frame black life in terms of the phrase "black is beautiful"? That phrase has been variously attributed to the black photographer Kwame Brathwaite's work in the 1950s and 1960s, and this legacy has been consecrated relatively recently in institutional art spaces.[2] However, the ethos of the phrase "black is beautiful" with which Brathwaite's work is commonly associated has more often been attributed to the teachings of the Negritude movement, (to a lesser degree) to the Harlem Renaissance and the perspectives of Marcus Garvey in the 1920s, and to the black consciousness movement for black indigenous South African liberation in the 1960s, and finally to the Black Arts Movement that I focus on in this chapter. My emphasis here is less on the origins or circulation of the phrase "black is beautiful" or specifically to the visual, and especially photographic, art that explicitly bore its message. As I have stated throughout this work and especially in the introduction, I am more interested in the form and conceptual tenets of making the world beautiful via blackness—that is, the aesthetic character of blackness that enacts this beautification—than I am in the content of specific forms of art. I stage my arguments this way to assert that the phrase "black is beautiful" was not simply about making black people beautiful, as it is often framed, but was more about making the world beautiful through blackness.

I do not provide a comprehensive (art) historical treatment or assessment of the Black Arts Movement, an artistic collection of politicized black poets, artists, theorists, and musicians who were all creating contemporary with, were intermixing with, and were inspired by the Black Power Movement from roughly the mid-1960s to the mid-1970s. Rather, I try to locate in the Black Arts Movement both one of the most radical and rigorous critiques and contestations of the aesthetic character of blackness—which is to say the regulative function of aesthetics as such—and one of its most tragically appropriated and vivifying justifications. This chapter assumes some familiarity with the extant but still too scant studies of the Black Arts Movement and instead reframes the movement in the context of my arguments about our aesthetic justification. On the one hand, I show how Black Arts Movement theoreticians and artists radically critiqued many of the goals, edicts, and pillars of the Harlem Renaissance and of course preceding issues within black aesthetic trajectories I have referenced thus far. On the other hand, I discuss how the Black Arts Movement struggled mightily with the regulative effects and force of black aesthetics and especially black beauty as a force for materializing the world against us even when it sounds like us.

First, I will discuss the philosophical and theoretical proclamations of the black aesthetic in the writing of Larry Neal, which details the Black Arts Movement's attempt to navigate and potentially synthesize ethics and beauty. I then discuss how the concept of black unity, poached from the Black Power struggle, was wedded to, theorized as, and conflated with black beauty by some Black Arts Movement writers. I complicate these aspirations and theorizations by the black artistic vanguard through the messy and complex sonic social dissonance of black music that flourished during the Black Arts Movement. The sonic invocations, the noisy bickering of black being together, provides a complex counter to the notions of synthesis, unity, and beauty being expounded at the time. Finally, I consider how black experimental artistic collectives navigated this theoretical tension between being accountable to black people and being accountable to black beauty. I specifically track how as the black beautiful was being theorized and expounded by artists in a theoretical register, black poor and working-class communities were being attacked by the violent aesthetic projects of city beautification programs and urban renewal. I offer this juxtaposition to theorize an ethic of our contemporary situation of "the black artist" and "black art" that I began this book with.

My earlier invocation of Frederick Douglass as the first black artist considered black music as evincing a similar beautifying capacity. By thinking through how black music humanizes or was invoked to humanize black people, I have emphasized the capacity of black music to humanize and liberate the world over black people. The Black Arts Movement potently and powerfully broached this predicament of the ethics of aesthetics precisely around questions of collective black esteem, affinity, representation, and beauty. The practiced theorizations of black life in the heart of blues performances, the improvisational music making that got caught up in jazz, and the kind of esteem James Van Der Zee's portraiture invokes were all conscious tenets and tendrils for the Black Arts Movement's conceptualizations of the black beautiful. Yet the black beautiful was, in the spirit of Langston Hughes's words that opened this chapter, not the only or even the primary altar at which Black Arts Movement participants worshipped. Black Arts Movement theorists and practitioners, inspired and informed by the Black Power Movement, sought to rigorously theorize and practice a kind of black ethics in relation to black life and black beauty. This tension or synthesis would form what Larry Neal proclaimed as the "Black aesthetic."

The Black Aesthetic

As Black Arts Movement cofounder Larry Neal so eloquently asserted in his short but seminal 1968 manifesto "The Black Aesthetic":

> When we speak of a "Black aesthetic" several things are meant. First, we assume that there is already in existence the basis for such an aesthetic. Essentially, it consists of an African American cultural tradition. But this aesthetic is finally, by implication, broader than that tradition. It encompasses most of the usable elements of Third World culture. The motive behind the Black aesthetic is the destruction of the white thing, the destruction of white ideas, and white ways of looking at the world. The new aesthetic is mostly predicated on an Ethics which asks the question: whose vision of the world is finally more meaningful, ours or the white oppressors'? What is truth? Or more precisely, whose truth shall we express, that of the oppressed or of the oppressors?

The aesthetic character of blackness is something the black aesthetic sought to move through and beyond as that which is thingified by whiteness, what Fred Moten elsewhere has called "the fucked-up whiteness at the essence of blackness."[3] How do we inter the regulative desire at the heart of aesthetics in us to make us more sociable to a world that wants us dead? Distinct even from the Harlem Renaissance, in which the primacy of aesthetics often capitulated to social and symbolic disciplinarity, comportment, respectability, aspirational uniformity and inclusion, the Black Arts Movement sought to abolish, destroy, steal, and steal back as much as it sought to "build up" black people and to restructure a kind of black togetherness for black life. This language of force in the Black Arts Movement is significant, for as I have discussed, it was often the essence or ontology of aesthetics to merely register the force of the storm from the shore. But one of the most radical gestures of the Black Arts Movement was its recognition and engagement with force that deeply informed its ethics and aesthetics.

What volatilizes the black aesthetic that Neal described is the drive for its art to be an endlessly ethical practice and not necessarily content to be curated. This objectified existence had besieged black music and culture since at least the nineteenth century. The collecting of black music in the decades preceding the 1960s, whether in the grooves of the record form or the pages of early ethnomusicologists, materialized and circulated black music as an intensely aesthetic generic materiality, "a sort of participation without belonging—a taking part in without being part of, without having membership in a set."[4] The Black Arts Movement, like the Harlem Renaissance and Negritude movement that preceded and occasioned it, sought to challenge this objectified history of black music and culture, largely by separating the sonic as a discursive mode of attachment from the sonic as a practiced territory. The slave society that Frederick Douglass found himself coercively liberated into or bonded to as "freedom" or the white family that could only conceive George W. Johnson's whistling as mimetic are part of the negation of the black cultural from which a positive assertion of black culture could be waged. The predicament of these first two examples in this book resonate with Alain Locke's earlier quoted contention that "the Old Negro, we must remember, was a creature of moral debate and historical controversy. His has been a stock figure perpetuated as an historical fiction partly in innocent sentimentalism, partly in deliberate reactionism."[5]

Black Arts Movement writers and artists sought to sever the hands that had for so long drawn them and made black art, music, and culture something that was mostly subjected to a hermeneutic circle from which its internal terms and energy were molded from without. Far more radically even than the Harlem Renaissance writers like Alain Locke, however, Black Arts Movement interventions challenged the very tenets from which black music and art could be valued and produced. The black aesthetic sought something beyond merely standing higher within an oppressive world order; it sought a whole new liberated world to stand up in altogether. The writings of Larry Neal and Amiri Baraka in particular, along with the theorizations of many black musicians and black music and black arts collectives, are among the most radical attempts to retheorize and practice the self-propriety and regulative form and function of something like black music and art. However, just as I complicated the captivity in Frederick Douglass's flight, I want to engage in this chapter how black beauty had an antagonistic effect and function within the black aesthetic that ultimately sublimated the ethics of black art against black life.

The Black Arts Movement faced the challenging task of aesthetics and ethics as an ongoing project of dismantling the legislative world that whiteness had built through the narrowed prism of the aesthetic character of blackness: "The new aesthetic is mostly predicated on an Ethics which asks the question: whose vision of the world is finally more meaningful, ours or the white oppressors'? What is truth? Or more precisely, whose truth shall we express, that of the oppressed or of the oppressors?" The black aesthetic called for a revolutionary artistic ethos that cut against the very dependency on the beautiful that would, unfortunately, become the period's most agreeable and enduring hallmark. The black nationalisms and Afrocentrisms that followed in the wake of the Black Arts Movement and which largely endured through and beyond the movement's ethical imagination substituted the practice of an ethics with the (aspirational) authority of (petty) sovereignty of and over the beautiful, the majestic, the masterly, the kingly/queenly. Black beauty and beautification, which had arguably started as or had been wedded to and woven in an ethical project around and in black life, reemerged as the aesthetic character of blackness, an aesthetic remainder of a larger diremption or forceful separation in which those lovely murals that open this book can contain the sonic image of black demand and dissent without, and even against, the force of black life, vengeance, and rage that sent them.

To this end I explicate some of the Black Arts Movement's more sustained contemplations by Larry Neal, Amiri Baraka, and Dingane Joe Goncalves (a somewhat lesser-known black San Franciscan poet and theorist of the Black Arts Movement) and think about how their provocations appear and disappear under the variegated practices by Black Arts Movement collectives, including the Black Artists Group of St. Louis and OBA-C/AfriCOBRA of Chicago. Beauty and beautification. The tangled relationship of these theorists and artists to value guide my selective treatment of their words and works here, which more richly draw out both the past and ongoing contours of the aesthetic character of blackness. As part of my critique of the romance of beauty as an allegedly careful and caring endeavor, I will interrogate simultaneously the forms and romances of community and unity tasked with black beauty and the realization and fabrication of black beautification. As with Ma Rainey and Dorcas Manfred in the previous chapters, I will not try to divulge a pure resistant or exceptional object to the onslaught of black representation (or representability) but will rather parse how value through beauty conscripted black collectivity such that its modes of care, accountability, and really its essential terms of being together became inextricably bound to practices of beautification.

Black Beauty's Vanguard

As I will demonstrate in the later stages of this chapter, black artistic collectives of the 1960s were recruited by state and private foundations to collect, unify, and curate poor black communities and neighborhoods to beautify the tactics used in the annihilation of black life. Part of what I am detailing is more overtly signaled under the work of gentrification by art or what is now more contemporaneously and colloquially called "artification," but I also once again theorize how this commonly realized "outer" spatial destruction also thrives in the internalized spaces of displacement in our psyches, sensibilities, and imaginations. Just as the (white) family, which houses the cruelty of its symbolic and propriety preconditions of connection, must be razed in critique, so too must "community," "collectivity," and indeed their presumptive registers of care and curation be treated with a ruthless analysis and criticism for how they house beauty inside us instead of housing us.[6] The liberation of our domination, as opposed to the liberation of us, requires an aesthetic regulation to humanize its force. And that force will, especially in the wake of the Black Arts Movement's violent appropriation by the forces of market and state power, look more black, more beautiful, and it will be composed of more and more sounds like us.

Black beauty, far from a precomprehension in my thinking, refers more to the capacity and process of beautification and increasingly to a productivity that liberates black beauty but cannot and could not liberate the black people over whom it established petty dominion.[7] On the one hand, black beauty structures and is structured by market forces in ways that the Black Arts Movement theorists and artists raised, especially through the forces of an emerging institutional black art market. However, I will also attempt to think of black beautification beyond being wholly precomposed by a consumer culture, although the petty dominion of petty capitalism plays a role that cannot be overstated. What I will argue is that a kind of originary accumulation, in Marx's terms (or what Derrida might just call art), determines the value of the consumer value of black beauty, black art, and black representation.

The liberation of beauty was secretly yet irrefutably raised as a weapon against the very peoples and peopling that were ferried through its material expansion, and this is something like the story of the value of black beauty that I will attempt to tell here, a story I bind in this chapter specifically to the Black Arts Movement and its intervening years with the relative present. The black beautiful as provision of the black avant-garde—the first ones out—and the prodigious capacity of city technocrats to "beautify" black neighborhoods with "community art projects" required a democratized participation in aesthetic regulation that drew both warring and at times overlapping renderings of "black community" or "black unity."

Just as numerous black artistic and political collectives founded black spaces as bastions of radical experimentation, private market entities from the Ford Foundation to state militias such as police foundations launched their own philanthropic and paternalist reform—which is to say fascist—"experiments" to "strengthen and modernize the exercise of the police function" in black neighborhoods.[8] The artistic or beautifying projects I am delineating here are a complement to the more overt confrontational violence of COINTELPRO, the author of FBI-driven counterintelligence programs that spied on, sabotaged, and killed radical organizers from roughly the mid-1950s to the 1970s. Alongside these more overtly militarized campaigns of state repression, governmental and private entities such as the Ford Foundation under the leadership of McGeorge Bundy actually sought to liberalize Black Power politics in the 1960s and 1970s to neutralize their representational and collective value. Instead of fighting against or directly warring with the majesty of black representation and beauty, institutional powers made these oppositional forces more fungible and (ironically) more representationally universal. There was no need to bar the door against black art, it was far more effective for oppressive institutions to go on the counteroffensive, manufacturing intimacy with black art both by infiltrating its centers of production and integrating its supposed vanguards into the very formations and systems of value they derided. If black revolutionary politics could be liberated into the ubiquity of beautiful and beautifying aesthetics, eventually the radical force of their demands would be liquidated through division and dilution, through being made more sociable to the very world they wished to demolish. The emerging market-integrated presence of what aesthetic remained would be emptied of its revolutionary ethical demands and could hence produce civil black subjects who comported themselves with dignity in the face of a world organized beautifully against their living. These antiblack counterorganizing projects often operated under the positive name of "community development."

The pseudo-community of institutional appropriation retrospectively drew upon and emerged from a radical and threating practice of black togetherness. Black Power activists and Black Arts Movement artists all found themselves volatilized by the black rebellions in urban cities across the United States in the mid-1960s that burned down commercial centers, state offices, and police stations; stoked work stoppages; frightened onlookers; and refashioned the black radical imagination against the austerity measures of mere civil rights. A latent and nascent black togetherness was being radically formalized from black life against the individuated forms of violent intimacy with the state that were and would increasingly be beautified in the language of civil rights. Not unlike the murals with which I opened this book, not long after its formalization, the black political and artistic vanguard was being riven and redirected to face an enemy disguised as the beautified character of its most vaunted and valued ideals. The avant-garde function of the black work of art was actively and effectively being mobilized against the vanguards of black movement.

Black Beauty as Black Unity

In the opening lines to the 1969 book *Black Arts Anthology*, exiled South African poet Keorapatse Kgositsile, quoting dramatist and poet Mari Evans, wrote, "'The beauty of blackness is not how many honkies and honky businesses you can rip off but how many black men you can support and build up.' . . . This anthology is one of our many attempts at self-examination (a process of building up) and self-assertion (an aspect of support)." The black avant-garde's guidance of an aestheticization of black life mirrored the grassroots leadership positions being taken in many black political groups. Black Power Movement groups organized the immanence of black liberation and collectivity, or "black unity." From this political unity, Black Arts Movement theorists attempted to configure an aesthetic unity. Reckoning with "the black self," black unity privileged beauty and the aesthetic "in building up" black social relations. Mari Evans's emphasis on not just ripping off "honkies and honky businesses" synthesized what would increasingly become the orientation of the Black Arts Movement and post–Black Arts Movement black aesthetics. Supporting and building up of black men extended the conflation of patrilineal ascension with aesthetic production I have previously discussed. The aspirational property, a future property, a musician of the future, of patriarchy runs in contradistinction to black needs located in "ripping off," which is implicitly cast as a denigratory and deviant behavior with respect to black unity.

Evans and Kgositsile's invocation of "ripping off" has at least two valances, the first of which might be "ripping off" in the sense of copying or imitating "white aesthetics," a practice of mimicry to which black aesthetics and the black aesthetic must never aspire. Black mimicry, as I have discussed in chapter 2, was never exclusively linked to formal derivativeness; instead, it was an affirmation of black subordination and white domination. Kgositsile's assertion suggests that black imitation was verification of the legitimacy of the dominant white order. George W. Johnson's whistling could be valued under such a subject-object relation only as an affirmation of dominion. However, Johnson's predicament, while it theoretically seems to be the obverse of the subject-full aspirations of Black Arts Movement writers, is not so easily distinct or separate, for Johnson was enlisted to beautify the ugly hiss of phonographic reproduction. Ultimately, the form and function of his sound were not a "rip-off" of white aesthetics but an (intentional) redress and an (unintentional) beautification of the force of a new regulative regime of black representation. Johnson's career was a blight on the record of the officially emerging black culture espoused by aesthetes of the Harlem Renaissance like Alain Locke. Similarly, when reduced to abject mimicry, Johnson's music was a point of condemnation for the self-determinant politics of the artists and theorists of the Black Arts Movement. Yet, as I will show, the beautifying function Johnson played (and played in) must not be so easily dismissed, as its dialectic recurs and unfolds anew in the perhaps seemingly unlikely bastion of black beauty and the dignity cast against the likes of Johnson. Already we can glean an inkling of such dignity in the esteem project of "supporting and building up" black men.

Alongside its conflation with mimicry, "ripping off" in Evans and Kgositsile's phrase, also has a perhaps more subtle or explicit implication: black beauty does not encompass or encourage stealing (back) from or "ripping off" the "honkies and honky businesses." Here beauty and policing, beauty and the legitimation of state, convene to produce antiblack categories like theft and crime. We can glean a lingering respectability and certainly a propriety that is similar to the aesthetic comportment Locke imagined in which black life ought not to be "deserving" of the criminalizing representation visited upon it, a legitimation that itself calls the police on the black life it claims to protect. It is the world we risk stealing from, and not the world that has been stealing from our living to make its wealth, about which we must be on guard in this invocation of "ripping off." The contemporary acknowledgment of (but also aversion to) the black radical politics of negation, stealing, theft, and demolition of a world that is not enough for us is embodied in the Kwame Nkrumah epigraph that opens the *Black Arts Anthology* and that occasions the "building up" it imagines: "A revolutionary ideology is not merely negative. It is not a mere conceptual refutation of a dying social order, but a positive creative theory, the guiding light of the emerging social order." I want to highlight this moment when this "positive creative theory" of black beauty will still be in tension and even at odds with the politics of stealing from, of ripping off and ripping down what stands in the way of what black folks need.

Black beauty increasingly capacitated and conditioned the understanding of black unity and black humanity. It was a new synthetic capacity that was speculated from our interiority and made to "build us up" or to "build up" as us. But the caution at the heart of this text must be raised again. For the aesthetic character of blackness can only "build up"; it can only accrue in the case files of the very law it attempts to refuse and that it cannot fully imagine tearing down. The ousting of "ripping off" in favor of "building up" subtly alludes to this broader tension and trajectory. Aesthetic judgment after all operates like legal accretion and hence cannot abolish the law that it appeals to and becomes a part of and a party to or enters into contracts with, as Dorcas's case illustrates in *Jazz*. The positive production and legislation of the work of art can only annul or make less relevant or amend what has come before by adding to the very structure that originally antagonized it. But no painting has ever removed the frame of another painting or even better, demolished the walls of the museum in which it was to be hung. Artists are rarely enlisted to explicitly tear down the space that exhibits their work or liquidate the coffers of the private foundations that fund them. In fact, from this moment in history forward, black artists were even less called upon to abolish representation, and were instead tasked with improving or "building up" representation and expanding it over black people. This litigious accretive work of black art further capacitates the already capacious space of display. It even expands its capacity to expand. The wish or hope for the Black Arts Movement was that black beauty could capacitate or facilitate our unity and not those spaces against us. But how did black beauty's architects propose this building up through beauty?

Building Up Black Beauty

In this same collection that Kgositsile wrote in, the late black San Francisco poet and activist Dingane Goncalves theorized "black beauty" in a pithy essay entitled "Natural Black Beauty." Goncalves elaborated the relationship between beauty and building up:

> This is an essay on natural beauty, natural Black beauty. Natural is the word. When we look toward nature for beauty, the thing that moves us most is the way nature complements itself. One rose on a rose bush complements—not imitates, complements—another. The leaves and branches complement the rose. One flower petal amens another, and

all the petals compliment the flower. Yank some petals off and you have a mess, trim some petals down and have a joke. When you destroy a forest, you destroy a natural beauty.[9]

After establishing a conception of "the natural" and Nature (in its almost authoritative nineteenth-century sense), Goncalves goes on:

> There is no question here of white standards of beauty. White culture projects itself as a standard of beauty, every culture does this except us, Black Americans.
>
> There is no question here of inward beauty vs. outward beauty. You are either beautiful or you are not. "Beauty begins when you lift your chin up," someone said. That's almost true, but it takes a revolution to lift a slave's chin up. When you understand the beauty that you are—everywhere—then you can be beauty, walk beauty, create beauty, spread beauty to your brothers and sisters—as much as a slave can.[10]

Dingane Goncalves's emphasis on beauty's complementary or perfecting function, its purposiveness toward "natural" perfection cannot be anchored without a comparativist logic of culture. Natural black beauty thus conjures, as did Alain Locke's or W. E. B. Du Bois's invocation of a Negro civilization, an essence sealed in and ferried through beauty. Goncalves contended that beauty could only come from a cultural totality from which a seemingly invisibilized subject's synthetic judgment of that beauty's "natural" perfection conveyed its authority. Beauty comes from authority; it conveys authority but can itself never hold authority or be authoritative. (This is overlooked when we say simply that beauty is "subjective." It is not; beauty is subjectivizing.) Put another way, authority wiggles its way into the social through beauty and never the other way around. The proprioception from which the beautiful is judged and realized is an (aspirationally) authoritative account because it does not have to realize, or linger in accountability with, relations so much as beauty gets to prescribe and bear value. Beauty is the account that can be given only by "the absolute free being" and not the complementary mechanization or sensuous relation of the world that Goncalves initially describes or something like what he is also very clearly interested in.[11]

The positive absolution of the realization of freedom in the subjectivized world as beauty is not a means to making these reciprocal organic floral relations, however. If anything, it is through or really against these floral relations that beauty can be extracted, realized, and represented against "nature." Plucking "the most beautiful blossom" is only about that flower's intrinsic relation to the other roses and the bush of its surround to the extent that their comparison facilitates the production of the authoritative value and judgment through which the plucking can make it beautiful. Soon beauty, not the rose, is plucked, out from among and against its relations. That is how the plucking can construct and legitimate its authority. Indeed, otherwise this plucking would be the terror, which Friedrich Schiller reminds us we are enmeshed in aesthetics precisely to get away from, precisely to disavow and deny that terror. Schiller writes of the value of aesthetics: "Man is superior to every terror of Nature so long as he knows how to give form to it, and to turn it into his object."[12] Beauty helps rationalize the violent force of plucking by transferring that force into the "passivity" of beauty and so offers a positive character to the violence it commits against those "floral relations" that threaten beauty's law. We might question whether beauty does anything for relationality other than be its product.

It is perhaps not surprising then that amid the climate of emerging Afrocentrisms and Black Nationalisms with their kingly and queenly registers and proclamations that "black is beautiful," Goncalves, true to the spirit of the Black Arts Movement, attempts to ground black beauty in the *telos* of representative capacity. For Goncalves beauty is almost (but not quite) a kind of production instead of being the mere object of an already extant normative representative capacity. On the one hand, the only true capacity for beauty is a productive capacity realized after revolution. Goncalves dramatically breaks from both the pontiffs of the Harlem Renaissance and a romantic idealist aesthetic tradition with this assertion. But imagining the kinds of relationality that might lead to revolution is complicated. What kinds of capacities do being together get us to the capacity to be and make beautiful and are the capacity to be and the capacity to make beautiful irreconcilable irreducible opposites? Being (together) beautifully is subordinated to and made possible by "making beautiful"; what is valuable about beauty is less its utility than its productive capacity. Black beauty loses its semblance character, "its mask of truth," and instead is conscripted into a productive and prescriptive "use value."[13]

This opens black life to a kind of recognition of its waywardness that Dorcas Manfred enacted and embodied in Morrison's *Jazz* because it founds a moment of original accumulation through which the black artist and black art will become the manager of the professionalized and productive utility of black life. What those concurrent and emerging discourses of "kings and queens" yoke to overt sovereignty Goncalves seems to attach to the regulative concept of humanity underwritten by the assumption that "in a word, Beauty must be exhibited as a necessary condition of humanity."[14] What the figure of the slave accomplishes for Goncalves is an illumination of the authority that constructs beauty by embodying, as he makes quite clear, its absolute lack: "For beauty comes with freedom. Slaves and dead people have no beauty. Beauty comes in the free walks of a woman, in the way she turns. Freedom begins in the mind, but only a fool thinks it runs its entire course there. Beauty is for free people. A slave is beautiful when the master says it is. We are ugly. . . . Beauty is when we come together and do great things together."[15]

The propriety of beauty or beauty as property and possession—if we take Goncalves's slave metaphor a bit more seriously—is simply the property of subjugated labor and a utility of perfection that elsewhere he describes as destroying what is "not useful." Black beauty grants value to black freedom. The good is beautified: "Beauty is when we come together and do great things together." Goncalves's claim "that beauty comes with freedom" seems to echo Frederick Douglass's sounding-image in which the capacity of the beautiful to legitimate the freedom-granting world, in which escape is captured, is conflated with freedom itself. Must freedom be beautiful for us to demand it, want it, fight for it? The obligatory floral relations disappear under the brush of freedom's beauty. Perhaps this is an oversight, a remainder of the plucked rose and the supposed need for the black artist and black art. Obligation and being together are thus replaced by the lonely freedom of a single plucked rose—the black artist and his black work of art.

Frederick Douglass on the stage of abolitionism—the black artist and black art—lives in isolation as a plucked rose. The Harlem Renaissance to a degree and the Black Arts Movement to far greater extent attempted to disband that lonely figure by instead privileging the collective as well as the ensemble, inspired by the improvisational musics that would later be called jazz. However, as I am tracking in this chapter, black beauty was an affront to or a complication of the black collectivity the Black Arts Movement privileged. Earlier I asked how black life starves to feed the efficiency of the concept of black beauty. It appears that again, but in a different way, the beauty of freedom is expanded over, through and ultimately at the expense of black life. The implication of Larry Neal's assertions that the Black Arts Movement would privilege an ethics to not just restrain but reconstruct what constituted its aesthetics implicitly raised this concern about the threat of beauty. Beauty still has the ability to trip up the incredibly deep class consciousness and class analysis of the Black Arts Movement. The assertion of this ethics as part of the black aesthetic emerged partially from and resonated with Langston Hughes's concerns about beauty that began this chapter.

The vanguardist and provincial impulses in the Harlem Renaissance did not as a whole seek to challenge this market logic of cultural consumption wherein the black beautiful could rise to the top. Instead, it sought to expand it. Alain Locke's championing of deeper class division within black society as the foundation and marker of a black civilization was symptomatic of Langston Hughes's critique that "the ordinary Negroes hadn't heard of the Negro Renaissance. And if they had, it hadn't raised their wages any. As for all those white folks in the speakeasies and night clubs of Harlem—well, maybe a colored man could find some place to have a drink that the tourists hadn't yet discovered."[16] Aspiring class ascension of course expanded upon and led to further ascensions of colorism and especially the symbolic "whitening" that Goncalves addressed in very contemporary terms: "When we try to change the natural beauty we are, we are left with a junkpile of broken promises; amens that never got there."[17]

The lines of Langston Hughes in the poem "To Beauty" foreshadowed Goncalves's lament and desire as well as his frustration: "To worship / At the altar of Beauty/ Is a pleasure divine, / Not given to the many many / But to fools / Who drink Beauty's wine." Making of beauty an altar defers the abundance of black life to the austere regulation of a concept, a Kantian logic thoroughly saturated the interdependent aspiration for beauty and class division of the Harlem Renaissance. It was as if, in Adorno's words, "the bourgeois want[ed] art voluptuous and life ascetic. He added, "The reverse would be better. Reified consciousness provides an ersatz for the sensual immediacy of which it deprives people in a sphere that is not its abode."[18] Indeed, making an altar, an "abode," a home for beauty has increasingly threatened the housing of black life and will continue to do so: Beauty's altars evict black life. The "promises" or "amens that never got there" of black perfection, of black beauty in the Harlem Renaissance, especially those made by the black elite, aspired to sublimate black life to an aesthetic comportment in which black music and art were domesticated in order to house black beauty. The impetus for black art was its reificatory function as the plenipotentiary of "the race" and black culture, which could now be black nature because it too could be made a demure property that upheld "the pregnant stillness of [proper] individuals."[19]

The possessive individualism and self-making that the Harlem Renaissance tried to instill however, was as much up for contestation as the content of black works of art in the Black Arts Movement. If the force and form of the properly comported individual was the bearer of the Harlem Renaissance, then it was the black collective that would be the force and form of the Black Arts Movement. Against the pitiful and piteous dignity of Lockean "aesthetic comportment," where black art made a proper black subject more sociable in both exogenous and increasingly endogenous codes of colonial civilization, Amiri Baraka called for "'poems that kill.' / Assassin poems, Poems that shoot / guns. Poems that wrestle cops into alleys / And take their weapons leaving them dead."[20] He called for "poems that shoot" that are also poems that will "love what you are." Black beautification that bumped against several related concepts and affected pride, esteem, dignity and humanity, and black aesthetics more broadly was closely theorized with notions of black autonomy, self-determination, force, political violence, freedom, and liberation. But the building up of all these positive affects struggled mightily against the horizontal ethical demands of the Black Arts Movement precisely when black beauty was enlisted to beautify black life.

Black Art as Black People

The intrepid Black Arts Movement founder Amiri Baraka took the implications of music centered on community and collectivity and proclaimed that "the song and the people is the same."[21] His words were delivered at least partially to rebuke the ascendance of black music and culture without the people that made it through the now-infamous appropriation of black music that arguably begins with the blackface minstrel stage. The underside of "the changing same" in particular was a refutation Baraka leveled at white jazz musicians and critics who were building careers from black music. In his only slightly less famous essay written three years prior, "Jazz and the White Critic," Baraka ruthlessly and expertly critiqued the appreciation and appropriation of the blues and jazz by the black bourgeoisie, white jazz musicians, and white critics. Baraka argued in this essay, in complement to his later concept of the changing same, that the formal appreciation (and denigration) of black music had led to a wholesale excision of its social context such that its meaning was now entirely genre-specific, white, and bereft of the black life that birthed it.[22] As if sparked by Nkrumah's plea that "a revolutionary ideology is not merely negative. It is not a mere conceptual refutation of a dying social order, but a positive creative theory," Baraka gave a positive grammar to this impressive negative critique. Baraka intended the gesture of the changing same in the spirit of the Black Arts Movement as a call for black unity, a unity of black people with black music and a unity even of black musics with each other despite wide-ranging practical and formal distinctions; despite the noise in and between them.

In "The Changing Same," perhaps his most famous essay, Amiri Baraka made one of his more daring and poetic distillations of the tensions around appreciation, curation, and imagining a new world derived from the ethical positions of black music: "The meeting of the practical God (i.e. the existent American idiom) (Sam Cooke, Aretha Franklin) and the mystical abstract God (Albert Ayler, John Coltrane etc.) is also the meeting of the tones, of the moods, of the knowledge, the different musics and the emergence of the new music, the really new music, the all-inclusive whole. The emergence also of the new people, the Black people conscious of all their strength, in a unified portrait of strength, beauty and contemplation."[23]

Baraka synthesized the force of nonresemblance between the gospel origins of Sam Cooke and Aretha Franklin and the angular tonal and harmonic experiments of Albert Ayler and spiritual cycles of John Coltrane into a proto-Hegelian "all-inclusive whole." While Larry Neal spoke of the refusal of "white ways of looking at the world," Baraka attempted to narrate, and to a great extent resolve, the nonresemblance between forms, re-sounding the earlier discussed demand for black unity. Specifically, he aspired to impart to the listener and impose on the music a kind of musical appreciative proprioception that would ensure the recognition of black cultural property, a fortress of spirit built against the forces of appropriation, an inclusivity that refuses inclusion in the white world it still holds at bay.

Ironically, the unity of black musics, purged of the power of their recognizable differences—at the very time when they were formally more distinct from one another—achieved a perhaps unintended consequence. That unification silenced the necessary bickering that Du Bois despised as an obstacle to nation formation. As black people were conflated with or made synonymous with black art, this space of the messiness of black life was collapsed into its product and depiction. Baraka's fear, after all, was the theft of the art form from the people who made it. He perhaps would have never thought to imagine, despite the overt irony, that the people and the variegated threat of their ways of living could become a new resource of appropriation, not that our art would be stolen but that our lives would be stolen as our art. Simply, Baraka perhaps could not see the danger of making more and more of black life into black art.

The impossible space of this living, the space whose living exceeds our life, is what Baraka called the "all-inclusive whole," a concept that synthesized a concordance between the musics that their differences and Baraka's original listening demands that we think dialectically beyond. The mythical mystical aesthetic thought of black music thinks the grounding of their unity against their practical and practiced (which is to say highly theoretical) compositional discord. His concept forced together the necessary disharmony between the queer/trans blues idioms of Ma Rainey and the sumptuary aesthetics of Alain Locke or its equally homophobic spiritual twin the black church into the same family once more. This synthesis was not only a violent reassertion of an internal domestic dominance; it was also the straightening and closeting of black queer musical traditions that pervaded mainstream post-1960s black musical cultures. Indeed, even the undeniable and flagrant queerness of the blues was suppressed within this trajectory. But equally perilous, an exogenous dominance lurked from "outside" the people and the music that benefited from this forcible unification.

A danger grew in the saving power of Baraka's synthesis, for what was necessarily antagonistic about the black queer blues to the enduring and predominating drives of secular and religious black aesthetic comportment, the policing not just from without but also from within, was subsumed under a collective whole—sublated, beautified for the herbarium of black unity. Paradoxically, this resolution by Baraka was nothing less than a capitulation to the quietude of the beautiful, "black people . . . in a unified portrait of strength, beauty and contemplation." The sublimation of black living under beauty's ground facilitated a kind of collection and curation of black people as black art. Black beauty put a kind of frame around black unity, a new structure of capture that facilitated a new site of value. The long history of the curation of black art as the curation of black people, to the extent that it relies on the aesthetic character of blackness, complicated the ethical projects of the Black Arts Movement. It was almost Warholian in its total artification of black life. We might ask what outside of the arting of black life remains for the living. Is there any future outside of us all being made black art?

Freddy Fixer and Black Aesthetic Comportment

There was no medium where the aesthetic character of blackness could not be pitched against black life. The lifeless void projected into the grooves of the record or the phonographic cabinet was also equally and increasingly liberated into the spaces where black folks lived and homed. Cities, especially black cities and neighborhoods, long the inhabited hinterland of exploitative labor, white flight, and engineered state and market abandonment, were increasingly being reconscripted into their original purpose of generating capital at the expense of black life. Cities were no longer a source of the centralization of labor and population, which was increasingly being exported to the Global South. Their purpose became to support the emerging economies of endless speculation and financialization that were unconstrained by the materiality of production that Marx had diagnosed. Ironically, in the context of Marx's "musician of the future," the constant speculation on "emerging markets" and "futures" would be increasingly hedged and wedged against labor; labor would be arted and expanded through the music and the musician. The hyperspeculation of increasingly financialized capital would take aim at the lands black folks lived on by priming these spaces and places to house valuations rather than traditional modes of labor and the lives of workers necessary for production and consumption. Black artists would progressively be anointed to art and manage this re-formation of original accumulation, exploitative labor, and extractive value. Because of its capacity to marketize more of the world (inhabited by black life) against black life, the black work of art would supersede more traditional forms of black work.

As Sidney Fine notes, most urban beautification projects, which sought to make black neighborhoods more "livable" through (cultural) landscaping and park-building campaigns, took place in areas and in cities, most famously Detroit, that during the 1960s had been hotbeds of black radicalism and race riots.[24] Black political activity was determined "from above" to be inherently anti-aesthetic and an encroachment on the beautiful. The dehumanizing and criminalizing implication that black neighborhoods, which were vibrant and vivified with revolutionary black political community, were actually "unlivable" was carried out primarily to aid in the state expansion of policing and prisons as a way to manage surplus black and immigrant labor that was fast being exported to expand global, structurally adjusted wealth inequality. This remixed rendering of *terra nullius* in the form of urban redevelopment and urban renewal programs would increasingly serve the purpose of generating our contemporary lifeless landscape of empty luxury condos, in which real estate (conveniently mischaracterized and euphemized as "housing") could, with state assistance and market voracity, be used to warehouse and proliferate the unlived values of capital at the direct expense of the lives of black poor and working-class people. The sign and authority of beautification expanded from disguising its overtly murderous aims and affects in the shroud of regulatory, improving, and developmental beautification. Beautifying blackness would not (at first) adopt the violent form of policing that had been directly used to brutalize and quell the race rebellions of the 1960s. Instead, beautification would reward from without the ersatz life and attendant forms of administration it hoped to install within black life—and against it. Here the aesthetic character of blackness displacing black life would ascend more powerfully than ever before.[25] Images of black people and black community began to be more insidiously and intricately implemented to disappear and destroy black ways of living, all in the name of beauty and improvement.

Genocidal antiblack redevelopment, from urban renewal to the contemporary YIMBY movement, would increasingly require a deeply artful politics to sneak in and actualize its violent force under the scurrilous aesthetics of city "beautification."[26] These death-driven aesthetics and politics often conscripted the domestic help of the black poor folks they sought to police, imprison, evict, and displace. Formal lines were drawn. City monies were directed toward classist antiblack "anti-poverty" campaigns that coercively conscripted groups of poor black youth as "Freddy Fixers," deputizing them into a voluntary proto-police force tasked with cleaning up or "beautifying" their cities by wiping them clean of the graffiti, littering, and vandalism that spoke messy language against state neglect in their name.[27] Black Power Movements and a bit later graffiti and hip-hop itself would revolt against these antiblack campaigns of extermination and gentrification with varying and sometimes overlapping tactics. However, all these insurgent black movements would struggle, not just because of the bearing down of state authority and market praxis from without but also because of the insidious and emerging internalized politics of "neoliberalism from below" enacted by black artists and art institutions from within black lifeworlds.[28]

Beautification projects like the "Freddy Fixer" pilot program in New Haven, Connecticut, which was funded by the federal Model Cities Program, began officially in 1963. This was an especially interesting aesthetic panacea for both the patriarchal black bourgeoisie focused on "respectability" and the paternalistic state officials who feared losing control over ongoing and emerging black working-class disaffection, rage, politicization, collectivizing, and revolt. All over New Haven, Freddy Fixer Clubs (similar versions of which existed in other black cities and neighborhoods throughout the United States under different names) encouraged children to imagine a fictional hero, a character named Freddy Fixer whom their beautification practices and anti-littering efforts brought to life. The reality of the federal funding and real estate interests embodied in "Freddy Fixer" were disguised in its singular heroic artificing, but they were frighteningly re-materialized in the deputizing of poor and working-class black youth into the aesthetic comportment of citizenship in a way that Alain Locke would have, and perhaps even Amiri Baraka might have, been fooled by in its majesty as "a unified portrait of strength, beauty and contemplation."[29]

But these forms of beauty, strength, and contemplation were being used to exterminate black life, not with the visceral force of antagonism from without but through asserting a positive aesthetic black character from within. Freddy Fixer vivified beautification efforts across historically black cities and neighborhoods and wielded them against blighted forms of black living. Indeed, the popular mythology of Freddy Fixer as it became inculcated into daily life, just like the community policing it embodied, became naturalized and normalized as a kind of culturally intrinsic celebration. The most commonly repeated popular myth is that the origins of the Freddy Fixer parade lie in the bravery and foresight of a middle-class black doctor, Dr. Fred Smith, who wanted to help senior citizens and disabled folks in the neighborhood fix up their houses and who wanted to draw on the inherent romantic diligence of the black community.[30] Indeed, every commemoration of the parade since 1963 has enfranchised the myth of Freddy Fixer as an intrinsically black cultural practice to be repeated almost ancestrally. But this was a synthetic artistic state-funded practice that was waged unsubtly against the messiness of black life. The "new life" the Freddy Fixer banner heralds (see figure 5.1) is an allusion to the new life of black art that would be increasingly used to displace the black life that peopled, flirted, fought, and raged against its own regulation.

While the predominance of "black is beautiful" or black beauty is only ever discussed in terms of an unflinching self-determinist logic in treatments of the Black Arts Movement, the inculcation of the Freddy Fixer character and its heir in the art of later urban interventionist black public art complicate the common conflation of black beauty with the felicity of black life. And this is an important prototype for domination even more than the specific program itself was. As an ironic final note, the annual Freddy Fixer parade was discontinued for the first time in its history in March 2022 because the parade committee could not raise the $65,000 the city of New Haven required to pay for the glut of police overtime for the parade. Both the nascence and burial of this putative or encoded cultural tradition and its beautifying character (the literal character of Freddy Fixer) were bounded by the aesthetic production of their policing; and now a vacancy lives where what was against black life was originally housed. This eviction of the black imagi-

5.1 A banner above the stage for a "Freddy Fixer" parade reads: "New Life for the Neighborhoods: Freddy Fixer 1977." Source: Public Art Archive, https://publicartarchive.org/art/Freddie-Fixer-Parade/e1780876.

nation was no accident; it was a careful strategy arts funding foundations used to regulate revolting black life into the austerity of potential market values. As the Ford Foundation head McGeorge Bundy, who was renowned for inventing creative ways to quell black unrest, said in 1968, "Picketing is better than rioting," and we can add from this logic that a parade is even better than picketing.[31] Even "better" than the de-radicalization embodied in the superficial spectacle of Freddy Fixer parades was the dispersion and suppression of the voluminous dissent that artistic acculturation could offer. Bundy's words would be the model for twentieth- and twenty-first-century campaigns of suppression, management, and extermination that saw black art as better than black life and black beauty as better than black rage.

The Black Artists Group and the Assault of "Beautification"

The success of Freddy Fixer and similar programs proved that cultural infiltration and promulgation were affectively beautiful approaches to policing. At the dawn of Black Power politics and the early rumblings of the

Black Arts Movement that precipitated collective organizing in black cities across the country, the Model Cities Program was initiated in 1966 as a part of Lyndon Johnson's genocidal War on Poverty programs, just one year after the Association for the Advancement for Creative Musicians (AACM) was founded and just two years before an ephemeral but intrepid St. Louis collective, the Black Artists Group (BAG), first decided to get together. The BAG, inspired by the AACM in Chicago and the emerging Black Power Movement nationally, was an interdisciplinary black collective of artists composed of more than twenty musicians, poets, painters, playwrights, and dramatists, among the most famous of which were Oliver Lake, Lester Bowie, Julius Hemphill, and Emilio Cruz. Distinct even from the AACM, the BAG included many different types of artists. However, the group's creative vigor, collaborative formation, and endurance for roughly four years was complicated, thrown into stark relief, and ultimately undone by funding from the emerging government arts and beautification programs, most notably from the Danforth Foundation in St. Louis and Model Cities Program funding nationally, the latter of which was responsible for the invention and financing of Freddy Fixer.

The Model Cities Program was designed to be the soft-handed liberal humanist arm of violent state repression. In the mold of fascist reform, the Model Cities Program used culture to identify populations it deemed either deserving of criminalization and death by incarceration or worthy of conscription and incorporation into the artistic production that labored largely to intensify this very oppressive divide-and-conquer strategy. The kind of class and moral division Alain Locke had hoped to stoke within black culture was now being collaboratively cultivated by forces from without, "the right kind of black people" or the "good black people." The former would be disciplined by the sociable world the latter were creating through these artistic initiatives. Like the properly comported black police in the Freddy Fixer parade, these programs drew upon the civilizing function of aesthetics through its regulative power instead of more abject force and overt discipline. Black art would be the new labor to till the "new" land of racist capitalist city redevelopment and urban renewal, making it more sociable for the world and a select few assimilable black people with it, at the expense of black life.

As the Ford Foundation heads confessed in the same spirit, there were too few police to declare a violent and openly antagonistic war against the mounting radicalized communities of black folks, poor folks, queer folks, indigenous folks; against participants in Third Worldist, communist, anarchist, situationist, anti-imperialists, and so many other revolutionary projects, who now increasingly understood cops and the state as the enemy. To declare such a naked conflict would be to instigate a war of attrition that the state could not risk inevitably losing. Indeed, a more effective strategy was to "integrate police" into the would-be radicalized black communities by using and appropriating the very languages of beauty, art, and esteem that black political and artistic collectives were fashioning.[32] The goal of many of these neoliberal anti-poverty art programs was to neutralize black life and counter-organize black revolutionary politics by making them conform to the singularly prescribed aesthetic character of blackness invading the neighborhoods in which such movements blossomed.

To extend the still-prescient work of Manning Marable on the Second Reconstruction, the aesthetic character of blackness was used to gentrify and genrify black politics into an increasingly and exclusively representational paradigm, a politics of value rather than a politics of ethics or force. Instead, black value would be reconfigured for how it can expand (and not weaken) the forces of their political enemies like the police. Not only was this intended to deepen black people's investment in the state, it was also intended to build up the density of the state by excavating black life and rendering it as the compacted building material of state power and its requisite façades. The aesthetic character of blackness thus contributed to the densification of representation and representational politics (verisimilar with rights in the law) through the simultaneous reliance on the poaching and appreciation of its paraded-out spectacle of black art.

For both the AACM of Chicago and the BAG of St. Louis, the introduction of this funding created tension about the formalization of the state's discursive rendering of the aesthetic character of blackness. The groups were quite aware from the moment these funds went on offer; their members knew that black artists would be simultaneously symbolically conflated with yet institutionally marked separate from the black communities they were conscripted to "improve." Black artists would increasingly become both the collectors and the collected, and the more complex task of building an ethical black collectivity organized against the state and against the forces against black life would prove more difficult through black aesthetics. The artistic practices of the BAG operated at a formal and material nexus of these conflicting relations. In St. Louis, some funds emerged from Model Cities federal money, but most of the money came from the local privately run but ideologically identical Danforth Foundation and to a lesser extent the Rockefeller Foundation. With the solicitation of city administrators, a program was developed to establish arts and cultural districts in poorer black cities (especially East St. Louis) and to dole out artist residencies to black artists through the Artist-In-Residence (AIR) Program. These grants would enlist black artists to, in the language of the Inner City Arts Project, "sophisticate" the misguided but "talented ghetto children" and "encourage creativity among a people deprived of it."[33]

The BAG had already formed before the enactment of these specific arts initiatives, although shortly after the group's first performance, BAG cofounder and chair, composer and saxophonist Julius Hemphill, was hired by the Arts and Education Council of St. Louis to administer these financial initiatives. Although the BAG had been inspired by the social and political initiatives of the Black Panther Party to get involved in black communities and by the AACM to find ways to do so through arts and music, the AIR Program drove a decisive philosophical wedge in the group's process of collectivization. Hemphill excitedly lobbied for BAG members to accept AIR Program money to finance their work, but several members expressed strong opposition to such an endeavor. Accepting AIR funding meant effectively allowing the interloping presence of the artistic administrator into their group. BAG members voiced their concerns, pointing out that "the program administrators had envisioned the AIR Program artists living in the vacant apartments at the Pruitt-Igoe housing project," the most infamous and institutionally neglected housing project in the United States at the time, as a way to symbolically vivify, animate, and beautify the blackness of Pruitt-Igoe. BAG painter Emilio Cruz roundly criticized this plan as an attempt to make Pruitt-Igoe appear to be a thriving and vibrant space by painting over the very kinds of black life that lived there. Cruz said, "What they were asking for was for people to be destroyed, because the people in Pruitt-Igoe were being destroyed." He added that the overarching structure of the initiative envisioned the black artist as a "cultural missionary."[34]

BAG's contemporaries in the AACM opted for a larger circumscribed self-reliance and refused similar funding options to the AIR Program in Chicago quite vehemently. However, BAG's navigation of the AIR Program's assimilationist agenda and the more self-determinist black liberation politics of the Black Arts and Black Power Movements illustrates the formal internalization of blackness as a to-be-collected. If, as Benjamin Looker wrote in his book-length treatment of the group, "BAG's commitment to its community functioned at a material as well as psychological and aesthetic level," then that materiality was under threat of discursive revision as institutional funding offered to turn it into simultaneously the index and weapon of gentrification.[35] The regulative form and function of the aesthetic character of blackness was precisely what the state and private foundations were furtively but intensely trying to integrate BAG into and coax it into reifying and reproducing.

Black collectivity as an index to beauty was the fulcrum upon which directives to exterminate black life turned, and this furrowed a contentious cleavage within BAG. Either BAG would be accountable to something like black representation, the aesthetic character of blackness, of black beauty and a discursive sense of official artistry, or they could make the risky choice of practicing outside the emerging and increasingly dignified genre of the black artist and not help destroy poor black communities that these programs ultimately targeted. BAG initially took the funding to get themselves an art performance and practice space on the outskirts of St. Louis, but things did not go as they planned. BAG opened an art space that it hoped would collectivize the majority black community into the relevancy of the cultural politics of liberation and the practices of official black culture and music. However, the housing crisis in the neighborhoods that BAG had through the AIR Program been enlisted to, in the words of Emilio Cruz, symbolically "clean up," became a more immanent materiality to the emerging prescribed and coercive sense of beautification. An upheaval of black life tripped up BAG's misguided quest for black beauty.

Low-income majority-black tenants from the Pruitt-Igoe housing projects in St. Louis were actively staging a rent strike—the largest in the history of the United States at that point—against degraded public housing conditions and eventually against threats of eviction from housing authorities. BAG had been aware of this but came more directly into conflict with the strike as its art space sought to entice black community members to attend its art performances. Instead, local tenant organizers pushed BAG to drop its curated bill of performances and instead provide resources for striking black tenants. In response, BAG opened its artists' center on the outskirts of town as a public forum around the strikes. Striking tenants and BAG members Julius Hemphill, Vincent Terrell, Oliver Lake, Charles Shaw, Pat Cruz, and Emilio Cruz collaborated on a mobile performance from a flatbed truck that drove around St. Louis to raise awareness of and engage activism around the Pruitt-Igoe rent strike. This collaborative endeavor was complicated by points in the performance when BAG members overstepped their bounds by trying to organize tenants who were already organizing themselves. For example, when Pat Cruz stepped up to the microphone to condemn the housing conditions at Pruitt-Igoe as abject and unlivable, Pruitt-Igoe tenants—breaking down the receptive barrier they had been given as an audience for BAG's potential vanguardism—interrupted to correct him. "The residents, feeling that the artists were condemning them rather than the municipal government, took offense and asked BAG to leave. In retrospect, [Pat] Cruz ascribes the incident to her being "earnest and naïve," but through both success and failures in dealing with the surrounding community, [BAG] members developed an acute sense of how they could participate in the development of political solidarity."[36]

BAG's engagement with the housing strike complicated its conscription by state and private arts funders as cultural missionaries of beautification and their own self-appointment as a vanguard of the beautiful. BAG turned on both the state that had partially financed them and against the representational façade they had been selectively plucked to beautify against the black life of Pruitt-Igoe. BAG instead chose the messy floral relations of actively organizing with black tenants, risking the bickering against the lie of unity and its implicit exaltation in the unified portrait of the black work of art. Such tensions initiate a material musical practice that must grapple with the speculative collecting of and being accountable to the aesthetic character of blackness in representation. The genres of state and institutional attachment correspond in some fashion to their processes of discursive subjectification via art's speculating on and in black life. BAG's tribulations with antiblack state funding signified the emerging tension from a conflicting mode of production of beauty that black artists had been enlisted to reify and produce. This Second Reconstruction (as Marable terms it) was similar to the first Reconstruction, when George W. Johnson's career bloomed and when state paternalism sought to generate black cultural production as a regulative force for managing black life. This time, however, private corporations, nonprofits, and the state mobilized black artists as highly individuated or specialized harbingers of its redevelopment programs. Far less as charity and far more under the guise of unity, autonomy, and beauty, these community art programs and projects built up a density and dignity of representation that would be difficult to distinguish from the integrity and esteem of black life. Any flower that sprang up would have to be plucked and made beautiful in the mounting black herbarium against black life.

The *Wall of Respect*

Before they were announced as the more famous and enduring Afri-COBRA, a collective of black artists worked together on various collaborative projects on the South Side of Chicago. The now-renowned collective that formed in 1968 was composed of Jeff Donaldson, Wadsworth Jarrell, Jae Jarrell, Barbara Jones-Hogu, Nelson Stevens, and Gerald Williams.[37] They began working together as the Organization of Black American Culture (OBA-C pronounced with Yoruba synonymity for leadership as *Oh-bah-shee*). This collective formed out of what was originally known as the Committee for the Arts founded by Hoyt W. Fuller, Conrad Rivers, and Abdul Alkalimat, which had begun as an expanding book club that met in people's apartments and that would later add Anne McNeil (who later became the group's drama director) and Ernest (Duke) McNeil before being rounded out by the eventual AfriCOBRA members. Although these people formed the "executive council" of the group, in contrast to the generic vanguardism attributed to some in the Black Arts Movement, OBA-C framed their principles in the service of the liberation of the already-ongoing liberatory actions taking place among black folks and the Black Power Movement.

OBA-C announced itself in the August 1967 issue of *Negro Digest* (which Hoyt Fuller co-edited) titled "Help for Tenants: Warriors on the Housing Front." The issue centered on tenant organizing and resistance and activism against landlords. Before the suffocating counterinsurgency of black class ascension, "black excellence," and black luxury that now pervades our barren black media landscape, *Negro Digest* in the 1960s started publishing grassroots black political and black artistic content, including articles about tenant strikes, essays by black activists and intellectuals, and feature pieces on the Black Power Movement. Moved by the seminal experimentalism of the AACM, which had been founded two years earlier, also in Chicago, OBA-C, like the AACM, became a membership-based collective that sought to work with, not merely work "on behalf of," other black folks in the neighborhoods and communities they lived in.

The brief announcement in *Negro Digest* under the heading "Cultural Consciousness in Chicago" reported on the group's recent multidisciplinary performance, which was directed by Anne McNeil and included nearly a dozen performers, musicians, visual artists, and researchers, including the emerging and incomparable Terry Callier. But the small article served primarily as an announcement of the group's artistic mission to promote "cultural revolution" that was rooted in what they termed "black experientialism." Perhaps most indicative that the group was intent on centering the experience of black folks instead of putting forth a purely prescriptive or prefigurative vanguardist mission statement, OBA-C (or later AfriCOBRA) never completely defined "black experientialism." Black experientialism was meant to remain something relatively undefined and instead largely be realized in the incompleteness and ongoingness of relations, processes, and practice among participating black folks.

Decades later, in a 2017 article, Abdul Alkalimat, a longtime member of OBA-C and AfriCOBRA, cited as an influence for the concept his independent studies as a teenager of Maurice Merleau-Ponty's phenomenological orientation that "we know not through our intellect but through our experience." For Alkalimat, black experientialism was that which would allow black folks to "escape" their formal, systematic, and institutional "miseducation."[38] Alkalimat's rare distillation of the group's working philosophy described a necessarily perpetually open and even self-negating force behind their practice rather than a prescriptive aestheticization that black beauty might at first seem to solely demarcate and behold. The group was far more rigorous in producing its own internal principles and analysis than they were in providing an external concept—even amid the early ascendance of conceptual art—or a genre or marketable gimmick or novelty.

Never aspiring to the voracious permanence of the institutionality of formal art or even to gallery status and never succumbing to the emerging vampirism and interlocution of the nonprofit model, OBA-C both began and ended (in the early 1990s) in the more poetically modest form of the creative workshop. OBA-C's disappearance might be mourned, like Dorcas Manfred's passing, as a presumed disappearance into ephemera, when the group could have morphed into the authoritative form of the nonprofit institution. Indeed, the aesthetic character of blackness adheres to just such an expectation. But OBA-C's refusal of the pseudo-sovereignty of representation and the petty governance over black life it signifies is a revolutionary ethic that is vital in the fight against the current bastion of our abundant representation.

Nowhere were OBA-C's ethics more challenged, transformed, and enriched than in the workshopping process for what would be the group's most famous early sonic-visual mural project, painted among some of Chicago's most dynamic music venues at the time. Roughly around the same time as the article in the *Negro Digest* was published, OBA-C and its Visual Arts Workshop began its most significant project, the *Wall of Respect*, on a two-story South Side Chicago bar located on 43rd and Langley. The *Wall of Respect* materialized as a fascinating presence in the neighborhood; sharing a formal and processual radical mode of appearance with its estranged (and perhaps later disowned) South Bronx relative, graffiti. Because despite the proclamations of the group of its intention to implant a formally prescribed notion of black beauty and "respect" in the community by painting the wall with prominent "black heroes" that "helped us honor ourselves," the wall's emergence and especially its sentiment were subject to various contestations and revisions, not just by the OBA-C artists but also by black folks living in the neighborhood: organizers, activists, workers, community members, and passersby.

The wall abutted an abandoned tavern that had already been marked for demolition by urban renewal, along with the public library down the street.[39] The mural was constructed not as a precedent or as a vehicle for redevelopment and real estate speculation, as so much black art has now increasingly been, but as a conscious act of contestation against the disappearance of the "defiant" spirit. A bold inscription on the wall read: "This Wall was created to Honor our Black Heroes, and to Beautify our Community." The name of the wall itself did not come from a generic notion of respect but was an acknowledgment of an ongoing process of revisable needs; many folks in the neighborhood and in OBA-C crossed out and painted over the proposed portraits throughout the years.

The wall mapped out distinct "sections" (planned out by Sylvia Abernathy, who had designed AACM member Roscoe Mitchell's landmark *Sound* album cover the year before) of its own distinct categorization of a black history waged against its disappearance: 1. Rhythm and Blues, 2. Religion, 3. Literature, 4. Theater, and 5. Jazz. It would contain figures who "1. Honestly reflect the beauty of Black life and genius in his or her style, 2. Does not forget his Black brothers and sisters who are less fortunate, 3. Does what he does in such an outstanding manner that he or she cannot be imitated or replaced."[40] Yet even these meticulously laid out aesthetic categories would become sites of complication through practices that included the interventions of neighborhood folks.

In the spirit of self-determination, the mural did not emerge from outside funding streams that were increasingly offered from the Ford Foundation through Model Cities and urban redevelopment programs, nor did it extort and extract resources from poorer folks in the community, including the kind of contemporary artistic "activating" of spaces as a mode of priming them for speculation and gentrification. Instead, funding was pooled from the twenty or so participating artists without an eye toward profit or an investment in developing some proto-nonprofit rooted in an aspirationally eternal funding stream or permanent branded presence within the neighborhood. The internal coherence of the work and the process of its production had a contingent relation to both its own realization, contestation, and even demolition, by both the community and even some of its participating artists.

The open, even interpenetrative, and transitory nature of the wall reflected the necessary contentiousness between the artists in composing a "unified portrait" that itself would be subject to layers of use. Alkalimat recalls,

> They agreed on the main political points, but lacked any unity on their art. These artists had diverged in many ways on the main issues of art—style and technique, color, representation versus abstraction, basic issues of media, and aesthetics in general.... The unity [was] expressed in the desire to find a project for the collective as a way to become agents of Black liberation, based on art as the basis for positive self-esteem and community values. This was a discussion aimed at the street and not the gallery scene, as it was an attempt by the artists to join the movement.[41]

These black artists privileging "join[ing] the movement" would be nearly unthinkable just a generation later from the perspective of rising black neoliberal institutional art; becoming "agents" of any movement limited the formal imagination of the collective and of course any marketized career the artists might have hoped to attain. However, working with rather than extracting from "the movement" seemed to create a meaningful prompt for the group. In the true spirit of the edicts of the Black Arts Movement, the demand for relationality as an end and not a means privileged an aesthetic practice rooted in ethical relations and not careerist networking, self-asserting performance, or endless production.

The wall was the backdrop for numerous organizing meetings and musical performances (including several by AACM luminaries), teach-ins, and additions and revisions by folks living in the neighborhood.

> The wall quickly became a symbol of pride in the neighborhood, indeed, throughout Chicago's black community; African Americans were rarely pictured in schoolbooks, in the media, or in museums and galleries. The mural informed and inspired: it served as a teaching medium and a gathering place. Its creation was celebrated with a month-long street festival—musicians jammed, actors performed, and poets recited. An undeclared landmark, the mural also became a tourist attraction, every day drawing up to a few hundred curious visitors who discussed the work with the artists. Street gangs supported the project, and the area became neutral turf. The mural drew rallies in support of civil rights and in opposition to urban renewal. Accord-

ing to the artists, it also attracted the attention of undercover police and FBI agents.⁴²

Here black representation was measured, reined in by the social relations that surrounded it and not the other way round. However partially, the wall achieved the threatening presence of black life itself rather than aiming to install within black life the kind of sociable internalized police station that so many black aesthetes and leaders had espoused. As Susan E. Cahan's book *Mounting Frustration: The Art Museum in the Age of Black Power* suggests, autonomous black counter- or anti-institutional art formation in the late 1960s and early 1970s was in varying ways a threat to both the state and to art institutions. Museums both had to lock their doors against black art collectives or, equally effectively, figure out a way to coercively and divisively let them in.⁴³

It may seem unimaginable to us in an era when black art is more commonly used to disorganize us that black art could acquire such a potent upheaval, one that amounted to more than a grievance or a petition to be better included in power's march against black life. Post-1970s aesthetics far more commonly enact a longer (even if at times latent) regulative form and function against the very black life they claim to represent. More often, the ascension of black art, especially in our contemporary post-1970s moment, ascends and achieves representation precisely through its exploitation, valuation, and sublimation of black life. Both BAG's artistic practices of messy and risky solidarity and OBA-C's work through the *Wall of Respect* represent a rare aesthetic occurrence: drawing a real picket line of refusal that staked out the fate of black art with black life. The *Wall of Respect* achieved, or was foisted into achieving through FBI surveillance, something approaching Amiri Baraka's demand for "poems that kill." While not quite as lethal as martial power, the *Wall of Respect* skirted valuation and attained a level of threat and scandal that is largely inconceivable in our own time, when black public arts projects (like the murals that opened this book) are more likely to be agents of the state and real estate against black liberation.

Black Beauty Makes No Enemies and No Friends

The scandal of the *Wall of Respect* lay in its attempt to name its enemies rather than celebrate itself as a representation. It was a piece of black art that aspired to name its heroes only and by necessity out of making and staging its actual enemies: the state, the city of Chicago, the real estate interests that primed it for urban renewal, and the FBI—indeed all the projects that sought to beautify and sanitize black Chicago. While it is easy, even in Alkalimat's appreciation of the work, to dismiss the dynamics of breaking down the framing and frame of the work as a mere product of the times, the openness of the work to being inhabited by the community to the abnegation of its enemies was a profoundly theorized and collectively constructed process. The workshop around which the *Wall of Respect* formed (and which the OBA-C and Visual Arts Committee would evolve into), as Jeff Donaldson and Geneva Smitherman recount, created three minimal but meaningful points of unity and agreement:

> First, there were to be no signatures affixed to the Wall to de-emphasize the artists as individuals and to advance the concept of collective activity in the struggle for Black liberation. Furthermore, this anonymity would serve to protect artists from media exploitation and from police harassment. A second course of action was the decision that all statements to Black media would be subject to approval by the entire group. Finally, the Wall belonged to the community, and as such, there was to be no individual or group attempt to capitalize on the celebrity status of the wall.[44]

Arguably the most profound principles, and certainly the most unthinkable to the black arts landscape that would emerge in the proceeding decades, was the robust processual horizontality in which and to which the Wall was conceived. The refusal of property—even the property of the ascription of the artists' proper names—and the refusal of visibility from the vertical structures that made the Wall's contestation necessary are among its most innovative gestures. OBA-C's decision to choose anonymity also openly acknowledged and critiqued the overlap between black artistic celebrity and surveillance and policing. The Wall's very form was what it refused. Less a perfect representation or product, it tentatively crystalized an ongoing process; among them a set of unevenly horizontal agreements between folks rooted in an aspirationally shared collective analysis against both their destruction by the state and exogenies produced by institutions of media, burgeoning art institutionality, and representation. Much of what would become even the contrarian impulses of conceptual nonrepresentative art would never achieve or aspire to achieve the Wall's disappearance of its framing that moved away from its status as the property of the artist (or the brand) and into something like the autonomy of the community. The

Wall attempted to move away from the adjunct ornamentation of the community that the framing of the work often initiates, invokes, and implies.

While Goncalves prescribed the black beautiful as the precondition or co-condition for black unity around black art—black art as black unity—the *Wall of Respect* attempted to construct itself directly against the social and economic verticalization sent to destroy it. It was at least partially rooted in the ripping off that Goncalves partially dismissed for the *Bildungs* of black beauty. This *Bildung*, as a kind of public institution or collective public ethic (abstracted and enshrined in the nation), is made possible by the kind of aesthetic education, refinement, rearing, or *Erziehung* (to us Friedrich Schiller's term).[45] Much like the Kantian or Schillerian project, black beauty makes no enemy and stages no enmity, because it emerges from a restrained domesticity, a good familial—as in a good family, from a good home—background that teaches black beauty a kind of restraint from ripping off, stealing from, antagonizing, or destroying the world that makes its stances of esteem, and its comportment and propriety, necessary. This is how we get beautiful black art and beautiful black people, who will never defend black life.

The *Wall* staked out a fight, an enemy; it hoped for friends and let relationships form, fail, and transform it.[46] What is sublimated in the reflective judgment of the Wall's "pure" concept, its arted-ness, was not left to the judgment of "the gallery," of the state upon whose stolen and denizen-traversed land it was painted. The "governing principle" of urban renewal and the emerging governance of the market—the art market, which would be expanded through gentrification, policing, and official black art as this book's preface shows—is robbed of the reflective power that reifies its authority.[47] In a rather powerful, and perhaps ironic, turn, this artistic project shows, as Assata Shakur famously reminded us, "It's that a wall is just a wall / and nothing more at all. / It can be broken down."[48] Goncalves's earlier demand that black art and black beauty "build up" is challenged with how the *Wall*'s painting has the effect of dressing it down, being torn down, getting tagged or marked by the community, disfiguring its purely reflective images, and exposing it to practice.

The *Wall* did not insert itself into the circuits of capital in black art that scholars such as Susan E. Cahan, Kellie Jones, and Darby English have documented as emerging and expanding at this time.[49] To the contrary, the Wall at least attempted to share the same fate as the neighborhood and the community it graced, as if the respect was not a condescending demand for dignity but instead the potential for organized refusal of a shared violation.

Distinct from the murals with which I began this book, the *Wall of Respect* adopted something like self-defense, in which the self was dislocated from the "ridiculous" form of its "self-enclosure" but instead defended a shared life as a collective defense.[50] The *Wall* embodied Larry Neal's provocation that the Black Arts Movement needed to imagine a new aesthetic challenged by the ethics of defending black life over the preservation of black art. Against the enduring romantic demand that we die for art, the *Wall of Respect* and the Black Arts Movement seemed to be asking if art is willing to die for us (too).

The good will of the artwork, which Kant insists it encloses and from which it releases beauty, is never about the practical freedom or defense of the object. In fact, that artwork's good will can never be so intrinsic, never so shared as a relation without being refracted through the prism of an increasingly litigious institutionally displaced judgment. The beauty of the artwork increasingly facilitates and upholds the initiation of more law. But even more dangerous than the law of genre, and the fabrication of the *Wall of Respect* alludes to this, is how art's original accumulation risks encircling black esteem with more law as "official" black culture. The aesthetic character of blackness requires these ongoing intrinsic and extrinsic relations in order to produce its valuation. From the internalization of the slave's borrowed humanity refracted by Frederick Douglass as black music to its the internalized representation and ideally externalized dignity of Alain Locke's black aesthetic comportment, a kind of danger grew in the presumed saving power of black art. The *Wall of Respect* is often described as one of the foundational works, if not the foundational work, of "black public art" and urban public murals across the United States. However, the threatening production of the public as a war against the black life it encircles more truly bears out the legacy of public art, more than it extends the profound relations fashioned through OBA-C's *Wall of Respect*. From this point forward, the "public" of public art would be enlivened and expanded precisely and solely at the expense of black life.

The Gentrifying Herbarium of Black Life

How do we get from the force of the Black Arts Movement, how do we move or more accurately how are we forced to move, how have we been evicted from the Black Arts Movement's homing of us over the homing of beauty? As Fred Moten and Stefano Harney have argued, "the public," at the heart of "public art," enacts a siege of "the self-accumulating individual's war, his total mobilization against the innumerable and against his fellows under the sign of ownership as improvement."⁵¹ Indeed, the siege brought by the individual black artist, now loosed of even the tangle of the black artists' collective—whose solemn ipseity is paralleled in contemporary popular music where increasingly there are no groups—has become the totem of the anti-social, antiblack "public" of public art. The genealogy of black public art or the black public of black art tells a story of an increasingly institutionally included, even "marginalized," black artist. Indeed, the language of marginalization dominates the lexicon of black art's institutionalization, from the late-twentieth-century writings of Charles Gaines to the twenty-first-century work of Darby English.⁵²

The legacy of the Black Art Movement's artist is now more as architect, a combination of the elevated voyeur of romantic art and the embedded managerial figure transfigured who operates as an ambassadorial financier to "the black community." "The black community" has become merely a source of aesthetic extraction at the least and the personal profit and property of the black artist at the most. The black artist has emerged more as a hustler of sorts, capitalizing meagerly on monumental consequences by poaching the ordinary language of black beauty from the substance of black life and verticalizing it into the economistic rationalization of black art. In the Euro-American context, Georgina Borne refers to this institutional ownership of the cultural as the late-twentieth-century "rationalizing of culture."⁵³ The beautification that transcends and ascends through black life only to be selectively and manipulatively waged against it emanates from a longer history of black music's "discovery," invention, and rationalization in the mid-nineteenth century.

The museum, the collection, the herbarium of black life disorganizes us as it categorizes and institutionalizes black culture into a force against us. I close this chapter with a partial explanation of how this book began. How do we go from the point where the very black neighborhoods that black arts collectives lived in and traversed decades ago, that were sites of black life and ongoing black revolutionary struggle against our extermination, were declared to be "blighted" by urban renewal programs, only to be beautified into "emerging" art markets populated by austere vacancies? This is to think more critically against what Fred Moten refers to as the "noisy" practice of contemporary black Chicago conceptual artist Theaster Gates's "thingly arrangements." Gates is an artist who symbolically works in and wields the massive legacy of the Black Arts Movement. His installation work in the last decade or so has involved "repurposing" allegedly empty or supposedly abandoned buildings on Chicago's South Side and "activating" them by improving, beautifying, and reforming them into nonprofit art spaces and art installations. This practice Gates calls "dark speculation," but we can, without much imaginative straining, simply understand this work as the curatorial underside of black capitalism.[54] The beauty and improvement of Gates's work installs a new sociable black character at the heart of structurally abandoned black lifeworlds. Gates's art emerges in the shadow of the Chicago and Midwest-based collectives I have discussed thus far, yet his work also enters and expands black art's neoliberal order wherein black community is both a token of and a cudgel against black living. Whether or not it is intended, the antisocial "impotence" admitted in a "good will" portends an unmistakable reification of class interests in the production of a world abundant with black art and vacant of black people; this is increasingly the structuring work of the black artist that emerges as the aesthetic character of blackness.[55]

Theaster Gates's recent architectural projects aestheticize the practice of gentrifying black urban neighborhoods through his memorialization of black life. Black neighborhoods become black memorials. Unlike Van Der Zee's personal memorial portraits, in Gates's work there is a sense of memorial removed of the life it allegedly celebrates yet ironically voluminous with the mere aesthetics of life. Gates leaves a symbolically curated and institutionally founded collection of the aesthetic character of blackness in the wake of the black social and political life that his highly institutionally funded and materially resourced projects help destroy. Gates's work romanticizes as it formalizes the structural violence of gentrification, or what is commonly called "artification." Gates's provocation of "repurposing" "unused" urban structures into a black archive full of what he calls "Negrobilia," such as old *Ebony* magazines or blackface kitsch, playfully images and institutionalizes a decentered, privatized form of a black middle-class quasi-cultural nationalist collection and collecting of the 1970s. The ubiquity of the popular black magazine form (*Ebony, Essence, Jet*, etc.) in Gates's collection embodies the 1970s celebration of the liberation of personal property, and Gates's archiving reifies its status by inserting personal propriety into a playful cultural-national archive. And not unlike the original reasons that drove the 1970s black elite's collection of minstrelsy figurines, Gates's archive emphasizes and overrepresents this rather basic monolithic form of exogenous racism, mostly created by white people, mostly to affirm that its specific modality of denigration is largely a thing of the past.

However, while the ironic presentation of blackface minstrelsy as a racist past is in a sense true, it denies the more urgent and complex ongoing structurally racist present of policing, gentrification, and intentional state-organized abandonment that allows for Gates's museumification of a selective official memorializing of racism in black communities and neighborhoods. It is a recurrence of Frederick Douglass's function on the stage of white abolitionism as the first black artist. A certain celebration (from without) of black culture or black humanity emerges by its opposition to the abject racism of the culture of the minstrel that conceals a form of more rationalized domination. The black artist facilitates the closing of minstrelsy's bodily schema while doing the originary accumulative work, the cultural labor and production, and the artwork of forming a new frontier of black culture (eventually) for those from without.

The integrity of Gates's buildings, down to the repurposed brick, is on the one hand a reassertion of Alain Locke's aesthetic comportment that formalizes the production of a selectively racist or celebratory racial past that it synthesizes as the building's cultural black archiving dignity. On the other hand, this dignity of Gates's archives is incidental to the essential memorial function of his public art's speculating on black neighborhoods where the framing of black life as a novelty of the past facilitates the present and future of its annihilation. The needs of Chicago's real estate speculators and the funding from private (art) foundations are the formal essential dignity of the building's construction. In this encroaching form of black art marketization, the long durée of black bourgeois cultural value and discipline convenes with the mid-twentieth-century programs of violent urban renewal.

The beautification aesthetic that Gates's work participates in emerges from both state-sanctioned and privately funded "beautification" and War on Poverty projects from at least the mid-twentieth century that sought to eradicate unwieldy, ugly, and wayward forms of black life in black urban centers like Chicago.[56] Beautification projects that have increasingly Trojan-horsed schemes aimed at eradicating black life through increased policing and real estate speculation have adopted the façade of asserting and centering coercively collectivized black representation, or more culturally sovereign conceptions of black art and the black artists who make it. However, projects that were once carried out with more state funding are now achieved by even cheaper means with the willful comportment of the black artist's entrepreneurial spirit. Now as a funded and more easily embedded entrepreneur, the black artist beautifies the dirty work of the real estate developer and does it much more cheaply.

In Gates's practice and projects, the "cultural missionary" function that the BAG ultimately eschewed or contested is openly celebrated. Gates's aestheticization of the South Side of Chicago (where he grew up) in his art practice, which adopts the language of "redeveloping," "reform," "renew," "speculation" or "redefining," plows a value-laden furrow into black life. Indeed as of 2024, the South Side of Chicago is being primed for the massive civilizing real estate project that is the Obama Presidential Center, which "represents a historic opportunity to build a world-class museum and public gathering space that celebrates our nation's first African American President and First Lady on the South Side of Chicago."[57] Gates's projects sadly resonate more with the form of this massive antiblack private real estate endeavor than with its Black Arts Movement antecedents who would have or should have fought against it. Whatever the referenced radical content, the form of Gates's *Bildungs* affectively relates or makes friends with the burgeoning real estate projects that commemorate the ultimate aestheticization of black value.

The museumification of black life requires and emerges from the same violent ventriloquism I have tracked throughout this work, from Frederick Douglass to George W. Johnson, because it prominently discloses the aesthetic, the humanized, the beautified, and the verified sound-image of blackness despite, and without, the sounds of black bickering it symbolically references. This cultural verticality of official black culture's founding does not liberate black people but instead liberates the white void into which a solitary black figure might stand, pointing into the future of eternal peopleless valuations. Black beauty and beautification facilitate this, first as what appears to be a dignified and sociable power transfer and then as what is revealed to be a more deadly sublation and subjugation to the black work in the service of power. What shelters Gates's work in black neighborhoods is the institutionalized performance of a black collectivity enshrined in the long legacy of black-being-collected, rooted in the appreciation of black music and art as the aesthetic character of blackness.[58] What forms and forces of black life can be lived and raised against the aesthetic character of blackness that will art the world with our living until there are none of us, only sounds like us, left?

Coda

SELF-DEFENSE AGAINST DENSITY

Five years have passed and the plywood images bearing radical slogans have been removed. Only the glass of the empty buildings they protected remains. This is the shore we washed up on, the husk of our shouts eaten with concrete lips. Now we no longer pose the threat of broken windows. The haunting suburban silence populating Downtown Oakland's new emptiness everywhere bears the grinning façade of black expulsion. We have been evicted. Only black images—"Our Stories"—affixed to lobby windows remain; the black past is now the empty luxury condo's future musician and its defensive architecture against us. (See figures C.1 and C.2.) The unpopulated image of "Black Joy" inaugurates a new parade, the "Black Joy Parade," a new Freddy Fixer with half the budget, almost none of the spectacle, and even more police. Such initiatives were funded to counter the black rage, the "death and destruction," of the summer of 2020 by flooding the streets of Oakland with "light, joy, pleasure, and celebration."[1] The positive character of black displacement, black art aiding in black deaths then paying its respects as black memorials,[2] is a material violence that arts the world.

You can't fight value with (more or different) value; you can only fight it with force. Vacant condo windows and their unpeopled lobbies house the needs of capital; they ferry the endless futurity of speculation through the mere aesthetics of life, of living, of dwelling as if they were ever only meant to be housing for the apparitions of black life as exploited labor and incarcerated surplus population that has been swept away in the public outcry over the spectacle of "darkening violence" in Downtown Oakland. These buildings have drowned out the whirring white noise of deadly mechanistic urban redevelopment; they are the inescapable architecture of scaffolding broadcasting an all-surrounding soundtrack of construction.[3]

The superficial publics of parklets, virtually populated developer renderings, and endless prostheses of hostile architecture "vanished from our cities. There are no longer any ghosts who can remind the living of reciprocity."[4] The latent potential of the work of art to manifest a shared interiority

C.1 (*top*) The windows of a vacant building that were once covered in plywood bearing murals that said "End All Racism" and "Black Lives Matter" are now covered with a slick advertisement featuring official black faces and official "Black joy stories" at a site where no black people can live. Downtown Oakland, January 25, 2024. Photo by the author.

C.2 (*bottom*) More photographs of smiling black folks cover the same vacant condo. Downtown Oakland, January 25, 2024. Photo by the author.

has been diffused into its refusal to make an enemy of anyone. And that is why hardly anyone lives here. The value of the condos in Downtown Oakland, decorated now with prolific black images, are much higher than they would have been if they had been occupied (and undone) by black life. The capacities of blackness in the images they bear bar the door against black living. Black art cannot cause these buildings' emptiness to "depart from their own character" because the fullness of black sound-imagining increasingly and automatically shares the productive function of that emptiness. Contrary to Kant, no living black person's labor or liking could be the subject of this automation, but black life's needs could certainly tear this windowed world down, against the surface of black art. After all, what kind of black art can fundamentally devalue the world? A world that lets black art be beautiful without black needs? What might it mean to squat these empty funeral plots with our living against and beyond this beautiful herbarium?

The sonic signature of black death has become its circulatory collectability. At the foot of the symbolic, its shout becomes its silence where a gentrifying art gallery's storefront window bears a sign that reads both "Black Lives Matter" and "No Public Restroom"—really saying to its occupied black neighborhood, "You can't come in but please don't break our windows."[5] In the streets, the aesthetic character of black death is depopulated of its living and merely ventriloquized, robbed of force, reinforced by an endless futurity against black life (and for capital), an aesthetic of endless on behalf of. This work has been an attempt to figure out why (however partially), how, and when we are just an "on behalf of" even with ourselves, even within ourselves. Adorno wrote simply, "Music says 'We' directly, regardless of its intention."[6] The contours of this "we" are undoubtedly inscribed by the reification of a discursively and institutionally bound symbolics of sound, of sounding blackness as its objectified aesthetic character. Yet the nonexistent social of a perpetually practicing black collectivity must be pointed to, met up for, practiced, and played in over and over and over again. And we need a spot to meet in, to home in, we need to squat the very emptiness of our image organized against the bickering of our being and living together.

We are no longer the terror of walked by or leaned against, caught cruising in, or loitered around and lived too nearby, but we are now a carefully curated procession and parade of "black joy" commissioned to beautify expanding downtown real estate. There is nowhere for black folks to hang around public for free and now nowhere for anyone to hang around public for free, partially because the only thing that has been liberated, the only thing that has been freed, is our sound-images. Instead of the threat of an incidental black look peering into the world populated against us, our images are all shield, all mirror, as reflective as a surveillance camera that makes sure one of us never looks in, makes sure one of us never lingers long enough to look in, never lives to linger long enough.

Mallarmé's windows were experimental media of memory, surfaces that imparted autonomous relations between life and death, and offered a fragile precipice where the prurience of a look and the waywardness of a reflection flirted and raged.[7] Why you are here and they are there was an unequal intimacy or an occasion for war. But the vacant condo windows across world cities have emerged as the experimental medium of the endless exchange between forms of state power and neoliberal capital sewn together by the work of art; an asymmetry so evacuated of its original opposition that it installs the suzerainty of its outside.

We live outside the surface of reflection, yet in the ubiquitous gleaming emptiness, against all this value, we could live, we could squat and steal—we could unmake it with the richness of our living. The voluntarist impulse of aesthetics need not stay shorebound to find a frame. We can reach each other, panic, swim, and storm too.

Acknowledgments

The passion motivating this project is explained in the preface, so here I will acknowledge the difficulties. Often the publication of a book is celebrated with romanticism projected onto the birthing of a new life, but writing this book cost me many important relationships, severely took a toll on my mental and physical health, and led to forms of isolation I wouldn't wish on anyone. Most of this occurred during and as revision, which is to say writing. And like many people publishing in academia, I needed to write this book to theoretically keep my job. Although if we're being honest, this is hardly enough to "keep" a job in a fascist-zionist, racist, transphobic, ableist career path in a glorified settler-colonial real estate hedge fund known as a university. Many more of us will sadly kill ourselves and ruin our lives to have "the life" a book's publication theoretically secures, even and especially when a book no longer secures that "life."

Despite the oppressive idea of "the life," I owe the life of this book's publication and my own survival to some truly incredible people.

Thank you first to my family and community, Eric and Tosh, for reading and supporting me with home, food, kind words, and critical eyes for revision over the years. Thank you Ralowe for being one of the most inspiring and challenging thinkers and organizers to shape many of my ideas, understanding, and practicing of the world. Thanks to Ollie (even though she can't read this) for being a dutiful writing companion. Thanks LaVelle for the sisterly love and conversations that kept me going toward the end. Thank you, Kira, for being a guiding light in struggle, in rage, and in care.

Thank you to Elizabeth Ault at Duke University Press, my editor who never gave up on this project and in fact always found ways to inject new belief into me and my words. Thank you to Craig Willse for your thorough developmental editing and coaching, which I highly recommend others seek out, that facilitated this work's organization and realization as a book. Thank you to faculty at UC Riverside, Dylan Rodriguez, Setsu Shigematsu, and the entire Black Studies Department who invited me for numerous critical talks that shaped this work's content. Thank you Petero Kalulé for reminding me of the floral relations of thinking, writing, and being and the inspiring chance encounters of ideas, which, like cats, can cross our path when we're open to them.

Early versions (which hardly resemble this final text) owe their realization to the advice of David Marriott, Gina Dent, and Eric Porter. Thank you to Hassan Khan, with whom my early conversations sculpted this aesthetic trajectory and my own.

Notes

Preface

I owe much of the framing of this preface and the text more broadly to my fifteen years of conversations with Hassan Khan about art and culture.

1. For some glimpses of this life, see three films by Marlon Riggs, *Long Train Running: A History of the Oakland Blues* (co-directed by Peter Webster); *Tongues Untied*; and *Black Is, Black Ain't*.
2. See these and many other racist screeds published in the *East Bay Times*: Burt, "Violence Darkening Oakland's Nightlife"; and Burt, "Violence Shutters Another Oakland Nightspot."
3. Two weeks after the George Floyd riots and about a week after all the murals went up, a celebratory piece about the murals was published: Webster, "Breathtaking Murals for Justice." This article did not mention those liberatory nights that required the art's arresting capacity. One of the many involved nonprofits was the Bay Area Mural Project (https://www.thebamp.org/), which worked in conjunction with several similar organizations and numerous local artists.
4. If you read one source cited in this work, let it be this one regarding the murder of unhoused black trans man activist Banko Brown: Levin, "A Walgreens Guard Killed a Black Trans Organizer. His Community Wants Answers."
5. Kant, *Critique of Judgment*, 67. In his formulation of the transcendental judgment, which the aesthetic serves and realizes, Kant wrote quite famously, "The beautiful is that which pleases universally, without a concept." My aim in this book is not to accept, imitate, or reproduce the systematic nature of Kant's thinking, particularly his distinction between "free beauty" (referenced in this quote) and what we can term conceptual beauty. I do not attempt to establish a "before concept," or an a priori, as Kant does, which is a reputed synthetic device. My emphasis is, however, very related to Kant's focus on judgment, on how black art justifies black life, and the role of the justificatory in regulating black life.
6. Marable, *Race, Reform, and Rebellion*; Spence, *Knocking the Hustle*.
7. Du Bois, "Criteria of Negro Art," 291.

Introduction

1. I take the phrase "slave society" from Binder, "The Slavery of Emancipation." In much resonance with Saidiya Hartman, Guyora Binder argues for a legal distinction between manumission and emancipation, denoting the distinction of manumitting enslaved black people into an enslaving society—that is, a reformed slave society, a society in which they are not truly emancipated but subordinated to beautified and reformed forms of bondage. I will explain this term more thoroughly later in this text.

2. Throughout this study, I will use the term "black" to designate all persons of black descent, although the style is to some extent illogical in light of contemporary trends. I believe that in our incalculable living we need and are entitled to much more than the placating gesture of symbolic sovereignty, dignity, and respectability and the lawful external relations they imply. It is worth noting that W. E. B. Du Bois was not the first black writer to capitalize the N in Negro (see *The Philadelphia Negro*, 1); black newspaper writers in the Chicago *Conservator* preceded him by two decades. The capital N was also used by the avowedly racist weekly paper *Vardaman's Weekly* (run by Mississippi senator James K. Vardaman) and in the condescending strands of liberal racism advocated by the Southern Sociological Congress in its literature. The aesthetics of the capital N implied no friends and no enemies, held no love and no rage. See Grant and Grant, "Some Notes on the Capital 'N.'"

3. Douglass, *Narrative of the Life of Frederick Douglass*, 47.

4. See the widely known opening pages of Hartman, *Scenes of Subjection* and of course the rejoinder in Moten, *In the Break*, 1.

5. Cruz, *Culture on the Margins*.

6. I am here deeply indebted to the still-too-understudied work of Barrett, *Blackness and Value*.

7. Henry Louis Gates Jr. in Charles Burnett's documentary film *Nat Turner: A Troublesome Property*.

8. Gray, *Cultural Moves*.

9. For a general history of enslaved revolts, see Aptheker, *American Negro Slave Revolts*.

10. "Vibrations: Archie Shepp Interview + Lecture."

11. Hartman, *Scenes of Subjection*, 7.

12. Douglass, *Narrative of the Life of Frederick Douglass*, 97.

13. Adorno, "The Curves of the Needle," 50. See also Okiji, *Jazz as Critique*.

14. Wynter, "Sambos and Minstrels," 149.

15. Hartman, *Scenes of Subjection*, 7.

16 Wynter, "Sambos and Minstrels," 154.

17 For "lawful external relations," see Kant, *Idea for a Universal History from a Cosmopolitan Point of View*, 18. The state this exact terminology applies to or its dialectical correspondent in the human will appear throughout this work. But these terms are interdependent and are often interchangeable or substitutable with one another since they converge in and (re)emerge from a totality. I will often substitute value and authority for this term. I will frequently reference these totalities, as this book is a critique of the coercion that makes possible a totality. Just as the categorical bounding of the human is made possible through an aesthetic, a critique of judgment, so is the categorical bounding of the state and its requisite coercion and paranoia endemic to and protected by the citizen-subject-police. These are all representational projects aimed at extending the authority of the imagination of dominance. Throughout this work, I will argue that being black ought never to cohere into anything like a state and that the desire or lament to do so, to be so, retrospectively and aesthetically overdetermines the contemporary discourse of black (non)being. This is why I do not (or rarely) rely on ontology. Another concession from Kant, even though it is possessed of a rigorously metaphysical outlook, admits: "Whatever concept one may hold, from a metaphysical point of view, concerning the freedom of the will, certainly its *appearances*, which are human *actions*, like every other natural event are determined by universal laws." Kant, *Idea for a Universal History from a Cosmopolitan Point of View*, 11. Kant's concession emerges from his engagement with and departure from Hume (who is an equally relevant origin of aesthetics for Nietzsche in the following footnote) acknowledges the thinness of metaphysics (which emerged from the pre-Socratic Ionian gestures of synthesis of various cosmologies that yielded the Greek logos and later the [law of the] Platonic forms) for collecting all our stories and all our judgments under one singular being. To this Athenian legacy of domination from without as the inheritance of within, Kant proposes autonomy teleologically driven toward "universal history." Autonomy is Kant's marriage of the customs of authority of Greek rationality with the moral authority of Jerusalem and the Christological traditions. A question that is never quite answered in Kant—but debatably answered in his successors—is whether there is an end to the production of law or autonomy and its law always requires and presumes the endless dialectical production of law.

18 Kant, *Critique of Judgment*, 356.

19 Hartman, *Scenes of Subjection*, 134.

20 I repeat Kant's point: "Whatever concept one may hold, from a metaphysical point of view, concerning the freedom of the will, certainly its *appearances*, which are human *actions*, like every other natural event are

determined by universal laws." Kant, *Idea for a Universal History from a Cosmopolitan Point of View*, 11.

21 Kant writes:

> Now the satisfaction in the Beautiful, like that in the Sublime, is not alone distinguishable from other aesthetical judgements by its universal communicability, but also because, through this very property, it acquires an interest in reference to society (in which this communication is possible). We must, however, remark that separation from society is regarded as sublime, if it rests upon Ideas that overlook all sensible interest. To be sufficient for oneself, and consequently to have no need of society, without at the same time being unsociable, i.e. without flying from it, is something bordering on the sublime; as is any dispensing with wants.

Kant, *Critique of Judgment*, 145.

22 Kant, *Critique of Judgment*, 356.

23 Davis, "Reflections on Black Women's Roles in the Community of Slaves."

24 I take the term "structuring antagonism" from Stanley's indispensable *Atmospheres of Violence* to describe a process that is not predestined or synthetically given but dialectically ongoing and unfolding and whose forms and contents carry and carried the capacity to undo the totality under and through which they are sublimated.

25 Quite terrifyingly, Schiller wrote: "When the mechanical artist sets his hand to the formless block, to give it the form that he intends for it, he does not hesitate to do it violence, for Nature, which he is fashioning, merits no consideration for herself, and his concern is not with the whole for the sake of the parts, but with the parts for the sake of the whole." I explain Schiller's broader obsession with the "formless" and its need to be violently corralled to form in chapter 1; here I only raise it as a caution. Schiller, *Letter upon the Aesthetic Education of Man* (2016 edition), 29. Unless otherwise noted, all subsequent citations are for this edition.

26 Schiller, *Letter upon the Aesthetic Education of Man* (1910 edition), 281. In the instance of this crucial paragraph I prefer this somewhat esoteric though very aesthetically minded translation of Schiller's text.

27 Schiller, *Letter upon the Aesthetic Education of Man*, 34. I must admit I am partial to Paul de Man's more succinct if provocative translation of this: "We are dealing only with the case where the object of terror actually displays its power, but without aiming it in our direction, where we know ourselves, in a condition where we know ourselves to be in safety." For this translation, see de Man, *Aesthetic Ideology*, 142–43.

28 De Man, *Aesthetic Ideology*, 142. For the Kantian allusion that de Man is making, see Kant, *Critique of Pure Reason*, 354–65, in which Kant writes:

> We have now not only traveled through the land of pure understanding, and carefully inspected each part of it, but we have also surveyed it, and determined the place for each thing in it. This land, however, is an island, and enclosed in unalterable boundaries by nature itself. It is the land of truth (a seductive name), surrounded by a broad and stormy ocean, the proper seat of semblance, where many a fog bank and rapidly melting iceberg misrepresents new lands and, ceaselessly deceiving with empty hopes the voyager looking around for new discoveries, entwine him in adventures from which he can never escape and yet also never bring to an end.

29 On the "unification" of form with "spirit" and the humanization of music, see Adorno's reading of Mozart in *Aesthetic Theory*.

30 Hegel, *Aesthetics: Lectures on Fine Art*, 28. I owe thanks to David Marriott for making me, making us, read (in part) this massive and oft-dismissed tome in his fascinating graduate course "Poetry, Language, Thought" at UC Santa Cruz in 2009, in which of course we also read Heidegger.

31 Schiller, *Letter upon the Aesthetic Education of Man*, 43.

32 Hartman, *Scenes of Subjection*, 3.

33 Many may notice the absence of Benjamin's work from this book. *The Aesthetic Character of Blackness* is certainly influenced by his work; however, I would hope a form of study and research that *The Aesthetic Character of Blackness* inspires is a consideration of how the arguments here trouble some of Benjamin's founding assumptions. See Benjamin, "Work of Art."

34 Moten, "Notes on Surrender."

35 For a distinct but equally influential conception of what troubles but is sifted through and so remains beyond "thought," see Chandler, *X—The Problem of the Negro*; and Adorno, *Negative Dialectics*.

36 Nietzsche, *The Birth of Tragedy*, 8.

37 I am paraphrasing or modifying Schiller's phrasing: "The man lacking in form despises all grace of diction as corruption, all elegance in social intercourse as hypocrisy, all delicacy and loftiness of demeanour as exaggeration and affectation." Schiller, *Letter upon the Aesthetic Education of Man*, 48.

38 Schiller, *Letter upon the Aesthetic Education of Man*, 105.

39 Hartman, *Scenes of Subjection*, 23.

40 At the roots of Nietzsche's demand or provocation of aesthetic justification and the assertive impact he imagines it making on and as the world

is the desire to see music achieve a level of development paralleling the authority of technoscientific rationality and the symbolic authority of the law. Nietzsche wrote: "We will have achieved much for the study of aesthetics when we come, not merely to a logical understanding, but also to the immediately certain apprehension of the fact that the further development of art is bound up with the duality of the Apollonian and the Dionysian, just as reproduction depends upon the duality of the sexes, their continuing strife and only periodically occurring reconciliation." Nietzsche, *The Birth of Tragedy*, 8.

41 Wynter, "The Ceremony Must Be Found," 31.

42 Nietzsche, *The Birth of Tragedy*, 18.

43 I am using "legal character" more in terms of how Adorno rightly contextualizes both Kant and Nietzsche: "This is what dialectics holds up to our consciousness as a contradiction. Because of the immanent nature of consciousness, contradictoriness itself has an inescapably and fatefully legal character. Identity and contradiction of thought are welded together. Total contradiction is nothing but the manifested untruth of total identification. Contradiction is nonidentity under the rule of a law that affects the nonidentical as well." Adorno, *Negative Dialectics*, 5. Adorno used the term "semblance character" referring to a work of art in numerous places in his writing, most extensively in his explicit writing on music and art. But for now, see Adorno, *Aesthetic Theory*; as well as Adorno, *Quasi Una Fantasia*; Adorno, "Music and Technique"; and Adorno and Simpson, "On Popular Music."

44 The phrase "cold heart" is from Friedrich Schiller's lines appealing to and arguing against the pure rationality of the law: "Hence the abstract thinker very often has a cold heart, since he analyses the impressions which really affect the soul only as a whole; the man of business has very often a narrow heart, because his imagination, confined within the monotonous circle of his profession, cannot expand to unfamiliar modes of representation." Schiller, *Letter upon the Aesthetic Education of Man*, 34. In general, however, the heart is a romantic trope perhaps most associated with the Rousseauean tradition. I will delve further into the role of Rousseauean pity and other romantic references in which the language of "the heart" is more commonly rooted and which (most importantly for this study) shaped Frederick Douglass's framing of black music in his writings and speaking. As a counter to this tradition, see Ebrahim N. Hussein's play about the Maji Maji Rebellion of 1905–1907, *Kinjeketile*.

45 Sterne, *The Audible Past*.

46 Foucault, *Discipline and Punish*, 23.

47 Foucault, *The Birth of the Clinic*, 121.

48 Du Bois, "Criteria of Negro Art," 103.

49 English, *How to See a Work of Art in Total Darkness*, 35.
50 Du Bois, "Criteria of Negro Art," 291.
51 Nietzsche, *The Birth of Tragedy*, 28.
52 Nietzsche rather famously wrote:

> The pre-condition of this Prometheus myth is the extraordinary value which a naïve humanity associates with fire as the true divine protector of that rising culture. But the fact that man freely controls fire and does not receive it merely as a gift from heaven, as a stirring lightning flash or warming rays of the sun, appeared to these contemplative primitive men as an outrage, a crime against divine nature. And so right there the first philosophical problem posed an awkward insoluble contradiction between man and god and pushed it right up to the door of that culture, like a boulder. The best and loftiest thing which mankind can share is achieved through a crime, and people must now accept the further consequences, namely, the entire flood of suffering and troubles with which the offended divine presences afflict the nobly ambitious human race.

Nietzsche, *The Birth of Tragedy*, 28.
53 Douglass, *Life and Times of Frederick Douglass*, 47.
54 Kalulé, "Being Right-With."

Chapter 1. Emancipating the Spaces of Sonic Capture

1 Hartman, *Scenes of Subjection*, 134.
2 What might be read as my awkward phrasing here is an attempt to think with David Marriot's work in *Haunted Life*, about how images of black objects always imply a consecrated practice of "looking" (extending from Fanon's notion of a "look" in *Black Skin, White Masks*). I glean this understanding from Marriott's reading of the (reflected) image of Narcissus in the pool, within a Fanonian lens. Indeed black images are not simply images but the freezing of white practices of looking that constructed them. This also accounts for how I talk about Hutchinson's hands in this chapter or Victor Emerson's hands in the next chapter.
3 Davis, "Reflections on Black Women's Roles in the Community of Slaves," 86.
4 Douglass, *My Bondage*, 265–66.
5 Brooks, *Bodies in Dissent*.
6 Berlant, "Genre Flailing."
7 Hartman, *Scenes of Subjection*, 19–21.
8 Adorno, *Aesthetic Theory*, 13.

9   As Sylvia Wynter has contended, "the bourgeois world found a source of cultural life on which to feed, if the barest minimum of an affective and emotional life were to be sustained in the wilderness of technological rationalization. . . . [Thus,] blacks function as the plantation subproletariat hidden in the raw material." Wynter, "Sambos and Minstrels," 149.

10 See Tate's formulation, which very broadly guides my concerns throughout this book, in *Everything but the Burden*.

11 Considering representations of black people that are purported to be liberating by virtue of their positivist rendering of a notion of freedom, even if largely from a configurational negation of explicitly imaged capture, such as Douglass's "Fugitive's Song," provides an interesting counter to the potentially liberating or meaningfully fugitive nonrepresentation of Harriet Jacobs/Linda Brent as discussed in McKittrick, *Demonic Grounds*.

12 Wynter, "Sambos and Minstrels," 152.

13 Douglass, *Narrative of the Life of Frederick Douglass*, 47.

14 Brooks, *Bodies in Dissent*, 27.

15 Hartman, *Scenes of Subjection*, 48.

16 I am here referring to an argument around Kant's "The Understanding," which I will discuss in the following chapter. This synthetic understanding houses the synthetic a priori that Kant discloses in the preface to *Critique of Judgment*: "It was then properly the *understanding* which has its special realm in the *cognitive faculty*, so far as it contains constitutive principles of cognition *a priori*." Kant, *Critique of Judgment*, 4.

17 Hartman, *Scenes of Subjection*, 17–18.

18 This is autonomy, in Kant's sense of the word from its sophist and platonic origins, as a legislative function of the will of comportment, of posture, of standing, of moral conduct that extends toward the representative force of universal reason actuated through the articulation of the will as the idealistic legislation of universal law. It is the posture, the comportment of Douglass and the notion that now, finally, he can possess or actualize a will as signifying the conversion to a liberated subject. Unquestionably, both by Douglass's imaging here and (as we will see) by his own fabrication of himself (and of course within its Kantian valences), this is an eminently aesthetic endeavor.

19 And its trajectories through the nineteenth, the twentieth, and, especially, the twenty-first centuries have perhaps increasingly illustrated this paradox. The reinterpretation of slave narratives as conditioning our current engagement with antiblackness as a preoccupation with "the slave" finds a fascinating and challenging interlocutor in Moses, *Liberian Dreams*. I

say paradox here to describe what I think is a relatively common synthesis when it is pinned to the object rather than wielded against the system that produces the object.

20 Buck-Morrs, *Hegel, Haiti, and Universal History*, 39.
21 James, *The Black Jacobins*, 196.
22 Wynter, "The Ceremony Must Be Found," 34. Wynter writes:

> A shift now took place. Since physical nature, knowledge of which had been freed from serving a verifying function the order/chaos dynamics of the system-ensemble, another mode of nature, *human nature*, would now be installed in its place. The representation of a naturally ordered distribution of degrees of reason between different human groups enables what might be called a homo-ontological principle of Sameness/Difference, figured as by/nature difference of superiority/ inferiority between groups, and could now function tautologically as the verifying proof of an infrasensory ontologized, naturally caused status-organizing principle, a principle based on differential endowment of Reason (rather than of Noble blood) and verified dynamically in empirical reality of the order.

23 For a broad historical treatment of New World slave revolts, see Aptheker, *American Negro Slave Revolts*; Genovese, *From Rebellion to Revolution*; Matthews, *Caribbean Slave Revolts*; and Reis, *Slave Rebellion in Brazil*.
24 Dabydeen, *Hogarth's Blacks*.
25 Hartman, *Scenes of Subjection*, 23.
26 For a critique of slavery's temporal ending or "post," see Hartman, "The Time of Slavery."
27 There are numerous examples, but Malcolm X's invocation in his seminal speech "Message to the Grassroots" is the first and most prominent in my mind: "You catch hell 'cause you're a black man. You catch hell, all of us catch hell, for the same reason. So we are all black people, so-called Negroes, second-class citizens, ex-slaves. You are nothing but an ex-slave. You don't like to be told that. But what else are you? You are ex-slaves. You didn't come here on the 'Mayflower.' You came here on a slave ship—in chains, like a horse, or a cow, or a chicken. And you were brought here by the people who came here on the 'Mayflower.' You were brought here by the so-called Pilgrims or Founding Fathers. They were the ones who brought you here." Malcolm X, "Message to the Grassroots," 4.
28 Cruz, *Culture on the Margins*.
29 Brooks, *Bodies in Dissent*, 74.
30 For the term "slave society," see Binder, "The Slavery of Emancipation." I am noting here how Binder in far more legally precise language discusses

manumission as an occasion for keeping intact the power relations of a world built on slavery while also further emancipating those forms of state and market power over the recently manumitted. Also of course see Saidiya Hartman's work in *Scenes of Subjection* for a closely related argument.

31 Hunter, *To 'Joy My Freedom*.

32 Marx responded to Adam Smith by asserting:

> Certainly, labour obtains its measure from the outside, through the aim to be attained and the obstacles to be overcome in attaining it. But Smith has no inkling whatever that this overcoming of obstacles is a liberating activity—and that, further, the external aims become stripped of the semblance of merely external natural urgencies and become posited as aims which the individual himself posits—hence as self-realization, objectification of the subject, hence real freedom, whose action is, precisely, labour. He is right, of course, that, in its historic forms as slave-labour, serf-labour, and wage-labour, labour always appears as repulsive, always as *external forced labour*; and not-labour, by contrast, as 'freedom, and happiness'. This holds doubly: for this contradictory labour; and, relatedly, for labour which has not yet created the subjective and objective conditions for itself (or also, in contrast to the pastoral etc. state, which it has lost), in which labour becomes attractive work, the individual's self-realization, which in no way means that it becomes mere fun, mere amusement, as Fourier, with *grisette*-like naïveté, conceives it. Really free working, e.g. composing, is at the same time precisely the most damned seriousness, the most intense exertion. The work of material production can achieve this character only (1) when its social character is posited, (2) when it is of a scientific and at the same time general character, not merely human exertion as a specifically harnessed natural force, but exertion as subject, which appears in the production process not in a merely natural, spontaneous form, but as an activity regulating all the forces of nature.

Marx, *Grundrisse*, 534. See also Stillman, "Scarcity, Sufficiency, and Abundance."

33 I try generally to avoid a positive discussion of "ugliness" as a contrarian or inherently transgressive hinge against "beauty"; I don't see them necessarily as opposites. But more important, for the management of surplus populations with criminality, see Schweik, *The Ugly Laws*, a historical record relatively contemporary to Marx; and of course Du Bois's *Black Reconstruction*.

34 Epstein, *Sinful Tunes and Spirituals*, 177.

35 Rankin, "How Slavery Honors Our Country's Flag," 13–14.

36 Marx, *The Poverty of Philosophy*, 122.

37 See, of course, Washington, "Address." For more critical rejoinders to the management of the landscape of black labor postemancipation, see Du Bois, *Black Reconstruction*, 128–81; Jones, "End to the Neglect"; Hunter, *To 'Joy My Freedom*; Woods, *Development Arrested*; and LeFlouria, *Chained in Silence*.

38 Marx, *Capital*, 169.

39 I am referring again to Sylvia Wynter's assertion that "the bourgeois world found a source of cultural life on which to feed, if the barest minimum of an affective and emotional life wern e to be sustained in the wilderness of technological rationalization. . . . [Thus,] blacks function as the plantation subproletariat hidden in the raw material." Wynter, "Sambos and Minstrels," 149. This is also a way to expand upon what is implicit in my early treatments of sonic technology, namely, the tendency within a longstanding Marxist materialist critique of the formal and rational tenets of artistic and technological modernity, particularly in the writings of Walter Benjamin, Theodor W. Adorno, and Friedrich Kittler, that has been rooted in a rigorous but all too limited ontology of the materiality of technological modernity, a materiality rooted primarily in the coercive production of wage-labor and not an understanding of the coercive and captive labors of the slave plantation, the colonies, and their all-encompassing echoes.

40 Wynter, "Sambos and Minstrels," 149.

41 Adorno, *Aesthetic Theory*, 227.

42 Douglass, *Narrative of the Life of Frederick Douglass*, 58.

43 Roberts, *Freedom as Marronage*, 59.

44 Here my thinking is shaped by Gaines, *The Theater of Refusal*, 12–21, which fully describes which marginalization within the imagination of the institution enables the expansion of the institution's dominance and how it does so. This point will become far more tense in the final chapter of this work, but for now suffice it to allow us to think of Douglass as a kind of model of a or *the* black artist as s/he/they becomes an increasingly intuitively idealized object of capture.

45 For "burdened individuality," see Hartman, *Scenes of Subjection*, 115–24.

46 Hartman, *Scenes of Subjection*, 43.

47 See Wynter, "Black Metamorphosis," 87. Wynter writes "It was alleged that a certain dance was danced at the funerals which incited slaves to rebellion. When planters were alerted to the danger of the seemingly harmless funerals, they soon woke up to the danger of the seemingly harmless drum, the harmless dance." I thank Professor Bedour Alagraa for bringing this indispensable reference to my attention.

48 See an important essay on Firmin by philosopher Russell, "Positivism and Progress in Firmin's Equality of the Human Races." Also see Firmin's

text (although it is still rather hard to obtain) *The Equality of the Human Races: Positivist Anthropology*.

49 Du Bois, *The Philadelphia Negro*, 351.
50 Du Bois, *The Philadelphia Negro*, 98.
51 Hartman, *Scenes of Subjection*, 134.
52 Adorno, *Aesthetic Theory*, 13.
53 Marx states in a somewhat anthropological way, "All mythology subdues, controls and fashions the forces of nature in the imagination and through imagination; it disappears therefore when real control over these forces is established." Later, grafting familial metaphors onto these, he adds,

> The difficulty we are confronted with is not, however, that of understanding how Greek art and epic poetry are associated with certain forms of social development. The difficulty is that they still give us aesthetic pleasure and are in certain respects regarded as a standard and unattainable ideal. An adult cannot become a child again, or he becomes childish. But does the naivete of the child not give him pleasure, and does not he himself endeavour to reproduce the child's veracity on a higher level? Does not the child in every epoch represent the character of the period in its natural veracity? Why should not the historical childhood of humanity, where it attained its most beautiful form, exert an eternal charm because it is a stage that will never recur? There are rude children and precocious children. Many of the ancient peoples belong to this category. The Greeks were normal children. The charm their art has for us does not conflict with the immature stage of the society in which it originated. On the contrary its charm is a consequence of this and is inseparably linked with the fact that the immature social conditions which gave rise, and which alone could give rise, to this art cannot recur.

Marx, *Grundrisse*, 43–44.

54 Du Bois, *The Souls of Black Folk*, 11.
55 Du Bois, *The Souls of Black Folk*, 13.
56 Du Bois came to realize and criticize this analysis later in his pathbreaking work *Black Reconstruction*.
57 Adorno, *Aesthetic Theory*, 12.
58 Adorno, *Aesthetic Theory*, 11.
59 For the common northern contemporary critique of slavery as merely a southern cultural custom rather than a foundational global pillar of "the slave society," see Binder, "The Slavery of Emancipation," 2063–102. Eric Lott proclaimed that the both contemporary and long-twentieth-century mischaracterization of minstrelsy as an exclusively "folk culture" belied its popularity in its cultural center of New York City. Lott, *Love and Theft*, 17.

Chapter 2. More Nearly Members of the Family

1. Brooks, *Lost Sounds*, 18.
2. Brooks, *Lost Sounds*, 18.
3. Brooks, *Lost Sounds*, 19.
4. For more on this, see Hartman, *Scenes of Subjection*; Spillers, "Mama's Baby, Papa's Maybe," 65–81; and Hunter, *To 'Joy My Freedom*. I am indebted for the treatment of these sources to a class I took with Professor Angela Davis and several graduate students at UC Santa Cruz entitled "Theories of Slavery."
5. Locke, "Enter the New Negro," 1.
6. Henry Louis Gates Jr. in Charles Burnett's documentary film *Nat Turner: A Troublesome Property*.
7. Du Bois, *The Souls of Black Folk*, 45–46.
8. Du Bois, *The Souls of Black Folk*, 227.
9. Brooks, *Lost Sounds*, 19.
10. Davis, "Reflections on Black Women's Roles in the Community of Slaves." Davis discusses the site of disinheritance as a lack of accrual, a hollowing out that primes black folks for the yoke of racial pathology but contends that this force of racial engendering also made possible especially black women's acts of rebellion and sabotage that were carried out under the cloak of the most violently forced intimacy. Davis argues that many black women and children "house slaves," in being characterized by their readiness-to-hand and possession at the hands of their disinheritance from their kin in the field, were the fulcrum of many poisonings and executions of the masters and their families.
11. Spillers, "Mama's Baby, Papa's Maybe," 80.
12. Here I am aided by one of Derrida's many engagements with Heidegger as a way of thinking beyond a Hegelian dialectic of history. Derrida wrote,

    Engaged in the opening up of this dissension, and above all by it, under its assignation, man is watched by what-is, Heidegger says, and such would be the essence (*Wesen*) of man "during the great Greek epoch." Man thus seeks to gather in saying (*legein*) and to save, to keep (*sozein, bewahren*), while at the same time remaining exposed to the chaos of dissension. The theater or the tragedy of this dissension is not yet seen as belonging either to the scenic space of presentation (*Darstellung*) or to that of representation, but the fold of dissension would open up, announce, send on everything that will afterward come to be determined as mimesis, and then imitation, representation, with the whole parade of oppositional couples that will form philosophical theory: production/reproduction, presentation/representation, original/derived, and so on. "Before" all these pairs, if one may say that, there will never have been presentative simplicity but another fold, another difference, unpresentable, unrepresentable, *jective* perhaps, but neither objective, nor subjective, nor projective. What of the unpresentable or the unrepresentable? How to think it? That is now the question.

Derrida, *Psyche*, 115.

13   Chandler, *X—The Problem of the Negro*, 140–41.

14   Davis, "Reflections on Black Women's Roles in the Community of Slaves."

15   For the concept of "shadow family," see Spillers, "Shades of Intimacy."

16   Wagner, *Disturbing the Peace*, 193.

17   The preceding insights and the quote are taken from Wagner, *Disturbing the Peace*, 195. Wagner noted that "maintaining that the phonograph was antithetical to black expression, collectors disowned the means that had enabled them to imagine a source for the tradition" (193).

18   Chandler, *X—The Problem of the Negro*, 140–41.

19   Saidiya Hartman thoroughly discusses the dangers of the illusion of equality (or we might say "likeness") in the construction of legal and extralegal emancipation discourses in the nineteenth century. In her central idea of "self-making," she addresses how forms of legal equality or ontological similitude, particularly during Reconstruction, attempted to efface the injurious and debilitating effects of slavery, even as they at base presumed their legal existence. See Hartman's chapter "Instinct and Injury: Bodily Integrity, Natural Affinities, and the Constitution of Equality" in *Scenes of Subjection*.

20   Baraka, *Blues People*, 3. Baraka's point that there was no human communication is sharply contradicted by Saidiya Hartman's work on sentimentality, humanity, and slavery in *Scenes of Subjection*.

21   Following the infamous trial that would define Johnson's later life in which he was accused of murdering his common-law wife, Roskin Stewart, newspapers stated that Johnson's "accomplishments are now being whistled and sung by slot machines from one end of the country to another." Brooks, *Lost Sounds*, 58.

22   Marx, *Capital*, 74.

23   Here Fred Moten's radical argument against a traditional conception of the avant-garde drives my thinking. In his chapter "The Sentimental Avant-Garde" in *In the Break*, he discusses how sentimentality is always already cut by a racial and sexual difference; blackness cuts the avant-garde even as it props it up. That Moten's point is provocatively temporal resonates with some of my own temporal claims here. It is particularly relevant considering how Moten understands the deconstructive relationship between part and whole in relation to black art and aesthetics.

24 Fanon, *Black Skin, White Masks*, 46.

25 My invocation of "the human" is significantly derived from Sylvia Wynter's work. Instead of invoking the discourses on the "post-human," I think with Sylvia Wynter's important critique of the concept rather than the "post-humanism." The post-human, as Wynter's work contends, does not significantly trouble the "overrepresentation" of man as human, which is part of the epistemological authority, and a "post-humanist" stance cannot account for the violence of such an overrepresentation. Nor does it, I might suggest, adequately trouble or address the symbolic currency of such a humanity, which was built on the capital or fungibility of blackness. I hope to confront this through the phonograph in this essay. Wynter, "Unsettling the Coloniality of Being/Power/Truth/Freedom," 257–337.

26 Weheliye, "After Man," 324. Also see Weheliye's book *Phonographies: Grooves in Sonic Afro-Modernity*.

27 In focusing primarily on Bell's "ear phonautograph," Jonathan Sterne seeks to differentiate it from Scott's (original) phonautograph in terms of each inventor's intentions. Whereas Bell's phonautograph, which sought more intentionally to imitate the tympanic aspects of the ear, was tied to an assimilationist politics that sought to "cure" deafness (and hence eradicate deaf culture), Scott's phonautograph fully invested in the majesty of *writing* sound, which he believed—not unlike Theodor W. Adorno almost a century later—would exalt music and restore it to its rightful place alongside writing. I will confront some of these aspects of Scott's phonautograph as well as Sterne's characterization of it shortly. Sterne, *The Audible Past*.

28 Bidwell, "Recent Inventions," 3.

29 Rosen, "Researchers Play Tune."

30 See Rilke, "Primal Sound."

31 Kittler, *Gramophone, Film, Typewriter*, 32.

32 While Derrida's focus in *The Politics of Friendship* is a notion of friendly love, his insight that such a notion of love is predicated on an ideal (albeit fabricated) notion of "symmetry" is helpful here. Specifically, Derrida establishes how concepts of political selfhood, among which we could include the human, depend on a kind of similitude to structure their field of recognition. Derrida, *The Politics of Friendship*, 297–99.

33 For the concept of body-reasoning, see Oyewumi, *The Invention of Women*.

34 Edison, "The Phonograph and Its Future," 536.

35 Dolar, *A Voice and Nothing More*.

36 For a critique of the failed analogy and conflation of automation with "the slave," see Eglash, "Broken Metaphor," 360–69.

37 Edison, "The Phonograph and Its Future," 530–33.
38 Dolar, *A Voice and Nothing More*. For Adorno's treatment of "his master's voice," see Adorno, "The Curves of the Needle."
39 Marriott, "Inventions of Existence," 61.
40 Derrida, *Specters of Marx*, 35.
41 Bidwell, "Recent Inventions," 5.
42 Bidwell, "Recent Inventions," 5.
43 Bidwell, "Recent Inventions," 2.
44 Kant, *Critique of Judgment*, 66.
45 Locke, "Book II of Ideas," 390.
46 Whether in philosophy's Ionian synthetization or our own contemporary "knowledge economies" of data, a material force always lives in, against, and beyond and makes these configurations possible. Jonathan Sterne's work on sonic technology in the middle of the nineteenth century brings this home quite precisely; he situates the macabre practice of robbing the graves of the poor to provide material resources for the experiments on the human ear that were instrumental in phonographic production. Sterne points out that this practice was equally important in portraying deaf cultures as characterized by the absolute lack of "hearing's" conceptual efficiency. Sterne, *The Audible Past*, 23.
47 Wynter, "The Ceremony Must Be Found," 27.
48 Wynter, "The Ceremony Must Be Found," 27, uses the term "vanished authority" to refer to and expand Heidegger's point in "The Word of Nietzsche" that the modern disappearance and substitution of the authority of god for the authority of reason was carried out by displacing the (fantastical) supersensory authority of god's omniscience with the rational.
49 Simpson, "Slave Songs of the United States," 341.
50 Here I am thinking of Clive Scott's thinking around the (internalized) rhythm of listening and the proper name, its attachment to a sound and a sensation. Scott points out that "if reading is listening, where interfering 'noise' amplifies with years, reading is also a process of self-enquiry and self-disclosure. . . . I respond to the oscillation between voiced and unvoiced. . . . I respond to a rhythmic and rhyming structure which tells me the third line is a climax, of certainty or defeat." Scott, *The Poetics of French Verse*, 84–85. Relatedly, the musicians' sounding threatens the phonological or what Derrida would have called the "phonologocentrism" of Simpson's assertions about the properness of the concept of music and the proper name. As Derrida puts it in his consideration of the trace: "The graphic image is not seen [does not appear]; and the acoustic image is not heard. The difference between the full unities of the voice re-

mains unheard. And, the difference in the body of the inscription is also invisible." Derrida, *Of Grammatology*, 65.

51   See one of my favorite books: Mudimbe, *The Invention of Africa*.

52   Cowen, "Earliest Known Sound Recording Revealed."

53   In *Of Grammatology*, Jacques Derrida coined the terms phonocentrism, phonologism, and phonologocentrism in his attempt to distinguish the ideality and materiality of writing from the logics of phonemes or simply of speech.

54   Bidwell, "Recent Inventions," 6. Bidwell attributes this lack to the phonautograph, but even more so to early phonographic and microphonic technology.

55   Bidwell, "Recent Inventions," 7.

56   Brooks, *Lost Sounds*, 27.

57   As it is famously told, turning the phonograph into a source of commercial entertainment grated against Edison's desire that the phonograph remain a kind of office tool for secretaries to dictate the words of their boss. This shift further complicated how the phonograph was gendered. Patrons paid a modest sum to consume the sound that emanated from the rubber-tube earpieces. While repeated listenings were the primary means of phonographic profit, the practice did not quite work with the material limitations of the wax cylinder format. Edison's wax cylinders could withstand only a limited number of reproductions—that is, both recordings and plays—before the paraffin wax they were made of would degrade to a level that rendered the recording unintelligible and or inaudible. Large-scale reproduction was then requisite in order to turn any profit. Repetition was simultaneously the basis for the recognition and reproduction of these phonographic hieroglyphs—how they could mean—and their point of sonic unintelligibility as they underwent the material degradation that was the partial recognition of their repetition. The Edisonian novelty of the ad infinitum repetition of the human voice through reproduction had become both a necessary possibility and an impossibility. Related to the desire for cheapness, loudness was an even more fantastical and perhaps powerful evocation of the ideal object of the phonograph. Prior to the 1920s, phonographic recording was entirely acoustical rather than electric. All objects of recording were sonically captured through a large acoustical recording horn. The possibility of graphical inscription in the record or cylinder required an acoustic force intense enough to be transmitted through the large recording horn and cause the recording stylus to make distinct enough impressions or grooves on the record. A somewhat famous issue of the phonograph is that certain instruments and certain sounds could not be faithfully inscribed on the cylinder and faithfully reproduced. High-pitched string instruments and

pianos were fairly difficult to record, as were highly percussive instruments (namely drums).

58 There is some discrete musical truth to the harmonic, tonal, and phonological distinctions implicit in phonographic recording. For example, symphonies and orchestras and some operatic music were afterthoughts due largely to the difficulty in recording the variety of instruments and frequency ranges. The brass instruments were more amenable to inscription: tubas, trombones, and trumpets allowed for more dynamic harmonic control and hence control of the movements of the cutting stylus during the recording process. Moreover, brass horn instruments could be more sharply focused in the direction of the recording horn, which allowed for a more faithful reproduction of their sound. Ultimately, what or who could or could not be recorded was as much a phenomenal distinction as it was a political or an ideological one and perhaps most consistently a psychic one. According to some theorists of the time, women's voices were impossible to record and reproduce. The cut of sexual difference here not only cuts the phonic coherence of the aforementioned instruments, it also reveals the instrumentalization of the body, the instrumentalization of the human through difference that had been under way in acoustic spaces like the field and the plantation long before it was mechanically recorded. This shows how the phonograph relied on and reinforced rigid phenomenal and symbolic conceptions of sexual difference.

59 Brooks, *Lost Sounds*, 27.

60 Brooks, *Lost Sounds*, 30.

61 Millard, *America on Record*, 27.

62 Concurrent with Johnson's recording career and the rise of the phonograph were the anthropological work of ethnologists such as J. Deniker and G. D. Gibb that emphasized the anatomical, physiological, and phrenological characteristics of Negroes and differentiated their speech among "the races of man" as a biological fact of the distinctness of the "Negro larynx" that made their voices and their sounds ideal for recording. This anatomization was tied to a phonic and phonological fetishization of the black body as the ultimate source of the black voice and even more as the ultimate source for all phonographic knowledge. The black voice was then embodied as it was instrumentalized in a manner reminiscent of Shelford Bidwell's earlier emphasis on the phonic and phonemic quality of the human voice as attributable to the qualities of the "cavity of the mouth." Hence, the black voice was assigned to a body with an excessive knowability and symbolization, a body presumed by ethnology, phrenology, phonology, and anthropology to be entirely known and knowable.

63 Maurice, "Cinema at Its Source." In this pathbreaking article, Maurice discusses a similar dynamic of the black voice in early sound synchroni-

zation of 1920s and 1930s cinema. Undoubtedly this story of the idealized essential reproducibility of the black voice is wrapped up in and perhaps to a degree attributable to its phonographic legacy.

64 Stadler, "Never Heard Such a Thing," 98.
65 This "tiny" quality, a common feature of early phonographic recording before the invention of electrical recording, was largely the result of the acoustic process via the recording horn, in which the amplitudes of both low and high tones were attenuated, if they were recorded at all. "Tiny" in fact became the sonic metonym for the phonograph, perhaps most famously harped on in Sousa, "The Menace of Mechanical Music." For a later complication of this "little sound," listen to the work of the Art Ensemble of Chicago, specifically Roscoe Mitchell's *Sound* (1966) and the piece "Little Suite," which uses the timbre of "little instruments" to explore the dynamic and chromatics of the audio space.
66 See Brooks, *Lost Sounds*, 28; and Gelatt, *The Fabulous Phonograph*, 49.
67 Listen to Arthur Collins's earlier "coon songs," particularly his ca. 1902 rendition of "Bill Bailey Won't You Please Come Home." The similarity of Collins's "minstrelized" voice to his announcing voice pervades nearly all of his songs. In fact, even songs that were not strictly "coon songs" bear this trait, perhaps further pointing to the contagious effects of the black voice in phonography.
68 For a greater discussion of Bert Williams's minstrelsy career and its role in the making of racialized stardom and notions of diaspora at the turn of the twentieth century, see Chude-Sokei, *The Last "Darky."*
69 Lott, *Love and Theft*, 147. For a further and more extensive critique of Lott's rather one-sided telling of minstrelsy, particularly its almost exclusive focus on male and male-on-male minstrelsy, see Brown, *Babylon Girls*.
70 Stadler, "Never Heard Such a Thing," 12.
71 For a sharp discussion of the relationship between inscription in more discursive terms, particularly in other forms of contemporary media, see Jackson, *Scripting the Black Masculine Body*.
72 Gelatt, *The Fabulous Phonograph*, 49.

> When the bankers arrived on the appointed day, Edison sat down before the instrument, set it in motion, and dictated a short letter into the mouthpiece. He then lowered the reproducing stylus into place and prepared to let the phonograph *sell itself* to his assembled guests. But instead of parroting the words he had just spoken, the phonograph emitted nothing more than an ugly hiss. Was it showing its contempt for the leaders of finance? Edison made some small adjustments, inserted a fresh cylinder, and dictated another letter—with the same humiliated result. After some further abortive tries, the Seligman

entourage took their leave, promising to return when Edison had the instrument in working order. The defect was quickly repaired, but the Seligman people never paid a second visit.

73   Wagner, *Disturbing the Peace*, 186; my italics.
74   See Johnson, "The Laughing Coon."
75   Wagner, *Disturbing the Peace*, 186.
76   See Homi Bhabha's well-known chapter on the stereotype, "The Other Question: Stereotype, Discrimination and the Discourse of Colonialism," in *The Location of Culture*.
77   Wagner, *Disturbing the Peace*, 194.
78   Wagner, *Disturbing the Peace*, 1.
79   Hunter, *To 'Joy My Freedom*, does an excellent job of detailing the gendered nature of Wagner's overlooking of the penetration of black women into the domesticity of "the white world" via their jobs as domestic wage laborers.
80   For Edison's early marketing campaign for the phonograph disguised largely as scientific research, see an abundance of articles at the turn of the twentieth century: Edison, "The Perfected Phonograph"; Edison, "The Talking Phonograph"; "Edison and the Kinetograph."
81   I am speculating that the older hand-cranked motor recorded Johnson's recordings of the early 1890s. Although Edison had technically developed a phonograph with a small electrical motor in the 1880s, such a mechanism was not available until the early 1900s. For commercial recordings, companies primarily used hand-cranked motors that ran on mechanical energy. One can hear the presence of the hand-cranked motor on Johnson's earliest recordings as an irregular hiss that is not exclusively the product of cylinder degradation but is also the product of Emerson's cranking hands. For more on the development of the various phonographic motors, see Millard's *America on Record*.
82   Derrida, *Of Grammatology*, 65.

Chapter 3. Ma Rainey's Phonograph

1   My retelling of this performance draws upon four versions: Albertson, *Bessie*, 113–15; Lieb, *Mother of the Blues*; McGinley, *Staging the Blues*; and O'Neal, "In Old Kay See." For a fleshing out of context also see Brooks, *The Bessie Smith Companion*.
2   Wynter, "On How We Mistook the Map for the Territory."
3   McMillan, *Embodied Avatars*.
4   Martin, "The Symbolic Nature of Chaos," 8.
5   Spillers, "Mama's Baby, Papa's Maybe," 68.

6   For treatments of iconicity, see Ellison, *Invisible Man*; Fleetwood, *Troubling Vision*, 47; and Brown, *Dark Matters*. Around the same time as this performance, iconicity was being built up through the circulated sonic and visual culture of black women blues artists via Paramount's advertisement campaign and by the prior and ongoing generation of black women in minstrel shows.

7   Brown, *Babylon Girls*.

8   Hammer, "'Just Like a Natural Man,'" 14.

9   Cheng, *Second Skin*.

10 Brooks, *Bodies in Dissent*, 132.

11 Adorno contributes to my meaning of this phrase here and my framing of the blackface minstrel stage—as he likely contributes similarly to the work of Eric Lott in *Love and Theft*—when he writes, "Clearly the immanent semblance character of artworks cannot be freed from some degree of external imitation of reality, however latent, and therefore cannot be freed from illusion either. For everything that artworks contain with regard to form and materials, spirit and subject matter, has emigrated from reality into the artworks and in them has divested itself of its reality: Thus the artwork also becomes its afterimage." Adorno, *Aesthetic Theory*, 103. The minstrel stage quite perilously, of course, sought to become the afterimage of slavery, antiblack racism through the surface of the skin, becoming the "afterimage" of black skin's legal and formal slavability.

12 Kheshti, *Modernity's Ear*.

13 From a 1957 article in the liner notes of the album *Prison Songs: Historical Recordings from Parchman Farm 1947–48*, vol. 1, *Murderous Home*, and vol. 2, *Don'tcha Hear Poor Mother Calling?*, Rounder Records, 1997. For a more focused treatment of the Lomaxes' exploitation of Lead Belly see Filene, "'Our Singing Country.'"

14 Wynter, "The Ceremony Must Be Found," 34.

15 See Lauren Berlant's treatment of the genre of subjects in *Cruel Optimism*. For a discussion of blackness and unknowability to the subject, see Crawley, *Blackpentecostal Breath*.

16 Phelan, *Unmarked*, 49.

17 If, as Theodor Adorno—well after Rainey's performative theorizations—worried, listening in the twentieth century would be divorced from the materiality of musical form and instead become indistinguishable from the instrumental rationality of the commodity form, then Rainey's performance critiques the representative economy that wrote the nineteenth-century consumption of (supposedly noncommodified) listening, the very form of listening Adorno wanted to defend from the impending audio commodification in the phonograph in the twentieth century.

18 Lewis, "Improvising Tomorrow's Bodies," 1–15.
19 Morrison, *Jazz*.
20 In his seminal work *Stompin' the Blues*, Albert Murray compared the blues to the craft of acting, suggesting that blues is constituted as much (if not more) by aesthetic artifice and performative technique as by some romantic "direct emotional expression in the raw." Murray's point presaged the work of McGinley by trying to think about the performativity of the blues lyric, which I will explicitly track in this chapter. Murray, *Stompin' the Blues*, 138.
21 The term "wilderness of technological rationalization" is taken from Wynter, "Sambos and Minstrels," 149. On the commodity that speaks, see Moten's chapter "Resistance of the Object: Hester's Scream" in *In the Break*, which works through and revises Marx's essay "Exchange" in *Capital*, 84.
22 Heidegger, *The Question Concerning Technology*, 21. For a further exposition of *Gestell*, see Ruin, "*Ge-stell*," 3. Ruin discusses Heidegger's deconstruction of the normative concept of being by invoking the term "readiness-to-hand," *Zuhandenheit*.
23 Heidegger, *Poetry, Language, Thought*, 179.
24 Edison promised that the phonograph would *capture* "sounds that were heretofore fugitive" and would thus ensure "their reproduction at will." Edison, "The Phonograph and Its Future."
25 Stott, *Documentary Expression and Thirties America*, 6.
26 Bateson, *Mind and Nature*.
27 Kant, *Critique of Judgment*.
28 Ferreira da Silva, "1 (life) ÷ 0 (blackness) = $\infty - \infty$ or ∞ / ∞."
29 Here I am helped by Moten, "Blackness and Nothingness."
30 Cruz, *Culture on the Margins*.
31 Moten, "Sonata Quasi una Fantasia," 110.
32 I am again driven by Oyewumi's phrase "body-reasoning" in *The Invention of Women*.
33 For Carby's work on the blues see "It Just Be's Dat Way Sometime." See also Angela Davis's indispensable work that guides my writing here, *Blues Legacies and Black Feminism*.
34 Beal, "Black Women's Manifesto."
35 Locke, "Enter the New Negro," 8.
36 Locke, "Enter the New Negro."
37 Douglass, *Narrative of the Life of Frederick Douglass*, 58.
38 The foreground of unemployed black men and the distant background of overemployed black women is a persistent and essential sociological ob-

ject of Du Bois's early and mid-career works, from the *Philadelphia Negro* to *Black Reconstruction*. This is the configuration around which Du Bois frequently contends that so much policing of black life is built up and so much possibility or measure of freedom for black folks can be detected. Saidiya Hartman's more recent work has provided a powerful critique of Du Bois's conflation of freedom for black people with the rights of black people to employment, as opposed to the complicated wayward autonomies and interdependencies among black folks, especially women, girls, and black queer folks. Hartman, *Wayward Lives*.

39 Molesworth, *The Works of Alain Locke*, 191.
40 Edwards, *The Practice of Diaspora*.
41 See my discussion of this Marx quote in chapter 5: "We pre-suppose labor in a form that is distinctly human. A spider conducts operations that resemble that of a weaver, and the bee puts to shame many an architect in the construction of her cells. But what distinguishes the worst architect from the best bees is this, that the architect raises his structure in imagination before he erects it in reality. At the end of every labor-process, we get a result that already existed in the imagination of the laborer at its commencement." Marx, *Capital*, 178.
42 Locke, "Enter the New Negro," 2; my italics.
43 Molesworth, *The Works of Alain Locke*, 222.
44 Barrett, *Blackness and Value*, 71.
45 Glissant, *Poetics of Relation*, 28.
46 Glissant, *Poetics of Relation*, 8.
47 Locke, "Values and Imperatives."
48 Locke, "The Ethics of Culture." This essay is from a speech Locke delivered at Howard University in 1923. In the "New Negro" and his explicit work on aesthetics (see Molesworth, *The Works of Alain Locke*), Locke wrote about intraracial class divisions and the construction of a black bourgeoisie as the precondition for black art.
49 Molesworth, *The Works of Alain Locke*, 183.
50 Molesworth, *The Works of Alain Locke*, 184.
51 Wynter, "Sambos and Minstrels," 149.
52 Cheng, *Second Skin*, 5.

Chapter 4. Music Against the Subject

1 Fanon, *Black Skin, White Masks*, 130.
2 Fanon, *Black Skin, White Masks*, 143.
3 Wilderson, *Red, White and Black*, 57.

4   For a treatment of the politics and ethics of intelligibility of the slave narrative, see, among others, Carby, *Reconstructing Womanhood*; Brooks, *Bodies in Dissent*; Hartman, *Scenes of Subjection*; and Diouf, *Servants of Allah*.

5   Moten, "Notes on Passage," 56.

6   Henry Louis Gates Jr. in Charles Burnett's documentary film *Nat Turner: A Troublesome Property*.

7   Fanon, *Black Skin, White Masks*, 134.

8   David Marriot distilled this formal movement in Fanon as

> the symptom of an epistemic bind, and one in which racism obligingly explains the taken-for-granted existence of races. We need, rather, to be prepared to find in the source of sociogeny the very resource on which Fanon draws for this thought on black existence; in the torsion between phylogeny and ontogeny, Fanon finds a precise means of addressing and critiquing racism as a discourse of time, and in the "failures" that are the object of his study, he presents his term as an advance on that of Freud's (a name completely missing from Wynter's account). In short, we need to ask why sociogeny was needed to explain the only possible creative mode of invention: that of a subject whose destiny is marked by something other than itself, a crossing of chance and necessity that is that subject's singular invention, according to which it is only black insofar as, paradoxically, it grasps its own impossible whiteness.

Marriott, "Inventions of Existence," 60.

9   Wynter, "The Ceremony Must Be Found," 27.

10 Fanon, *Black Skin, White Masks*, 2.

11 Fanon, *Black Skin, White Masks*, 217–18.

12 Crawley, *Blackpentecostal Breath*, 2.

13 See Ricoeur, *Time and Narrative, Volume 1*, 75.

14 Wilderson, announcing his work, wrote: "My analysis of socially engaged feature films insists on an intellectual protocol through which the scholarship of preconscious interests and unconscious identifications are held accountable to grammars of suffering—accountable, that is, to protocols of structural positionality." Wilderson, *Red, White and Black*, 31. Putting a finer point on his claim, Wilderson added: "The Afro-pessimists are theorists of Black positionality who share Fanon's insistence that, though Blacks are indeed sentient beings, the structure of the entire world's semantic field—regardless of cultural and national discrepancies—'leaving' as Fanon would say, 'existence by the wayside'—is sutured by anti-Black solidarity" (58).

15 Morrison, *Jazz*, 220.

16 Berlant, *Cruel Optimism*, 99.

17 I am here of course referring to Foucault's conception of biopower in *Society Must Be Defended*.

18 Edison, "The Phonograph and Its Future," 533.

19 Here I am referring to Cheryl Harris's central conceptual claim in "Whiteness as Property" (which even allows her skepticism about the lasting efficacy of affirmative action legislation, which she is strategically and necessarily defending) that whiteness is a juridical property relation fundamentally constructed vis-à-vis capitalism by the acquisition of property. Or put another way, whiteness is founded on the authority to speculatively accumulate and convert objects into property (under the law) as a set of legal relations *as social relations*.

20 Berlant, "Big Man," 1. I thank Ralowe Trinitrotoluene Ampu for bringing this text to my attention and for all the rigorous intellectual conversation that has found life in and, most important, life beyond this essay.

21 Wynter, "Human Being as Noun?"

22 The term "transparency of the subject" is taken from Spivak's canonical essay "Can the Subaltern Speak?," 278.

23 Morrison, *Jazz*, 63–65.

24 Shakur, "Pathology of Patriarchy."

25 Davis, "Reflections on Black Women's Roles in the Community of Slaves"; Spillers, "Mama's Baby, Papa's Maybe."

26 Suékama, "Dispatches from Among the Damned."

27 Morrison, *Jazz*, 8.

28 Wagner, *Disturbing the Peace*, 4.

29 Moten, "The Case of Blackness," 180.

30 Berlant, "On the Case," 663.

31 Kingsley, "Whence Comes Jass?"

32 Mackey, "Other: From Noun to Verb," 269.

33 Morrison, *Playing in the Dark*, x.

34 Here I am referring to Derrida and Ronell, "The Law of Genre," 59.

35 Morrison, *Jazz*, xix.

36 Moten, "Blackness and Nothingness," 739; my italics.

37 Hartman, "The Belly of the World," 169.

38 Alexander, *Pedagogies of Crossing*.

39 Hartman, *Wayward Lives*, 218.

40 Hartman, *Scenes of Subjection*, 176–79.

41 Roach, "What Jazz Means to Me," 3.

42 Van Der Zee, Dodson, and Billops, *The Harlem Book of the Dead*, 39.
43 Gray, "Necrophagy at the Lynching Block."
44 Marriott, *On Black Men*, 10.
45 Marriott, *On Black Men*, 10.
46 Gray, "Necrophagy at the Lynching Block."
47 Raiford, *Imprisoned in a Luminous Glare*.
48 Ruin, "Ge-stell," 186. Ruin argues that the concept of *Zuhandenheit* suggests that things, "their understanding and their meaningfulness presupposes precisely that they are not objectified, but rather lived through in a spontaneous referential context." See "Ge-stell," 186.
49 Van Der Zee, Dodson, and Billops, *The Harlem Book of the Dead*, 30.
50 Derrida's words convey something like what I am after: "Loving belongs only to a being gifted with life or with breath (*en empsúkô*). Being loved, on the other hand, always remains possible on the side of the inanimate (*en apsúkhô*), where a *psukhé* may already have expired." Derrida, *The Politics of Friendship*, 12–13.
51 Derrida, *The Politics of Friendship*, 12–13.
52 Jones, *Theatrical Jazz*, 23.
53 I thank Stasha Lampert for reminding me that work, which cannot acknowledge the entangled complexity of blackness and black life as infinitely contradictory overlapping realities, ain't shit.
54 By comfort I mean something like what Lauren Berlant has brushed against here: "Comfort in proximity to a vague object or scene that promises to deliver some ballast in sociality is not the same as enjoying supremacist pleasure, just as psychoanalytically speaking, misrecognition is not the same as being mistaken." Berlant, *Cruel Optimism*, 185.
55 Adorno, *Philosophy of New Music*, 55. Against art's living beyond life, Adorno writes, "It is precisely its origin in subjectivity that becomes the contingency of arbitrary pronouncement as soon as the rule stands in the way of the subject, positively, as a regulative system." Adorno, *Aesthetic Theory*, 27.
56 Adorno writes: "Artworks were always meant to endure; it is related to their concept, that of objectivation. Through duration art protests against death; the paradoxically transient eternity of artworks is the allegory of an eternity bare of semblance. Art is the semblance of what is beyond death's reach." Adorno, *Aesthetic Theory*, 27.
57 Adorno, *Aesthetic Theory*, 52.
58 For the language of the slave ship, see Hartman, "The Belly of the World," 167. For the grammar of blackness, see Edwards, *The Practice of Diaspora*.

59   Marriott, *Haunted Life*.
60   Morrison, *Jazz*, 4.
61   Morrison, *Jazz*, 74.
62   Dolar, *A Voice and Nothing More*, 19.
63   Marriott, *On Black Men*; Raiford, *Imprisoned in a Luminous Glare*; Iton, *In Search of the Black Fantastic*.
64   Derrida, *Monolingualism of the Other*.

Chapter 5. Sounds Like Us

1   I am referring to Langston Hughes's rather ambivalent framing in his pithy 1926 poem "To Beauty":

> To worship
> At the altar of Beauty,
> To feel her loveliness and pain,
> To thrill
> At the wonder of her gorgeous moon
> Or the sharp, swift, silver swords
> Of falling rain.
>
> To walk in a golden garden
> When an autumn sun
> Has almost set,
> When near-night's purple splendor
> Shimmers to a star-shine net.
>
> To worship
> At the altar of Beauty
> Is a pleasure divine,
> Not given to the many many
> But to fools
> Who drink
> Beauty's wine.
> Not given to the many many
> But to fools
> Who seek no other goddess
> Nor grapes
> Plucked from another's
> Vine.

Hughes, "To Beauty," 75.

2   See Brathwaite, *Kwame Brathwaite*. This publication was part of the launch of a significant national exhibit, *Black Is Beautiful: The Photography of Kwame Brathwaite* at the New York Historical Society from August 19, 2022 to January 15, 2023.

3   Moten, *In the Break*, 70.
4   Derrida and Ronell, "The Law of Genre," 59. Derrida refers to the secondary eruption of invagination as emerging from its previousness (its what-is-made-transgressive), as "unarrestable," and as invoking "the commitment made no longer to give an account" (70).
5   Locke, "Enter the New Negro," 1.
6   Joseph, *Against the Romance of Community*. I am guided even more here by Hwang, "Deviant Care for Deviant Futures."
7   Derrida, *The Truth in Painting*, 101.
8   Collings-Wells, "From Black Power to Broken Windows, " 739. For a general expansion of these policies, see the Ford Foundation's *Annual Report* for 1969–1970.
9   Goncalves, "Natural Black Beauty," 19.
10 Goncalves, "Natural Black Beauty," 20.
11 Goncalves's position here shares some qualities of the mythological function of beauty and the aesthetic: "Before we make ideas aesthetic, i.e., mythological, they hold no interest for the people, and conversely, before mythology is reasonable, the philosopher must be ashamed of it. Thus finally the enlightened and unenlightened must shake hands; mythology must become philosophical, and the people reasonable, and philosophy must become mythological in order to make philosophy sensual. Then external unity will reign among us." Anonymous, "The Oldest Systemic Programme of German Idealism," 1.
12 Schiller, *Letter upon the Aesthetic Education of Man*, 96.
13 The truth content of artworks, which is indeed their social truth, is predicated on their fetish character. The principle of heteronomy, apparently the counterpart of fetishism, is the principle of exchange, and in it domination is masked. Only what does not submit to that principle acts as the plenipotentiary of what is free from domination; only what is useless can stand in for the stunted use value. Artworks are plenipotentiaries of things that are no longer distorted by exchange, profit, and the false needs of a degraded humanity. In the context of total semblance, art's semblance of being-in-itself is the mask of truth. Marx's scorn of the pittance Milton received for *Paradise Lost*, a work that did not appear to the market as socially useful labor, is, as a denunciation of useful labor, the strongest defense of art against its bourgeois functionalization, which is perpetuated in art's undialectical social condemnation. A liberated society would be beyond the irrationality of its *faux frais* and beyond the ends-means-rationality of utility.

    Adorno, *Aesthetic Theory*, 227.
14 Schiller, *Letter upon the Aesthetic Education of Man*, 37.

15 Goncalves, "Natural Black Beauty," 21.
16 Hughes, *The Big Sea*, 123.
17 Goncalves, "Natural Black Beauty," 19.
18 Adorno, *Aesthetic Theory*, 12.
19 Adorno, "The Curves of the Needle," 50. See also Okiji, "Jazz, Individualism, and the Black Modern."
20 Baraka, "Black Art," 219.
21 This famous adage by Amiri Baraka, then LeRoi Jones, appeared in "The Changing Same," *Jones/Baraka Reader*, 191.
22 Baraka, "Jazz and the White Critic."
23 Baraka, "The Changing Same," *Black Music*, 220.
24 Fine, *Violence in the Model City*, 433.
25 I am guided again by Adorno's highly influential framing here that "the bourgeois want art voluptuous and life ascetic; the reverse would be better. Reified consciousness provides an ersatz for the sensual immediacy of which it deprives people in a sphere that is not its abode." *Aesthetic Theory*, 13.
26 For a succinct definition of the "Yes In My Backyard," or YIMBY, astroturf campaign, see Szeto and Meronek, "YIMBYs."
27 For an important treatment of this subject, see Jackson, *Model City Blues*, 75.
28 Gago, *Neoliberalism from Below*.
29 I am here reframing Baraka's earlier-cited quote to show its sublimation of its kind of thinking within the kinds of black aesthetic projects it would potentially have imagined itself to be fighting against. Baraka, "The Changing Same," *Black Music*, 220.
30 Contrary to Mandi Isaac Jackson's earlier study, the popular mythology of Freddy Fixer pervades. See "History of the Lower Dixwell Neighborhood," Walk New Haven Cultural Tours, n.d., https://walknewhaven.org/lower-dixwell-history, one of many popular retellings of Dr. Fred Smith as the grassroots originator despite the Model Cities Program and state funding.
31 McGeorge Bundy, Ford Foundation president, quoted in Meyer, "Washington's Grant to the Ford Foundation."
32 For this specific piece of organizing and or counterinsurgency history, see Collings-Wells, "From Black Power to Broken Windows."
33 Looker, *"Point from which creation begins,"* 65.
34 Looker, *"Point from which creation begins,"* 65.
35 Looker, *"Point from which creation begins,"* 67.
36 Looker, *"Point from which creation begins,"* 83.

37 For an important in-depth treatment of the *Wall of Respect*, see Margo Natalie Crawford's works "Black Light on the Wall of Respect" and *Black Post-Blackness*.
38 Alkalimat, "Black Liberation," 96–98.
39 Campkin, Mogilevich, and Ross, "Chicago's Wall of Respect."
40 Alkalimat and Zorach, "The Heroes and Heroines of the Wall of Respect."
41 Alkalimat, "Black Liberation," 104.
42 Huebner, "The Man Behind the Wall."
43 Cahan, *Mounting Frustration*.
44 African American Historical and Cultural Museum, *The People's Art*, 105.
45 Here I am referring to the original German title of Schiller's *Letter upon the Aesthetic Education of Man*, which I have been citing throughout: *Über die ästhetische Erziehung des Menschen in einer Reihe von Briefen*.
46 Bergman and Montgomery, *Joyful Militancy*.
47 On the "governing principle" of art's reflective judgement, see Adorno, *Aesthetic Theory*: "There is no aesthetic refraction without something being refracted; no imagination without something imagined. This holds true particularly in the case of art's immanent purposiveness. In its relation to empirical reality art sublimates the latter's governing principle of sese conservare as the ideal of the self-identity of its works; as Schoenberg said, one paints a painting, not what it represents" (4).
48 Shakur, "Affirmation."
49 Cahan, *Mounting Frustration*; Jones, *South of Pico*; and English, *1971*.
50 For a critique of the self-enclosure of bourgeois art, see Adorno, *Aesthetic Theory*, 119.
51 Harney and Moten, *All Incomplete*, 41.
52 Gaines, *The Theater of Refusal*. A related argument, which I glossed in the introduction to this book, is conveyed in English, *How to See a Work of Art in Total Darkness*.
53 Borne, *Rationalizing Culture*.
54 Gates, *To Speculate Darkly*.
55 I am here referring to Marx and Engels's famous disputation of Kant's notion of goodwill as entirely located within the class project of the European bourgeoisie, specifically the owning class, or burghers. Marx and Engels, *The German Ideology*, 97.
56 Hartman, *Wayward Lives*, has been an indispensable and beautiful influence here.
57 Robinson, "With Art Hubs and Performances"; Chan, "Theaster Gates"; Moore, "How Theaster Gates Is Revitalizing Chicago's South Side";

Dingwall, "How to Renew the Color of Bricks"; Evans, "Theaster Gates' Arts Incubator." All of these articles praise Gates's beautification work of structure and conflate that "revitalization" with expanding the vitality of black life and the black lifeworlds. I took this quote about the Obama Presidential Center came from the center's website (https://www.obama.org/the-center/) on November 3, 2021.

58 "We could adorn a figure with all kinds of spirals and light, but regular lines, as the New Zealanders do with their tattooing, if only it were not the figure of a human being. And again this [ornamentation] could have much finer features and a more pleasing and gentle cast of countenance provided it were not intended to represent a man, much less a warrior." Kant, *Critique of Judgment*, 82.

Coda

1. The curator of the project, Ashara Ekundayo, stated: "It's not been all death and destruction. There has been light, joy, pleasure, and celebration in the streets of Oakland." Rasilla, "In Downtown Oakland, 30+ Storefronts Display Art Celebrating Black Joy."

2. A popular saying in Arabic comes to mind: "يقتل القتيل ويمشي بجنازته," which is commonly translated as "He kills the deceased and walks in his funeral" or similarly "He kills the victim and then attends his funeral."

3. See the countless publications that aestheticize the violence of downtown internecine harm and relations to justify the systematic harm of urban redevelopment. See also the fearmongering in Burt, "Violence Darkening Oakland's Nightlife"; and Burt, "Violence Shutters Another Oakland Nightspot." Like a lot of papers in major cities throughout the United States whose corporatization rebranded them as cultural arbiters in the 1990s, the *East Bay Times* criminalizes black cultures and lauds and supports the fictitious valuations of the properly and propertied artistic cultures that call the police and fill the emerging void with properly marketizable life and eventually with condos that remain vacant.

4. Certeau, *The Practice of Everyday Life*, 27.

5. For this insight about lack of access to public restrooms, I am indebted to a conversation with Ralowe T. Ampu.

6. Adorno, *Aesthetic Theory*, 167.

7. Mallarmé, "Le Fenêtres/The Windows," 10–11. For the origins of Mallarmé's windowed fascination see Descartes, "Meditations on First Philosophy."

Sources

Discography

Abrams, Muhal Richard. *Levels and Degrees of Light*. Delmark Records, 1967.
The Art Ensemble of Chicago. *Certain Blacks*. America Records, 1970.
Cage, John. "Cartridge Music." Composition. Bremen, September 15, 1960.
Cage, John. "4'33." Composition. Woodstock, NY, August 29, 1952.
Cage, John. "Living Room Music." Composition. 1940.
Cage, John. "Music for ___." New Milford, CT, August 15, 1984.
Coleman, Ornette. *Free Jazz*. Atlantic, 1960.
Coleman, Ornette. *The Shape of Jazz to Come*. Atlantic, 1959.
Coleman, Ornette. *Tomorrow IS the Question*. OJC, 1959.
Collins, Arthur. "Bill Bailey Won't You Please Come Home." Columbia Phonograph, 1902.
Collins, Arthur. "My Josephine." Berliner Gramophone, 1899.
Jarman, Joseph. *Song For*. Delmark Records, 1966.
Johnson, George W. "The Laughing Coon." Columbia Phonograph, 1898.
Johnson, George W. "The Whistling Coon." North American Phonograph, 1891.
Lomax, Alan. *Prison Songs: Historical Recordings from Parchman Farm 1947–48*. Vol. 1, *Murderous Home*. Rounder Records, 1997.
Lomax, Alan. *Prison Songs: Historical Recordings from Parchman Farm 1947–48*. Vol. 2, *Don't cha Hear Poor Mother Calling?* Rounder Records, 1997.
Rainey, Ma. *Ma Rainey*. Milestone Records, 1974.
Roscoe Mitchell Sextet. *Sound*. Art Ensemble of Chicago Series Volume 1. Delmark Records, 1966.
Smith, Bessie. *Bessie Smith: Any Women's Blues*. Columbia Records, 1971.
Smith, Bessie. *Bessie Smith: Empty Bed Blues*. Columbia Records, 1973.
Smith, Bessie. *Bessie Smith: Nobody's Blues but Mine*. Columbia Records, 1972.
Smith, Bessie. *Bessie Smith: The World's Greatest Blues Singer*. Columbia Records, 1970.
Wade, Steven. *A Treasury of Library of Congress Field Recordings*. Rounder Records, 1997.
Williams, Bert, and George Walker. "My Little Zulu Baby." Victor Talking Machine, 1901.

Films

Ahearn, Charlie. *Wild Style*. Directed by Charlie Ahearn. Wild Style, 1982.
Burnett, Charles. *Nat Turner: A Troublesome Property*. Directed by Charles Burnett. Subpix, 2003.
Harris, Christopher. *Still/Here*. Directed by Christopher Harris. Rosegra Films, 2000.
Riggs, Marlon. *Black Is, Black Ain't*. Directed by Marlon Riggs. Signifyin' Works, 1994.
Riggs, Marlon. *Tongues Untied*. Directed by Marlon Riggs. Signifyin' Works, 1989.
Riggs, Marlon, and Peter Webster. *Long Train Running: A History of the Oakland Blues*. Directed by Marlon Riggs and Peter Webster. University of California, Berkeley, 1981.

Interviews

Khan, Hassan. Interview with the author, August, 22, 2010, Cairo, Egypt.
Khan, Hassan. Interview with the author, September 24, 2012, Istanbul, Turkey.
Mitchell, Roscoe. Interview with the author, November 20, 2012, Mills College, Oakland, CA.
Terreffe, Selamawit. "What Exceeds the Hold? An Interview with Christina Sharpe." *Rhizomes* 29, no. 1 (2016). Accessed December 13, 2016. http://www.rhizomes.net/issue29/terrefe.html.
"Vibrations: Archie Shepp Interview + Lecture (WFSU, 1978)." YouTube video. Accessed June 22, 2024. https://www.youtube.com/watch?v=DMoomZ_bFjE.

Bibliography

Adorno, Theodor W. *Aesthetic Theory*. Translated by Robert Hullot-Kentor. Minneapolis: University of Minnesota Press, 1997.
Adorno, Theodor W. "The Curves of the Needle." 1928. In *Essays on Music*, edited by Richard Leppert, translated by Susan H. Gillespie. Berkeley: University of California Press, 2002.
Adorno, Theodor W. "Music and Technique." In *Sound Figures*, translated by Rodney Livingstone. Stanford, CA: Stanford University Press, 1999.
Adorno, Theodor W. *Negative Dialectics*. Translated by E. B. Ashton. New York: Bloomsbury Academic, 2015.
Adorno, Theodor W. *Philosophy of New Music*. Translated by Robert Hullot-Kentor. Minneapolis: University of Minnesota Press, 2006.
Adorno, Theodor W. *Quasi Una Fantasia: Essays on Modern Music*. Translated by Rodney Livingstone. New York: Verso, 1992.

Adorno, Theodor, and George Simpson. "On Popular Music." 1941. In *Essays on Music*, edited by Richard Leppert, translated by Susan H. Gillespie. Berkeley, CA: University of California Press, 2002.

African American Historical and Cultural Museum. *The People's Art: Black Murals 1967–1978*. Philadelphia: African American Historical and Cultural Museum, 1986.

Albertson, Chris. *Bessie*. New Haven, CT: Yale University Press, 2003.

Alexander, M. Jacqui. *Pedagogies of Crossing: Meditations on Feminism, Sexual Politics, Memory, and the Sacred*. Durham, NC: Duke University Press, 2004.

Alkalimat, Abdul. "Black Liberation: OBAC and the Makers of Respect." In *The Wall of Respect: Public Art and Black Liberation in 1960's Chicago*, edited by Abdul Alkalimat, Romi Crawford, and Rebecca Zorach. Chicago: Northwestern University Press, 2017.

Alkalimat, Abdul, and Rebecca Zorach. "The Heroes and Heroines of the Wall of Respect." In *The Wall of Respect: Public Art and Black Liberation in 1960's Chicago*, edited by Abdul Alkalimat, Romi Crawford, and Rebecca Zorach. Chicago: Northwestern University Press, 2017.

Anonymous. "The Oldest Systematic Programme of German Idealism." In *The Early Political Writings of the German Romantics*, edited by Frederick C. Beiser. New York: Cambridge University Press, 1996.

Aptheker, Herbert. *American Negro Slave Revolts*. New York: International Publishers, 1983.

Baraka, Amiri. "Black Art." In *The Leroi Jones/Amiri Baraka Reader*, edited by William J. Harris in collaboration with Amiri Baraka. New York: Thunder Mouth Press, 1999.

Baraka, Amiri. *Blues People: The Negro Experience in White America and the Music that Developed from It*. New York: Morrow Quill Books, 1963.

Baraka, Amiri. "The Changing Same (R&B and New Black Music)." 1963. In *The LeRoi Jones/Amiri Baraka Reader*, edited by William J. Harris in collaboration with Amiri Baraka. New York: Thunder Mouth Press, 1999.

Baraka, Amiri. "The Changing Same (R&B and New Black Music)." 1966. In *Black Music: Essays by LeRoi Jones (Amiri Baraka)*. New York: Akashic Books, 2010.

Baraka, Amiri. "Jazz and the White Critic." 1963. In *Black Music: Essays by LeRoi Jones (Amiri Baraka)*. New York: Akashic Books, 2010.

Barrett, Lindon. *Blackness and Value: Seeing Double*. New York: Cambridge University Press, 1999.

Bateson, Gregory. *Mind and Nature: A Necessary Unity*. New York: Hampton Press, 2002.

Beal, Francis M. "Black Women's Manifesto; Double Jeopardy: To Be Black and Female." 1969. In *The Black Woman: An Anthology*, edited by Toni Cade Bambara. New York: New American Library, 1970.

Benjamin, Walter. "The Work of Art in the Age of Mechanical Reproduction." In *Illuminations: Essays and Reflections*. New York: Mariner Books, 2019.

Bergman, Carla, and Nick Montgomery. *Joyful Militancy: Building Thriving Resistance in Toxic Times*. Oakland, CA: AK Press, 2017.
Berlant, Lauren. "Big Man." *Social Text*, January 19, 2017. Accessed June 14, 2018. http://socialtextjournal.org/big-man/.
Berlant, Lauren. *Cruel Optimism*. Durham, NC: Duke University Press, 2011.
Berlant, Lauren. "Genre Flailing." *Capacious: A Journal of Emerging Affect Inquiry* 1, no. 2 (2018): 156–62.
Berlant, Lauren. "On the Case." *Critical Inquiry* 33, no. 4 (2007): 663–72.
Bhabha, Homi K. *The Location of Culture*. New York: Routledge, 1994.
Bidwell, Shelford. "The Recent Inventions for Reproducing the Sounds of the Human Voice." In *Proceedings of the Musical Association*, Fifth Session, 1878–1879, 1–14. Reprinted by Kraus Reprint, 1966.
Binder, Guyora. "The Slavery of Emancipation." *Cardozo Law Review* 17 (1996): 2063–102.
Borne, Georgina. *Rationalizing Culture: IRCAM, Boulez, and the Institutionalization of the Musical Avant-Garde*. Berkeley: University of California Press, 1995.
Brathwaite, Kwame. *Kwame Brathwaite: Black Is Beautiful*. Edited by Tanisha C. Ford and Deborah Willis. Reading, PA: Aperture Press, 2019.
Brooks, Daphne A. *Bodies in Dissent: Spectacular Performances of Race and Freedom: 1850–1910*. Durham, NC: Duke University Press, 2006.
Brooks, Edward. *The Bessie Smith Companion: A Critical Detailed Appreciation of the Recordings*. New York: Da Capo Press, 1982.
Brooks, Tim. *Lost Sounds: Blacks and the Birth of the Recording Industry, 1890–1919*. Chicago: University of Illinois Press, 2004.
Brown, Jayna. *Babylon Girls: Black Women Performers and the Shaping of the Modern*. Durham, NC: Duke University Press, 2008.
Brown, Simone. *Dark Matters: On the Surveillance of Blackness*. Durham, NC: Duke University Press, 2015.
Buck-Morrs, Susan. *Hegel, Haiti, and Universal History*. Pittsburgh, PA: University of Pittsburgh Press, 2009.
Burke, Greg. "The Father of Harmolodics." *Los Angeles Times*, February 18, 2007. Accessed April 15, 2023. https://www.latimes.com/archives/la-xpm-2007-feb-18-ca-ornette18-story.html.
Burt, Cecily. "Violence Darkening Oakland's Nightlife." *East Bay Times*, November 12, 2007. Accessed September 28, 2020. https://www.eastbaytimes.com/2007/11/12/violence-darkening-oaklands-nightlife/.
Burt, Cecily. "Violence Shutters Another Oakland Nightspot." *East Bay Times*, February 26, 2008. Accessed September 28, 2020. https://www.eastbaytimes.com/2008/02/26/violence-shutters-another-oakland-nightspot/.
Cahan, Susan E. *Mounting Frustration: The Art Museum in the Age of Black Power*. Durham, NC: Duke University Press, 2016.
Campkin, Ben, Mariana Mogilevich, and Rebecca Ross. "Chicago's Wall of Respect: How a Mural Elicited a Sense of Collective Ownership." *The*

Guardian, December 8, 2015. Accessed January 15, 2025. https://www
.theguardian.com/cities/2014/dec/08/chicago-wall-of-respect-collective
-ownership-organisation-black-american-culture#:~:text=The%20
Wall%20of%20Respect%20claimed,collective%20ownership%2C%20
by%20local%20people.

Carby, Hazel. "It Just Be's Dat Way Sometime: The Sexual Politics of Women's Blues." *Radical America* 20, no. 4 (1986): 9–22.

Carby, Hazel. *Reconstructing Womanhood: The Emergence of the Afro-American Woman Novelist*. New York: Oxford University Press, 1987.

Certeau, Michel de. *The Practice of Everyday Life*. Berkeley: University of California Press, 1984.

Chan, T. F. "Theaster Gates: London, Urban Reform and Exemplars of Black Excellence." *Wallpaper*, October 12, 2021. https://www.wallpaper.com/art/theaster-gates-interview.

Chandler, Nahum Dimitri. *X—The Problem of the Negro as a Problem for Thought*. New York: Fordham University Press, 2014.

Cheng, Anne Anlin. *Second Skin: Josephine Baker and the Modern Surface*. New York: Oxford University Press Chapters, 2010.

Chude-Sokei, Louis. *The Last "Darky": Bert Williams, Black-on-Black Minstrelsy and the African Diaspora*. Durham, NC: Duke University Press, 2006.

Cocteau, Jean. *The Blood of a Poet*. Paris: Vicomte de Noailles Studio, 1932.

Collings-Wells, Sam. "From Black Power to Broken Windows: Liberal Philanthropy and the Carceral State." *Journal of Urban History* 48, no. 4 (2022): 739–59.

Cowen, Ron. "Earliest Known Sound Recording Revealed: Researchers Unveil Imprints Made 20 Years before Edison Invented Phonograph." *Science News*, June 1, 2009. Accessed February 4, 2011. http://www.usnews
.com/science/articles/2009/06/01/earliest-known-sound-recordings
-revealed.html.

Crawford, Margo Natalie. "Black Light on the Wall of Respect: The Chicago Black Arts Movement." In *New Thoughts on the Black Arts Movement*, edited by Lisa Gail Collins, Margo Natalie Crawford, and Alondra Nelson, 23–43. New Brunswick, NJ: Rutgers University Press, 2006.

Crawford, Margo Natalie. *Black Post-Blackness: The Black Arts Movement and Twenty-First-Century Aesthetics*. Champagne: University of Illinois Press, 2017.

Crawley, Ashon. *Blackpentecostal Breath: The Aesthetics of Possibility*. New York: Fordham University Press, 2016.

Cruz, Jon. *Culture on the Margins: The Black Spiritual and the Rise of American Cultural Interpretation*. Princeton, NJ: Princeton University Press, 1999.

Dabydeen, David. *Hogarth's Blacks: Images of Blacks in 18th-Century English Art*. Athens: University of Georgia Press, 1987.

Davis, Angela. *Blues Legacies and Black Feminism: Gertrude "Ma" Rainey, Bessie Smith, and Billie Holiday*. New York: Vintage Books, 1998.

Davis, Angela. "Reflections on Black Women's Roles in the Community of Slaves." *Massachusetts Review* 13, no. 1/2 (1972): 81–100.
de Man, Paul. *Aesthetic Ideology*. Translated by Andrzej Warminski. Minneapolis: University of Minnesota Press, 1996.
Derrida, Jacques. *Monolingualism of the Other: or, The Prosthesis of Origin*. Translated by Patrick Mensah. Palo Alto, CA: Stanford University Press, 1998.
Derrida, Jacques. *Of Grammatology*. Translated by Gayatri Charkrovorty Spivak. Baltimore, MD: Johns Hopkins University Press, 1997.
Derrida, Jacques. *The Politics of Friendship*. Translated by George Collins. New York: Verso, 1997.
Derrida, Jacques. *Psyche: Interventions of the Other, Volume 1*. Translated by Peggy Kamuf and Elizabeth Rottenberg. Stanford, CA: Stanford University Press, 2007.
Derrida, Jacques. *Specters of Marx: The State of the Debt, the Work of Mourning and the New International*. Translated by Peggy Kamuf. New York: Routledge, 2006.
Derrida, Jacques. *The Truth in Painting*. Translated by Geoffrey Bennington and Ian McCleod. Chicago: University of Chicago Press, 1987.
Derrida, Jacques, and Avital Ronell. "The Law of Genre." *Critical Inquiry* 7, no. 1 (1980): 55–81.
Descartes, René. "Meditations on First Philosophy in Which Are Demonstrated the Existence of God and the Distinction between the Human Soul and the Body (1639)." In *Descartes: Meditations on First Philosophy: With Selections from the Objections and Replies*, translated by John Cottingham. Cambridge: Cambridge University Press, 1996.
Dingwall, Chris. "How to Renew the Color of Bricks." *Gagosian Quarterly*, June 9, 2020.
Diouf, Sylviane A. *Servants of Allah: African Muslims Enslaved in the Americas*. New York: New York University Press, 2013.
Dolar, Mladen. *A Voice and Nothing More*. Cambridge, MA: MIT Press, 2006.
Douglass, Frederick. *Life and Times of Frederick Douglass*. 1892; repr., New York: Collier, 1962.
Douglass, Frederick. *My Bondage and My Freedom*. New York: Penguin Classics, 2003.
Douglass, Frederick. *Narrative of the Life of Frederick Douglass, an American Slave*. New York: Penguin Classics, 2014.
Du Bois, W. E. B. *Black Reconstruction in America: 1860–1880*. New York: The Free Press, 1935.
Du Bois, W. E. B. "Criteria of Negro Art." *The Crisis* 32 (October 1926): 290–97.
Du Bois, W. E. B. *The Philadelphia Negro: A Social Study*. Philadelphia: University of Pennsylvania Press, 1899.
Du Bois, W. E. B. *The Souls of Black Folk: On Our Spiritual Strivings*. 1903. New York: Oxford University Press, 2009.

Edison, Thomas A. "The Perfected Phonograph." *North American Review* 146, no. 379 (1888): 641–51.

Edison, Thomas A. "The Phonograph and Its Future." *North American Review* 126, no. 262 (1878): 527–36.

Edison, Thomas A. "The Talking Phonograph." *Scientific American* 37, no. 25 (1877): 384–85.

"Edison and the Kinetograph." *Montreal Daily Star*, April 20, 1895. Reprinted in *Film History* 4, no. 11 (1999): 404–7.

Edwards, Brent Hayes. *The Practice of Diaspora: Literature, Translation, and the Rise of Black Internationalism*. Cambridge, MA: Harvard University Press, 2006.

Eglash, Ron. "Broken Metaphor: The Master-Slave Analogy in Technical Literature." *Technology and Culture* 48, no. 2 (2007): 360–69.

Ellison, Ralph. *Invisible Man*. New York: Vintage Press, 1994.

English, Darby. *How to See a Work of Art in Total Darkness*. Boston, MA: MIT University Press, 2010.

English, Darby. *1971: A Year in the Life of Color*. Chicago: University of Chicago Press, 2016.

Epstein, Dena J. *Sinful Tunes and Spirituals: Black Folk Music to the Civil War*. Champaign: University of Illinois Press, 2003.

Evans, Maxwell. "Theaster Gates' Arts Incubator and Garden Will Prove 'There Is Life' in South Side's Vacant Properties." *Block Club Chicago*. September 7, 2021.

Fanon, Frantz. *Black Skin, White Masks*. Translated by Charles Lam Markmann. New York: Grove Press, 1967.

Feaster, Patrick, ed. "Édouard-Léon Scott de Martinville's 1861 Communication to the Academie des Sciences de l'Institut de France: A Critical Edition with English Translation and Facsimile." Working Paper No. 4, FirstSounds.org, rev. May 22, 2009. https://www.firstsounds.org/publications/working-papers/First-Sounds-Working-Paper-04.pdf.

Ferreira da Silva, Denise. "1 (life) ÷ 0 (blackness) = $\infty - \infty$ or ∞ / ∞: On Matter Beyond the Equation of Value." *E-flux Journal* 79 (February 2017). Accessed March 14, 2018. https://www.e-flux.com/journal/79/94686/1-life-0-blackness-or-on-matter-beyond-the-equation-of-value/.

Filene, Benjamin. "'Our Singing Country': John and Allen Lomax, Leadbelly, and the Construction of an American Past." *American Quarterly* 43, no. 4 (1991): 602–24.

Fine, Sidney. *Violence in the Model City: The Cavanagh Administration, Race Relations, and the Detroit Riot of 1967*. East Lansing: Michigan State University Press, 2007.

Firmin, Joseph-Anténor. *The Equality of the Human Races: Positivist Anthropology*. 1885. New York: Garland Publishing, 2000.

Fleetwood, Nicole R. *Troubling Vision: Performance, Visuality, and Blackness*. Chicago: University of Chicago Press, 2011.

Ford Foundation. *Ford Foundation Annual Report, October 1, 1969 to September 30, 1970*. New York: Ford Foundation, 1970.

Foucault, Michel. *The Birth of the Clinic: An Archeology of Medical Perception*. Translated by Alan Sheridan. New York: Routledge Press, 1973.

Foucault, Michel. *Discipline and Punish: The Birth of the Prison*. Translated by Alan Sheridan. New York: Vintage Press, 1977.

Foucault, Michel. *Society Must Be Defended: Lectures at the College de France, 1975–1976*. Translated by David Macey. New York: Picador Books, 2003.

Gago, Véronica. *Neoliberalism from Below: Popular Pragmatics and Baroque Economies*. Durham, NC: Duke University Press, 2014.

Gaines, Charles. *The Theater of Refusal: Black Art and Mainstream Criticism*. Edited by Rhea Anastas, Charles Gaines, Jamillah James, and Eric Golo Stone. Brooklyn: Dancing Fox Press, 2025.

Gates, Theaster. *To Speculate Darkly: Theaster Gates and Dave the Potter*. Exhibit at the Milwaukee Art Museum, Milwaukee, WI, April 16 to August 1, 2010.

Gelatt, Roland. *The Fabulous Phonograph: From Edison to Stereo*. New York: Appleton-Century, 1965.

Genovese, Eugene. *From Rebellion to Revolution: Afro-American Slave Revolts in the Making of the Modern World*. Baton Rouge: Louisiana State University Press, 1979.

Glissant, Edouard. *Poetics of Relation*. Translated by Betsy Wing. Ann Arbor: University of Michigan Press, 2010.

Goncalves, Dingane Joe. "Natural Black Beauty." In *Black Arts: An Anthology of Black Creation*, edited by Ahmed Alhamisi and Harun Kofi Wangara, 19–22. Detroit, MI: Black Arts Publications, 1969.

Grant, Donald L., and Mildred Bricker Grant. "Some Notes on the Capital 'N.'" *Phylon* 36, no. 4 (1975): 435–43.

Gray, Erin. "Necrophagy at the Lynching Block." *GLQ: A Journal of Gay and Lesbian Studies* 21, no. 1 (2015): 13–15.

Gray, Herman. *Cultural Moves: African Americans and the Politics of Representation*. Berkeley: University of California Press, 2005.

Hammer, K. Allison. "'Just Like a Natural Man': The B. D. Styles of Gertrude 'Ma' Rainey and Bessie Smith." *Journal of Lesbian Studies* 23, no. 2 (2019): 1–16.

Harney, Stefano, and Fred Moten. *All Incomplete*. New York: Minor Compositions Press, 2021.

Harris, Cheryl I. "Whiteness as Property." *Harvard Law Review* 106, no. 8 (1993): 1707–91.

Hartman, Saidiya. "The Belly of the World: A Note on Black Women's Labors." *Souls: A Critical Journal of Black Politics, Culture and Society* 18, no. 1 (2016): 166–73.

Hartman, Saidiya. *Scenes of Subjection: Terror, Slavery and Self-Making in Nineteenth-Century America*. New York: Oxford University Press, 1997.

Hartman, Saidiya. "The Time of Slavery." *South Atlantic Quarterly* 101, no. 4 (2002): 757–77.

Hartman, Saidiya. *Wayward Lives, Beautiful Experiments: Intimate Histories of Riotous Black Girls, Troublesome Women, and Queer Radicals*. New York: W. W. Norton, 2019.

Hegel, George Wilhelm Friedrich. *Aesthetics: Lectures on Fine Art, Volume 1*. 1835. Translated by T. M. Knox. London: Oxford University Press, 1998.

Heidegger, Martin. *Poetry, Language, Thought*. Translated by Albert Hofstadter. New York: Perennial, 1975.

Heidegger, Martin. *The Question Concerning Technology and Other Essays*. Translated by William Lovitt. New York: Garland Publishing, 1977.

"History of the Lower Dixwell Neighborhood." Walk New Haven Cultural Tours, n.d., https://walknewhaven.org/lower-dixwell-history.

Huebner, Jeff. "The Man Behind the Wall." *Chicago Reader*, August 28, 1997. Accessed April 12, 2021. https://chicagoreader.com/news-politics/the-man-behind-the-wall/.

Hughes, Langston. *The Big Sea: An Autobiography of Langston Hughes*. New York: Hill and Wang, 1940.

Hughes, Langston. "To Beauty." In *The Collected Poems of Langston Hughes*, edited by Arnold Rampersad and David E. Roessell. New York: Vintage Press, 1995.

Hunter, Tera W. *To 'Joy My Freedom: Southern Black Women's Lives and Labors after the Civil War*. Cambridge, MA: Harvard University Press, 1997.

Hussein, Ibrahim N. *Kinjeketile*. Dar es Salaam, Tanzania: Oxford University Press, 1969.

Hwang, Ren-Yo. "Deviant Care for Deviant Futures: QTBIPOC Radical Relationalism as Mutual Aid Against Carceral Care." TSQ: *Transgender Studies Quarterly* 6, no. 4 (2019): 559–78.

Iton, Richard. *In Search of the Black Fantastic: Politics and Popular Culture in the Post–Civil Rights Era*. New York: Oxford University Press, 2009.

Jackson, Mandi Issacs. *Model City Blues: Urban Space and Organized Resistance in New Haven*. Philadelphia, PA: Temple University Press, 2008.

Jackson, Ronald L. *Scripting the Black Masculine Body: Identity, Discourse, and Racial Politics in Popular Media*. Albany: State University of New York Press, 2006.

James, C. L. R. *The Black Jacobins: Toussaint L'Ouverture and the San Domingo Revolution*. New York: Vintage Press, 1963.

Jones, Claudia. "An End to the Neglect of the Problems of Negro Women." In *Claudia Jones: Beyond Containment*, edited by Carole Boyce Davies. London: Ayebia Clarke Publishing, 2011.

Jones, Kellie. *South of Pico: African American Artists in Los Angeles in the 1960s and 1970s*. Durham, NC: Duke University Press, 2017.

Jones, Omi Osun Joni L. *Theatrical Jazz: Performance, Ase, and the Power of the Present Moment*. Columbus: Ohio State University Press, 2015.

Joseph, Miranda. *Against the Romance of Community*. Minneapolis: University of Minnesota Press, 2002.

Kalulé, Petero. "Being Right-With: On Human Rights Law as Unfreedom." *Feminist Legal Studies* 31, no. 2 (2023): 243–64.

Kant, Immanuel. *Critique of Judgment*. Translated by J. H. Bernard. New York: Hafner Press, 1914.

Kant, Immanuel. *Critique of Pure Reason*. Edited by Allen W. Wood. Translated by Paul Guyer. New York: Cambridge University Press, 2013.

Kant, Immanuel. *Idea for a Universal History from a Cosmopolitan Point of View*. Translated by Lewis White Beck. New York: Macmillan Publishers, 1963.

Kheshti, Roshanak. *Modernity's Ear: Listening to Race and Gender in World Music*. New York: New York University Press, 2015.

Kingsley, Walter. "Whence Comes Jass? Facts from the Great Authority on the Subject." In *Keeping Time: Readings in Jazz History*, edited by Robert Walser. New York: Oxford University Press, 1999.

Kittler, Friedrich. *Gramophone, Film, Typewriter*. Translated by Geoffrey Winthrop-Young and Michael Wutz. Stanford, CA: Stanford University Press, 1999.

LeFlouria, Talitha L. *Chained in Silence: Black Women and Convict Labor in the New South*. Chapel Hill: The University of North Carolina Press, 2013.

Levin, Sam. "A Walgreens Guard Killed a Black Trans Organizer. His Community Wants Answers." *The Guardian*, May 10, 2023. https://www.theguardian.com/us-news/2023/may/10/banko-brown-death-san-francisco-walgreens.

Lewis, George. "Improvising Tomorrow's Bodies: The Politics of Transduction." *E-misferica* 4, no. 2 (2007): 1–15.

Lieb, Sandra. *Mother of the Blues: A Study of Ma Rainey*. Amherst: The University of Massachusetts Press, 1981.

Locke, Alain. "Enter the New Negro." *Survey Graphic*, 1925.

Locke, Alain. "The Ethics of Culture." In *The Philosophy of Alain Locke: Harlem Renaissance and Beyond*, edited by Leonard Harris. Philadelphia, PA: Temple University Press, 1989.

Locke, Alain. "Values and Imperatives." In *The Philosophy of Alain Locke: Harlem Renaissance and Beyond*, edited by Leonard Harris. Philadelphia, PA: Temple University Press, 1989.

Locke, John. "Book II of Ideas: Chapter XXIII Of our Complex Ideas of Substances, No. 14." In *An Essay Concerning Human Understanding*. 1690. New York: Penguin Classics, 1998.

Looker, Benjamin. *"Point from which creation begins": The Black Artists' Group of St. Louis*. St. Louis: Missouri Historical Society Press, 2004.

Lott, Eric. *Love and Theft: Blackface Minstrelsy and the American Working Class*. New York: Oxford University Press, 1993.

Mackey, Nathaniel. *Nod House*. Cambridge, MA: New Directions Publishing, 2011.

Mackey, Nathaniel. "Other: From Noun to Verb." In *Discrepant Engagement: Dissonance, Cross-Culturality and Experimental Writing*. Cambridge: Cambridge University Press, 1993.

Malcolm X. "Message to the Grassroots." In *Malcolm X Speaks: Selected Speeches and Statements*, edited by George Breitman, 3–17. New York: Grove Press, 1994.

Mallarmé, Stéphane. "Le Fenêtres/The Windows." In *Collected Poems and Other Verse*, translated by E. H. and A. M. Blackmore. New York: Oxford University Press, 2006.

Marable, Manning. *Race, Reform, and Rebellion: The Second Reconstruction and Beyond in Black America, 1945–2006*. Jackson: University of Mississippi Press, 2007.

Marriott, David. *Haunted Life: Visual Culture and Black Modernity*. New Brunswick, NJ: Rutgers University Press, 2006.

Marriott, David. "Inventions of Existence: Sylvia Wynter, Frantz Fanon, Sociogeny, and 'the Damned.'" *CR: The New Centennial Review* 11, no. 3 (2011): 45–89.

Marriott, David. *On Black Men*. New York: Columbia University Press, 2000.

Martin, Dawn Lundy. "The Symbolic Nature of Chaos." In *A Gathering of Matter*. Athens: University of Georgia Press, 2007.

Marx, Karl. *Capital: A Critical Analysis of Capitalist Production*. Edited by Friedrich Engels. Translated by Samuel Moore and Edward Aveling. New York: International Publishing, 1967.

Marx, Karl. *Grundrisse: Foundations of the Critique of Political Economy*. 1858. Translated by Martin Nicolaus. New York: Penguin Classics, 1993.

Marx, Karl. *The Poverty of Philosophy*. Translated by H. Quelch. Chicago: Charles H. Kerr, 1913.

Marx, Karl, and Friedrich Engels. *The German Ideology*. 1846; repr., New York: International Publishers, 1947.

Matthews, Gelien. *Caribbean Slave Revolts and the British Abolitionist Movement*. Baton Rouge: Louisiana State University Press, 2013.

Maurice, Alice. "Cinema at Its Source:" Synchronizing Race and Sound in the Early Talkies." *Camera Obscura* 17, no. 1 (49) (2002): 31–71.

McGinley, Paige A. *Staging the Blues: From Tent Shows to Tourism*. Durham, NC: Duke University Press, 2013.

McKittrick, Katherine. *Demonic Grounds: Black Women and the Cartographies of Struggle*. Minneapolis: University of Minnesota Press, 2006.

McMillan, Uri. *Embodied Avatars: Genealogies of Black Feminist Art*. New York: New York University Press, 2015.

Meyer, Martin "Washington's Grant to the Ford Foundation." *New York Times*, November 13, 1966.

Millard, Andre. *America on Record: A History of Recorded Sound*. New York: Cambridge University Press, 1995.

Molesworth, Charles, ed. *The Works of Alain Locke*. New York: Oxford University Press, 2012.

Moore, Natalie. "How Theaster Gates Is Revitalizing Chicago's South Side, One Vacant Building at a Time." *Smithsonian Magazine*, December 2015. https://www.smithsonianmag.com/innovation/theaster-gates-ingenuity-awards-chicago-180957203/.

Morrison, Toni. *Jazz*. New York: Vintage Books, 2004.

Morrison, Toni. *Playing in the Dark: Whiteness and the Literary Imagination*. New York: Random House, 1992.

Moses, Wilson Jeremiah. *Liberian Dreams: Back-to-Africa Narratives from the 1850s*. University Park: Pennsylvania State University Press, 1998.

Moten, Fred. "Blackness and Nothingness: (Mysticism in the Flesh)." *South Atlantic Quarterly* 112, no. 4 (2013): 738–80.

Moten, Fred. "The Case of Blackness." *Criticism* 50, no. 2 (2008): 177–218.

Moten, Fred. *In the Break: The Aesthetics of the Black Radical Tradition*. Minneapolis: University of Minnesota Press, 2003.

Moten, Fred. "Notes on Passage (The New International of Sovereign Feelings)." *Palimpsest: A Journal on Women, Gender, and the Black International* 3, no. 1 (2014): 51–74.

Moten, Fred. "Notes on Surrender." *The Brooklyn Rail*, November 2020. Accessed September 29, 2023. https://brooklynrail.org/2020/11/criticspage/Note-on-Surrender.

Moten, Fred. "Sonata Quasi Una Fantasia." *Hambone* 19 (Fall 2009): 110–33.

Mudimbe, V. Y. *The Invention of Africa: Gnosis, Philosophy, and the Order of Knowledge*. Bloomington: Indiana University Press, 1988.

Murray, Albert. *Stompin' the Blues*. New York: Vintage Press, 1976.

Nietzsche, Friedrich. *The Birth of Tragedy: Out of the Spirit of Music*. 1872. Translated by Shaun Whiteside. New York: Penguin Books, 1994.

Okiji, Fumi. "Jazz, Individualism, and the Black Modern." In *Jazz as Critique: Adorno and Black Expression Revisited*. Palo Alto, CA: Stanford University Press, 2018.

Okiji, Fumi. *Jazz as Critique: Adorno and Black Expression Revisited*. Palo Alto, CA: Stanford University Press, 2018.

O'Neal, Chas. "In Old Kay See." *Chicago Defender*, July 18, 1925.

Oyewumi, Oyeronke. *The Invention of Women: Making an African Sense of Gender Discourses*. Minneapolis: University of Minnesota Press, 1997.

Phelan, Peggy. *Unmarked: The Politics of Performance*. New York: Routledge Press, 1996.

Raiford, Leigh. *Imprisoned in a Luminous Glare: Photography and the African American Freedom Struggle*. Chapel Hill: University of North Carolina Press, 2013.

Rankin, John. "How Slavery Honors Our Country's Flag." *Anti-Slavery Record* 1 (February 1835): 13–23.

Rasilla, Azucena. "In Downtown Oakland, 30+ Storefronts Display Art Celebrating Black Joy." *The Oaklandside*, July 16, 2021. Accessed January 29, 2024. https://oaklandside.org/2021/07/16/downtown-oakland-30-storefronts-display-art-celebrating-black-joy/.

Reis, Joã José. *Slave Rebellion in Brazil: The Muslim Uprising of 1835 in Bahia.* Baltimore, MD: Johns Hopkins University Press, 1995.

Ricoeur, Paul. *Time and Narrative, Volume 1.* Translated by Kathleen McLaughlin and David Pellauer. Chicago: University of Chicago Press, 1983.

Rilke, Rainer Maria. "Primal Sound." In *Selected Works of Rainer Maria Rilke,* vol. 1, *Prose,* translated by C. Craigh Houston. London: Hogarth Press, 1954.

Roach, Max. "What Jazz Means to Me." *The Black Scholar* 3 (Summer 1972): 3–6.

Roberson, Ed. "the puzzle in bundles." In *Voices Cast Out to Talk Us In.* Iowa City: University of Iowa Press, 1995.

Roberts, Neil. *Freedom as Marronage.* Chicago: University of Chicago Press, 2015.

Robinson, Evita. "With Art Hubs and Performances, Theaster Gates Is Redefining Chicago's South Side." *Condé Nast Traveler,* February 18, 2021.

Rosen, Jody. "Researchers Play Tune Recorded before Edison." *New York Times,* March 27, 2008. Accessed January 24, 2011. http://www.nytimes.com/2008/03/27/arts/27soun.html?_r=2.

Ruin, Hans. "*Ge-stell*: Enframing as the Essence of Technology." In *Martin Heidegger: Key Concepts,* edited by Bret W. Davis. Montreal, Canada: McGill-Queen's University Press, 2010.

Russell, Camisha. "Positivism and Progress in Firmin's Equality of the Human Races." *Journal of Pan-African Studies* 7, no. 2 (2014): 45–67.

Schiller, Friedrich. *Letter upon the Aesthetic Education of Man.* 1795. In *The Harvard Classics,* vol. 32, *Literary and Philosophical Essays: French, German and Italian,* edited by Charles W. Eliot. New York: P. F. Collier and Son, 1910.

Schiller, Friedrich. *Letter upon the Aesthetic Education of Man and Letters to Prince Frederick Christian von Augustenburg.* 1795. Translated by Keith Tribe. New York: Penguin Classics, 2016.

Schweik, Susan M. *The Ugly Laws: Disability in Public.* New York: New York University Press, 2010.

Scott, Clive. *The Poetics of French Verse: Studies in Reading.* London: Oxford University Press, 1998.

Shakur, Assata. "Affirmation." In *Assata: An Autobiography.* Chicago: Lawrence Hill Books, 2001.

Shakur, Sanyika. "Pathology of Patriarchy: A Search for Clues at the Scene of the Crime." *Kersplebedeb,* March 2, 2013. Accessed October 20, 2023. https://kersplebedeb.com/posts/pathology-of-patriarchy/.

Simpson, A. "Slave Songs of the United States." *Lippincott's Magazine of Literature, Science and Education*, March 1868, 341–43.

Sousa, John Phillip. "The Menace of Mechanical Music." *Appleton's Magazine* 8 (1906): 278–84.

Spence, Lester K. *Knocking the Hustle: Against the Neoliberal Turn in Black Politics*. Santa Barbara, CA: Punctum Books, 2015.

Spillers, Hortense. "Mama's Baby, Papa's Maybe: An American Grammar Book." *Diacritics* 17, no. 2 (1987): 65–81.

Spillers, Hortense. "Shades of Intimacy." Lecture given at The Flesh of the Matter: A Hortense Spillers Symposium, Ithaca, NY, March 18, 2016. https://www.cornell.edu/video/hortense-spillers-shades-of-intimacy-eighteenth-century.

Spivak, Gayatri Chakravorty. "Can the Subaltern Speak?" In *Marxism and the Interpretation of Culture*, edited by Cary Nelson and Lawrence Grossberg, 271–316. Chicago: University of Illinois Press, 1988.

Stadler, Gustavus. "Never Heard Such a Thing: Lynching and Phonographic Modernity." *Social Text* 28, no. 1 (102) (2010): 87–105.

Stanley, Eric. *Atmospheres of Violence: Structuring Antagonism and the Trans/Queer Ungovernable*. Durham, NC: Duke University Press, 2021.

Sterne, Jonathan. *The Audible Past: The Cultural Origins of Sound Reproduction*. Durham, NC: Duke University Press, 2003.

Stillman, Peter G. "Scarcity, Sufficiency, and Abundance: Hegel and Marx on Material Needs and Satisfactions." *International Political Science Review/Revue Internationale de Science Politique* 4, no. 3 (1983): 295–310.

Stott, William. *Documentary Expression and Thirties America*. Chicago: University of Chicago Press, 1973.

Suékama, Nsámbu Zu. "Dispatches from Among the Damned: On the History and Present of Trans* Survival." *Pinko*, September 29, 2022. Accessed October 19, 2023. https://pinko.online/web/trans-survival.

Szeto, Andrew, and Toshio Meronek. "YIMBYs: The Darlings of the Real Estate Industry." *Truthout*, May 10, 2017. Accessed January 29, 2024. https://truthout.org/articles/yimbys-the-alt-right-darlings-of-the-real-estate-industry/.

Tate, Greg. *Everything but the Burden: What White People Are Taking from Black Culture*. New York: Crown Press, 2003.

Van Der Zee, James, Owen Dodson, and Camille Billops. *The Harlem Book of the Dead*. Introduction by Toni Morrison. New York: Morgan and Morgan, 1978.

Wagner, Bryan. *Disturbing the Peace: Black Popular Culture and Police Power*. Cambridge, MA: Harvard University Press, 2009.

Washington, Booker T. "Address by Booker T. Washington, Principal." At opening of Atlanta Exposition. September 18, 1895. Recorded speech: https://www.loc.gov/exhibits/civil-rights-act/multimedia/booker-t-washington.html.

Webster, Emma. "Breathtaking Murals for Justice Proliferate on the Streets of Downtown Oakland." 7 × 7, June 12, 2020. https://www.7x7.com/downtown-oakland-murals-black-lives-matter-2646168310.html.

Weheliye, Alexander G. "After Man." *American Literary History* 20, no. 1–2 (2008): 321–36.

Weheliye, Alexander G. *Phonographies: Grooves in Sonic Afro-Modernity.* Durham, NC: Duke University Press, 2004.

Wilderson, Frank B. *Red, White and Black Cinema and the Structure of U.S. Antagonisms.* Durham, NC: Duke University Press, 2010.

Woods, Clyde. *Development Arrested: The Blues and Plantation Power in the Mississippi Delta.* New York: Verso Press, 2017.

Wynter, Sylvia. "Black Metamorphosis: New Natives in a New World." Unpublished manuscript, 1971.

Wynter, Sylvia. "The Ceremony Must Be Found: After Humanism." *boundary 2* 12, no. 3–13, no. 1 (1984): 19–70.

Wynter, Sylvia. "Human Being as Noun? Or *Being Human* as Praxis? Toward the Autopoetic Turn/Overturn: A Manifesto." Unpublished manuscript.

Wynter, Sylvia. "On How We Mistook the Map for the Territory, and Reimprisoned Ourselves in Our Unbearable Wrongness of Being, of *Désêtre*." In *A Companion to African-American Studies,* 107–69. Malden, MA: Blackwell Publishing, 2006.

Wynter, Sylvia. "Sambos and Minstrels." *Social Text* 1 (Winter 1979): 149–56.

Wynter, Sylvia. "Unsettling the Coloniality of Being/Power/Truth/Freedom: Towards the Human, After Man, Its Overrepresentation, an Argument." *CR: The New Centennial Review* 3, no. 3 (2003): 257–337.

Index

Page numbers in italics refer to figures.

Abernathy, Sylvia, 197
abjection, 17–18, 69, 97, 113–14, 118, 142–44, 151, 163
abolitionism: and blackface minstrelsy, 36–38; and black labor, 52–54; and black music, 7, 10, 14–15, 24, 31, 56, 70; and documentary embodiment, 118; and Douglass, 33–34, 40–41, 58–60, 69, 181, 205; and the family, 68; Garrisonian, 13, 35, 50; and the law, 43–44; in Oakland, ix, xi; and photography, 65; and "the slave," 39, 45–51. *See also* humanization
Adorno, Theodor, 39, 57–58, 62, 64, 82, 104, 160, 182, 209, 218n43, 233n17; *Aesthetic Theory*, 103, 233n11, 238n55–56, 241n25, 242n47
aesthetic comportment (*Gleichgültigkeit*), 64, 107, 134–35, 139, 151, 157, 162, 177, 182–83, 185–89, 202, 205
aesthetic justification: and the Black Arts Movement, 169; and black music, 2, 29, 60, 73; definition of, 11, 19–24; and the family, 74; and Fanon, 136–37, 140; and Nietzsche, 20, 22, 27, 217–18n40; and performance, 121–22; and the slave society, 4–6, 15, 51
aesthetic labor, xvii, 3, 8, 56
aesthetic regulation: and beauty, 165, 174–75; and black art, 15, 26–27; and black music, 2–3, 5; and blackness, 11, 13–14, 19, 69–70, 96, 105, 158; and Fanon, 139; and *Jazz*, 22, 143, 149; and Locke, 21
aesthetics, definition of, 9–13

AfriCOBRA. *See* Organization of Black American Culture (OBA-C)/AfriCOBRA
Afrocentrism, 173, 180
Ahearn, Charlie, 6
Alexander, M. Jacqui, 106, 150–51
Algeria, 137
Alkalimat, Abdul, 195–96, 198, 200
antiblackness: and black art, xv–xvii, 116; and black beauty, 177; and black music, 4; and cisheteropatriarchy, 146; and racism, 116, 128, 156, 233n11; and the slave narrative, 220n19; and urban renewal, x–xi, 175, 187, 194, 203, 206; and Van Der Zee's images, 153, 155–56
Anti-Slavery Record, 53–54, 57, 81
Art Ensemble of Chicago, 133, 231n65
artification, 174, 185, 204
artist collectives. *See* Association for the Advancement of Creative Musicians; Black Artists Group (BAG); Organization of Black American Culture (OBA-C)/AfriCOBRA; *individual collectives*
Artist-In-Residence (AIR) Program, 192
Association for the Advancement of Creative Musicians (AACM), 161, 190–92, 195, 197–98
autonomy, 28, 45, 57, 108–10, 194, 220, 220n18; black, 33, 151, 183
autopoiesis, 55, 144
Ayler, Albert, 184

Babylon girls, 105, 109, 111–12
Baker, Houston, 128
Baker, Josephine, 105, 111, 113, 131

Baraka, Amiri, 25, 29, 72, 172–73, 188, 199; *Blues People*, 4, 77, 226n20; "Changing Same, The," 184–85, 241n29; "Jazz and the White Critic," 183–84
Barrett, Lindon, 127, 129
Bateson, Gregory, 118
beautification: and aesthetics, 9, 59, 177; and the black artist, 27; and black beauty, 173–74, 206; of black labor, 52, 54; of blackness, 71, 165, 168–69, 183; and the New Negro, 127, 130; projects, ix, 29, 99, 170, 186–90, 193–94, 203, 205, 243n57
beauty. *See* beautification; black beauty
beauty, definition of, 12
Bell, Alexander Graham, 80, 227n27
Benjamin, Walter, 105, 217n33, 223n39
Berlant, Lauren, 143, 147, 238n54
Bethune, Thomas, 70
Bidwell, Shelford, 84, 91, 230n62
Bildung, 201, 206
Billops, Camille, 134, 158
Binder, Guyora, 214n1
black (use of term), 214n2
"Black Aesthetic" (Neal), 171–73
black art, definition of, 24–30
black artist, definition of, 24–30
Black Artists Group (BAG), 29, 173, 189–94, 206
Black Arts Movement: and aesthetics, 9, 12; and beautification projects, 99, 188, 190, 195, 198, 202, 206; and black aesthetics, 171–73; and black art, 25, 181–83; and black beauty, 29, 165, 168–71, 174–76, 180; and the black community, 203; and black enjoyment, 28; and black unity, 176–78, 184–85
black beauty: and artist collectives, 193, 196, 199, 203; and the Black Arts Movement, 169–73, 183; and black life, 29, 86, 206; and black unity, 176–78, 185; definition of, 165, 174–76; and Freddy Fixers, 188–89; and Goncalves, 178–82, 201; and Hughes, 168, 182
black bourgeoisie, 28, 71, 110, 137, 165, 183, 187, 205, 235n48
black death: and aesthetics, 143, 209; and black art, 207; and black life, 140; in *Harlem Book of the Dead*, 134, 141, 152–58; in *Jazz*, 137, 144, 147, 161–63. *See also* lynchings
black enjoyment, 28–29
black experientialism, 195–96
blackface minstrelsy. *See* minstrelsy (blackface)
black imagination, xv, 11, 16, 21, 27, 126, 153–54
"black is beautiful" (phrase), 169, 180, 188
black labor: and black music, 8, 51–58, 60, 65; and Du Bois, 61, 63; extraction of, xv; and jazz, 152; and Marx, 62; and minstrelsy, 37; and slavery, 6–7, 20, 49
Black Lives Matter, xi, *xiii*, 208, 209
black music. *See* black song; blues music; jazz music; *individual artists*
black music, definition of, 2–4
black nationalisms, 173, 180
Black Panther Party, 192
Black Power Movement, 29, 169–71, 175–76, 187, 189–90, 192, 195
black representation: and aesthetics, 11, 29, 58–59, 96; and beautification projects, xiv-xvi, 173–75, 177, 199, 205; and black life, 164, 168; and the black voice, 69; and the black work of art, 26–27; Fanon on, 135–36, 138; and the Harlem Renaissance, 23, 106–7, 122–25, 128, 153; and performance, 109; and phonography, 101, 113, 120
black song: and aesthetic justification, 19–21; and beautifying black labor, 51–58; development of, 2, 4, 7–9, 15; and Douglass, 5, 12–13, 17, 40, 48, 61
black sounding, x, 4, 25, 27–28, 54, 103, 114, 141
black study, 10, 138
black unity, 170, 175–76, 178, 184–85, 201
black voice: and anthropology, 230n62; and chattel slavery, 67; and cinema, 230–31n63; definition of, 40, 69; and Douglass, 38, 124; and Fanon, 138; and "his master's voice," 76–79, 83; and Ma Rainey, 105, 108, 115, 119, 127, 141; phonographic, 65, 87, 91–98, 100–101, 107, 121, 165, 231n67
black work of art, definition of, xvii, 2–3, 24–30

blues music: appropriation of, 144, 183; black queer, 22, 103, 107, 115, 122, 129, 185; and documentary embodiment, 116; instrumental, 113; and jazz, 165; in Oakland, ix; performances of, 111, 170; phonographs of, 100, 104, 119; scholarship on, 21, 25, 61, 106, 234n20; work songs of, 121. *See also* Rainey, Gertrude "Ma"
Borne, Georgina, 203
bourgeoisie (black). *See* black bourgeoisie
Brathwaite, Kwame, 169
Brazil, 88–89, 106
Brooks, Daphne A., 35, 50, 111
Brooks, Tim, 67–68, 70–74, 76
Brown, Banko, xiv, 213n4
Brown, Henry Box, 35
Buck-Morss, Susan, 46
Bundy, McGeorge, 175, 189
burdened individuality, 60, 99
Burlin, Natalie Curtis, 112
Burnett, Charles, 136–37

Cahan, Susan E., 199, 201
Callier, Terry, 195
capitalism, 39, 55, 61–63, 78, 237n19; black, 127, 204; petty, 128, 130, 174; racial, xv, 6–7, 27, 138, 190
captivity: and aesthetic regulation, 14; beautified, xv, 18; and black music, 10, 33–34, 45; fugitive, 114; and Ma Rainey, 108, 110; of representation, 104; and slavery, 4, 12, 41, 124
capture: and abolition, 33, 39, 41, 45, 181; aesthetic, 13, 22–23, 59, 110, 164; and aesthetic justification, 64; of black music, 2, 4–5, 7–9, 11, 18, 24, 28, 119; and black unity, 185; documentary, 134; fugitive, 81, 99; and jazz, 151, 165; and narrative, 144–45; and the New Negro, 129; phonographic, 66, 76, 82, 96, 106, 114–15, 117–18, 143, 234n24; sonic, 21, 104, 108, 229n57; technological, 65, 69
Carby, Hazel, 121, 128
Cardinal, Marie, 149
Certeau, Michel de, ix
Chandler, Nahum Dimitri, 75–76
chattel slavery, 4, 67–68, 73, 78, 151

Cheng, Anne Anlin, 111, 131
Chicago, IL: art groups in, 29, 173, 190–92, 195; South Side, 194, 196, 204, 206; and Theaster Gates, 203–4, 205; and Wall of Respect, 198–200
cinema, 23, 105, 109, 117, 120, 131, 135–37, 154, 231n63
civil rights, 155, 176, 198
class: black, 21–22, 112, 121–22, 129, 195; Locke on, 110, 116, 128, 182, 190, 235n48; and Marxism, 52, 242n55; middle, 188, 204; working, xvi, 28, 170, 186–88
Cocteau, Jean, 1
Coleman, Ornett, 67
Collins, Arthur, 95, 231n67
colonialism, 39, 58, 86, 88–89, 112–13, 117, 137, 140, 146, 150, 183, 223n39
colorism, 44, 112, 116, 182
Coltrane, John, 184
Columbia Phonograph Company, 91
Committee for the Arts. *See* Organization of Black American Culture (OBA-C)/AfriCOBRA
commodification, 5, 38, 58, 78, 92, 97, 100, 104, 108, 233n17
condos, ix–xv, 26, 59, 186, 207–10, 243n3. *See also* gentrification; real estate
Cooke, Sam, 184
"coon songs," 94–95, 231n67
Cowper, William, 43–44
Cox, Ida, 122
Crawley, Ashon, 25, 140
Cruz, Emilio, 190, 192–93
Cruz, Jon, 4, 50, 119
Cruz, Pat, 193–94
cultural production, 5, 18, 21, 39, 51, 59–61, 105–6, 113, 128, 139, 194

Dabydeen, David, 49
dance, 5, 17, 145, 148, 223n47
Danforth Foundation, 190–91
Davis, Angela, 21, 33–34, 75–76, 106, 121, 146, 225n10
deadly bribes, xvii
death. *See* black death; lynchings; social death
defensive architecture, xiv, 27, 207
dehumanization: and blackness, 17–19, 186; and minstrelsy, 34, 64, 116; and slavery, 2–3, 8, 13, 17, 43. *See also* humanization

de Man, Paul, 10, 16, 216n27
de Martinville, Édouard-Léon Scott, 79–80, 87, 91, 227n27
Deniker, J., 230n62
Derrida, Jacques, 80, 148, 174, 225–26n12, 227n32, 228–29n50, 229n53, 238n50, 240n4
Detroit, MI, 186
différance, 84, 90
displacement, x, xv, xvi, 78, 149–50, 207. *See also* condos; gentrification; real estate; redevelopment/urban renewal
documentary embodiment, 41, 105, 114, 116–19, 125–26, 153–54
Dodson, Owen, 134, 155, 159
Dolar, Mladen, 82
Donaldson, Jeff, 195, 200
Dorcas (*Jazz* character). *See* Manfred, Dorcas (*Jazz* character)
Douglass, Frederick: and abolitionism, 58–63, 68–69, 86, 181; and aesthetic justification, 20–24; and aesthetics, 9–13, 65–66, 206; and the black aesthetic, 172; and black art, 24, 28–29; and black music, 2–8, 20, 42–45, 54, 64, 202, 218n44; and black representation, 104–5, 107, 122; and documentary embodiment, 119; as the first black artist, 11, 170, 205, 223n44; on "Fugitive's Song" cover sheet, 31–34, 220n11; and humanization, 13–19, 56–57; and the New Negro, 124, 134; and phonographic sound, 70–72, 82–83, 96, 116; and racial pathology, 135, 138; sound-imaging of, 35–42, 88, 120, 159, 168, 220n18; and "the slave," 45–51, 98–99
Du Bois, W. E. B.: and Alain Locke, 122, 124, 126, 128, 135, 137, 179; and black art, 20, 22, 25, 121, 184; *Black Reconstruction*, 46, 234–35n38; "Criteria of Negro Art," 26–29; and the "fight," xvii, 12; and individuation, 72–74; *Philadelphia Negro, The*, 61, 214n2, 234–35n38; and "race men," 70, 116; and slavery, 11; and "souls of black folks," 4, 35, 61, 63

Edison, Thomas: and fugitive sounds, 81, 117, 119, 234n24; and great men, 84, 98, 143; and immortality, 80–81; and the phonograph, 82, 87, 159, 229n57, 231–32n72, 232n81; and the ugly hiss, 96, 100
Edison Phonograph Company, 91
Edwards, Brent Hayes, 125, 128
Ekundayo, Ashara, 243n1
Ellington, Duke, 20
Ellison, Ralph, 4, 20, 25
emancipation, 14, 33, 39–40, 44, 51, 56, 59, 62–63, 66, 69, 124; legal, 8, 60, 81, 226n19; vs. manumission, 214n1
Emerson, Victor H., 91–92, 94, 100–101, 219n2, 232n81
empathy, 33, 40, 44–45, 48, 68, 70, 118, 124, 154; empathic identification, 8, 43, 162
English, Darby, 25–26, 201, 203
enslaved labor, 2, 5, 7–8, 34, 51–54, 56, 58, 73
escape: and black experientialism, 196; and black music, 4, 62; Douglass's, 12, 14, 33–35, 41–42, 45–46, 57, 181; and the family, 73; and jazz, 149; and the New Negro, 126; and Rainey, 114; from slavery, 164
ethnomusicology, 4, 10, 15, 25, 42, 70, 110, 112, 126, 172
Evans, Mari, 176–77
exposure (paid in), xvi–xvii

Fanon, Frantz: and a "look," 219n2; and Morrison, 149; and narcissism, 83; and narrative, 134–40; and postural schema, 78–79; and racism, 97–98, 236n14; and sociogeny, 137, 143, 236n8
Federal Bureau of Investigation (FBI), 175, 199
fetishism, 57, 62, 148, 163, 230n62, 240n13
Filene, Benjamin, 113
Fine, Sidney, 186
Firmin, Joseph-Anténor, 17
flesh: captive, 108, 110, 131; and Douglass, 43; fungibility of, 33; and *Jazz*, 145–46, 152; and Ma Rainey, 21, 103, 106–11; and minstrelsy, 95; and Van Der Zee, 160, 163
Floyd, George, ix, 213n3
Floyd, Samuel, 4
Ford Foundation, 175, 189–90, 197

Foucault, Michel, 26
Franklin, Aretha, 184
Freddy Fixers, 185–90, 207, 241n30. See also beautification
Freud, Sigmund, 138, 236n8
fugitive sounds, 18, 117, 119
"Fugitive's Song" sheet music, 69–70, 74, 76–79, 81–88, 144, 172, 225n12
fugitivity, 10, 31–37, 40, 59–60, 81, 98–99, 114, 117–18, 220n11, 234n24
Fuller, Hoyt W., 195
fungibility, 33, 38, 48, 78, 115, 175, 227n25

Garrison, William Lloyd, 13, 35, 40, 50, 59. See also abolitionism
Garvey, Marcus, 152, 169
Gates, Henry Louis, Jr., 5, 8, 23, 71–72, 120, 136–37
Gates, Theaster, 203–6, 243n57
Gelatt, Roland, 231–32n72
gender: and the blues, 121; and jazz, 148; and the New Negro, 127, 130; and performance, 21, 108–11, 123; and race, 53, 105–6, 113, 150; and voice, 84, 90–91, 229n57. See also patriarchy
genre: black life as, 22, 104, 113, 141, 143, 193–94; development of, 16, 25, 114; and documentary, 119; of the human, 118; and jazz, 142, 144–45, 148–52, 165, 183; law of, 11, 149–50, 202; and Ma Rainey, 115; and photography, 117, 153–54, 158, 164. See also individual genres
genrefication, 22, 104, 109, 137, 151
gentrification, xi, 7, 174, 187, 192, 197, 201, 204–5. See also condos; displacement; redevelopment/urban renewal
Gibb, G. D., 230n62
Giovanni, Nikki, 25
Gleichgültigkeit, 64
Glissant, Édouard, 128, 130
Goncalves, Dingane Joe, 12, 29, 173, 178–82, 201, 240n11
gospel music, 184
graffiti, xi, 6, 187, 196
grand patriarchy, 146–47
Gray, Erin, 154
Gray, Herman, 25, 40, 154
Great Migration, 120

Haiti, 48
Hammer, K. Allison, 21, 106, 110, 127
Harlem Book of the Dead, The (Van Der Zee), 23, 134–35, 137, 140–41, 152–64, 170, 204
Harlem Renaissance: and aesthetic justification, 20–23, 64; and black aesthetics, 9, 71–72, 121–22, 171–72; and the black artist, xvii; and black beauty, 28–29, 168–69, 180–83; and black culture, 127–28, 137, 177; and black music, 56, 165; and black representation, 120–23; and Ma Rainey, 104, 106–7, 110, 116; and photography, 134. See also Du Bois, W. E. B.; Locke, Alain; Negro civilization; New Negro; Van Der Zee, James
Harney, Stefano, 71, 202
Harris, Cheryl, 237n19
Hartman, Saidiya: and Douglass, 3, 17–18, 31–32, 44–45; and Du Bois, 235n38; and gender, 150; and mastery, 39–40, 60, 62; and Reconstruction, 226n19; *Scenes of Subjection*, 5; and self-mastery, 10; and slavery, 21, 38, 49, 82, 151, 161
Hegel, Georg Wilhelm Friedrich, 16, 140, 184, 225n12
Heidegger, Martin, 67, 113, 117, 225n12, 228n48
Hemphill, Julius, 190, 192–93
Herskovitz, Melville, 17
His Master's Voice, 82
Hughes, Langston, 20, 25, 167–68, 170–71, 182, 239n1
humanization: and abolitionism, 36, 44, 48, 51–52, 69, 118; and aesthetics, 23, 174; and black music, 1, 3–4, 34, 41–42, 54, 56–57, 59, 61, 65, 170; and blackness, 11, 13–17, 28, 35, 50; and the black voice, 70–72, 74, 82, 88, 113; and Kant, 85–86; and slave narratives, 10, 136, 140. See also dehumanization
Hunter, Tera W., 52, 55, 121
Hutchinson, Jesse, Jr.: "Fugitive's Song" sheet music, 69–70, 74, 76–79, 81–88, 144, 172, 225n12
Hutchinson Family Singers, 31, 40

imagination (black). See black imagination

imperialism. *See* colonialism
individuation, 27, 43, 60, 62, 72, 74, 81, 83, 146, 151
Inner City Arts Project, 192
interiority: in art, 207; black, 39, 42, 119; and black beauty, 178; and black music, 20, 40–41, 115, 119; evacuative, xiv, 144; in photographs, 156; and slavery, 69; in writing, 149
Iton, Richard, 25

James, C. L. R., 46
Jarrell, Jae, 195
Jarrell, Wadsworth, 195
Jazz (Morrison novel): and aesthetic justification, 20, 178; and black art, 23, 139, 180; and black death, 140, 147, 153, 155, 161; and black representation, 106; and genre, 22, 104; and jazz music, 133, 141–45, 148–52; and racial pathology, 134–35, 146. *See also* Manfred, Dorcas (*Jazz* character)
jazz music: and black history, 197; and black relationality, 159–60; genre of, 148–52, 161, 165; gentrification of, 22, 104; and improvisation, 161, 170, 181; and *Jazz* (novel), 133, 141–45, 148; and white musicians, 183
Jim Crow, 120
Johnson, George W.: and beauty, 165, 177; life and career of, 18–19, 21, 66–76, 116, 194, 226n21; and mimesis, 77–79, 81–82, 88, 172, 206; phonography of, 91–101, 106–7, 111, 120–21, 141, 159, 232n81
Johnson, Samuel, 67, 78
Jones, Claudia, 55, 121
Jones, Kellie, 201
Jones, LeRoi. *See* Baraka, Amiri
Jones, Omi Osun Joni L., 159–60
Jones-Hogu, Barbara, 195

Kalulé, Petero, 29
Kant, Immanuel: and aesthetics, 6, 15–16, 59, 112, 217n28; and aesthetics of judgment, 118, 128, 215n21, 220n16; and autonomy, 220n18; and beauty, 182, 201–2, 213n5; and black art, 209; and the figure of the human, 84–85; and goodwill, 242n55; and lawful external relations, 215n17; and luxury, 12; on the Māori, 85–86, 88, 243n58; metaphysics of, 10, 215n20
Kgositsile, Keorapatse: *Black Arts Anthology*, 176–78
Kheshti, Roshanak, 112
Kittler, Friedrich, 80, 223n39

labor. *See* aesthetic labor; black labor; enslaved labor
Lake, Oliver, 190, 193
Lampert, Stasha, 238n53
law of genre, 11, 149–50, 202
Lead Belly, 100, 113
Ledbetter, Huddie Williams "Lead Belly," 113
LeFlouria, Talitha L., 55
Lewis, George, 115
liberation: and aesthetics, 9; and beautification projects, 192–93, 195, 198–200; and beauty, 168, 174, 176, 183; of black music, 3–4, 34–35, 40–41, 44; of blackness, 14, 39; and the Harlem Renaissance, 120, 124; and *Jazz*, 139, 151; of personal property, 204; and the phonograph, 81, 88; and slavery, 45–46, 55, 57; of the slave society, 8, 10, 17, 99
Locke, Alain: and aesthetic comportment, 64, 139, 177, 183, 188, 202, 205; and aesthetic justification, 20–22; and aesthetics, 11, 14, 72, 112, 164, 185, 235n48; and black art, 25, 120, 130, 137; and the Black Arts Movement, 172; and black beauty, 179, 182; and black culture, 190; and Ma Rainey, 104, 131; and the New Negro, 4, 71, 106–7, 110, 113, 122–29, 134–36, 153; and property, 85; and race men, 70, 116
Lomax, John and Alan, 100, 112–13, 126, 144
Looker, Benjamin, 192
Lott, Eric, 9, 95, 224n59, 233n11
L'Ouverture, Toussaint, 46
lynchings, 93, 95–97; photography of, 109, 154–55, 163

Mackey, Nathaniel, 25, 31, 148
Mailer, Norman: *White Negro, The*, 148–49
Malcolm X, 221n27
Mallarmé, Stéphane, 210

Manfred, Dorcas (*Jazz* character), 20, 23, 106, 133–35, 141–54, 159, 161–65, 173, 178, 180, 196. See also *Jazz* (Morrison novel)
Māori people, 85–86, 88, 243n58
Marable, Manning, 191, 194
Marriott, David, 83, 154, 219n2, 236n8
Martin, Dawn Lundy, 103, 106
Marx, Karl: and art, 52, 54–58, 63, 174, 186, 224n53, 240n13; and Kant, 242n55; and labor, xvii, 39, 62, 125, 222n32, 235n41; and social hieroglyphics, 78
Marxism, 39, 58, 62, 223n39
mastery: aesthetic, 19, 44, 56, 86; Hartman on, 39–40, 60, 62; and *Jazz*, 142–43; self-, 10; and slavery, 6, 38, 49–51, 65; small, 9, 11; and sonic reproduction, 79, 81–83, 95, 101, 107; white, 36, 48
Mathes, Carter, 25
Maurice, Alice, 230–31n63
McNeil, Anne, 195
McNeil, Earnet (Duke), 195
Merleau-Ponty, Maurice, 196
Middle Passage, 17, 19
Millard, Andre, 92
Miller, Sodarisa, 122
mimesis, 69–70, 74, 76–79, 81–88, 144, 172, 225n12
mimicry, xvii, 70, 80, 118, 123, 176–77
minstrelsy (blackface): and black music, 183; black women in, 110, 233n6; dehumanizing character of, 34, 64, 116; and Douglass, 4–5, 18, 39–40, 44, 71; and George W. Johnson, 21, 94–97, 101, 107; introduction to, 35–38, 224n59; and Ma Rainey, 109–12; and mastery, 9, 65; and the New Negro, 123, 127; and slavery, 6, 10, 233n11; and sonic reproduction, 88, 105, 120, 231n67; and Theaster Gates, 204–5
misrecognition, 84, 135, 143–45, 148, 152, 156, 159–62, 238n54
Mitchell, Roscoe, 197, 231n65
Model Cities Program, 187, 190–91, 197, 241n30
Moore, Samuel, 67
Morrison, Toni: and black aesthetics, 25; and *The Harlem Book of the Dead*, 134, 137, 152, 155, 161, 163–64; *Jazz*, 20, 22–23, 104, 106, 133, 135, 139, 180; and *Jazz* narrator, 144–48, 153; and narrative, 140–41; *Playing in the Dark*, 149–50; and sovereignty, 143. See also *Jazz* (Morrison novel)
Moten, Fred, 3, 25, 71, 117, 119, 136, 145, 147, 171, 202–3, 226n23
murals: and aesthetic justification, 11–12; in Oakland, xi–xv, xvii, 6, 27, 160, 173, 176, 208, 213n3; *Wall of Respect* (OBA-C project), 194, 196–202
Murray, Albert, 4, 20, 25, 116, 234n20
museumification, 205–6
music. *See* black song; *individual genres*

narcissism, 82–83, 91, 219n2
Neal, Larry, 25, 29, 170–73, 181, 184, 202
Negritude movement, 128, 169, 173
Negro civilization, 70–71, 75, 126, 128, 153, 179
Negro Digest, 195–96
neighborhoods. *See* beautification; gentrification; urban renewal/redevelopment
neoliberalism, 55, 99, 168, 187, 191, 198, 204, 210
New Haven, CT, 187–88
New Negro, 4, 71, 106–7, 110, 113, 122–29, 134–36, 153
New World, 38, 46, 48, 117
New York City, NY, 6, 60, 224n59; Harlem, 120; South Bronx, 196
Nielsen, Aldon Lynn, 25
Nietzsche, Friedrich: and aesthetic justification, 20, 22, 27, 217–18n40; and aesthetics, 15, 215n17, 218n43; and the artist, 23, 27, 106; and the Prometheus myth, 219n52
Nkrumah, Kwame, 177, 183
noise, x, 7, 10, 16, 53, 184, 207, 228n50; noise ordinances, ix, xiv
North American Phonograph Company, 91

Oakland, CA, ix–xiv, 207–9, 243n1, 243n3
Oakland Art Murmur, x, *xii*, 27
Obama Presidential Center, 206, 243n57
Odum, Howard, 112
Okiji, Fumi, 25

Organization of Black American Culture (OBA-C)/AfriCOBRA, 29, 173, 194–200, 202. See also *Wall of Respect* (OBA-C project)

Paramount Records, 104, 108, 233n6
paternalism, 63, 123, 130, 146, 175, 187, 194
pathology (racial). *See* racial pathology
patriarchy: black, 110–11, 121–22, 162–63, 187; and black unity, 176; and family, 63, 72, 74–76, 159; grand, 146–47; in *Jazz*, 134, 151; and Locke, 21–22, 130; and voice, 82–83, 92. *See also* gender
performance. *See* minstrelsy (blackface); Rainey, Gertrude "Ma"; vaudeville
personhood, 55–56, 60, 66
Phelan, Peggy, 114
phonautographs, 79–88, 90–91, 227n27, 229n54
Phonogram, 92
phonographs: Adorno on, 160, 233n17; and aesthetic justification, 11; and black song, 6, 15, 41–42, 44–45, 51; and black voice, 65, 69, 87–88, 107, 226n17, 231n67; development of, 79–83, 228n46, 229–30nn57–58, 231n65, 231n72, 232n81; and documentary embodiment, 116–19; and George W. Johnson, 18–19, 67, 72–73, 76, 78–79, 91–96, 106, 121; and the Harlem Renaissance, 23, 113, 123–26, 131; and jazz, 143; and Ma Rainey, 21, 103–5, 108–9, 112, 114–15, 134, 141, 165; and mimesis, 83–84; and racist pathology, 136, 138; and the ugly hiss, 97–101, 177
photography. *See* documentary embodiment; *Harlem Book of the Dead, The* (Van Der Zee)
photography (lynching), 109, 154–55, 163
plantations: and aesthetics, 5, 51, 60; and black music, 16, 38, 69, 81, 108; and the black song, 2–3, 8, 43, 53, 118; decline of, 35, 40, 45, 49; and the family, 68, 75–76, 78; and George W. Johnson, 67; of the mind, 6; and minstrelsy, 9, 34, 36, 65, 88, 110; Wynter on, 14, 31, 42, 48, 220n9, 223n39

police power, 23, 97, 99, 147
police violence, ix–xiii, 190–91, 199–200, 207
policing (Wagner concept), 98–99
property: and abolition, 45–46; of aesthetics, 11–12; and beauty, 176, 181–82; and black art, 24, 27, 29, 62–63, 184, 200, 203; and black life, 66, 121; and the black voice, 77, 79; of enslaved labor, 5; and the family, 69, 73, 76, 98, 160; investment, xvii; and jazz, 148; Lockean, 85; and the New Negro, 127; personal, 81, 204; private, 7–8; slave, 18, 23, 33, 35, 38, 55, 60; and subjectification, 138–41; whiteness as, 237n19. *See also* real estate
Pruitt-Igoe housing project, 192–94
psychoanalysis, 39, 238n54
public art projects. *See* beautification; *Wall of Respect* (OBA-C project)

queerness: and black art, 30, 134; and black performers, 109–10, 114; and the blues, 21–22, 103, 106–7, 115, 122, 129–30, 185; and jazz, 148, 150; and the New Negro, 126–27; and urban renewal, ix, 190

race men/women, 70, 111, 116
racial capitalism, xv, 6–7, 27, 138
racial pathology, 10, 21, 134–39, 146, 153, 225n10
racism: aesthetics of, 23; anti-, xi–xiii, *208*; antiblack, 116, 128, 156, 233n11; and capitalism, 190; Fanon on, 236n8; language of, 214n2; and lynchings, 154; and minstrelsy, 21, 64, 120, 205–6; and narcissism, 83; and the New Negro, 123, 135–37; rationalization of, 106; and slavery, 2–3, 18, 66; structural effects of, 112
Raguet, Condy, 89–90
Raiford, Leigh, 155
Rainey, Gertrude "Ma": and aesthetic justification, 20–22; and black representation, 173; and blues music, 61, 185; performances of, 106–12, 114–17, 121–24, 129–30, 136, 153–54, 164, 233n17; phonography of, 103–5, 111–12, 119, 126, 131, 134, 141, 165
Rankin, John, 54

rationalization: aesthetic, 3, 65; and black music, 34, 42, 45, 64, 203; and documentary embodiment, 126; and the family, 72, 75; and the imagination, 6, 18, 66; legal, 23–24; and mastery, 143; and minstrelsy, 109; and racial pathology, 138, 153; and skin, 111–12; and slavery, 46, 122; technological, 22, 40, 51, 65, 69, 101, 104–6, 117, 220n9, 223n39, 234n21; and voice, 83, 121

real estate: and beautification projects, 186–87, 197, 199, 205–6, 209; in Oakland, x–xiv, xvi, 168. *See also* condos; gentrification

Reconstruction, 10, 46, 61, 69, 78, 97, 191, 226n19; Second, 194

redevelopment/urban renewal, 170, 186–87, 190, 197–98, 199, 201, 203, 205. *See also* displacement; gentrification

regulation: and abolition, 38–39, 51; and aesthetic justification, 136–37; and black art, 29, 116, 188; and black life, 18, 23, 71, 111–12, 182; and black music, 4, 7, 52, 56, 65; and the imagination, 6; and phonography, 76, 82; and representation, xvii, 164; self-, 10, 62; sexual, 106, 120, 148. *See also* aesthetic regulation

representation (black). *See* black representation

resistance: and black art, xvi; and black culture, 75–76; and black music, 2–3, 15, 20, 28, 44, 65; and black representation, 173; and death, 155, 163; and public art, xi, 195; to slavery, 34, 46, 59–60, 64; and the subject, 139, 152

restraint, xi, xvii, 2, 9–10, 12–13, 22, 27, 181, 201

Ricoeur, Paul, 133, 140
Rilke, Rainer Maria, 80
Rivers, Conrad, 195
Roach, Max, 151–52
Roberson, Ed, 1, 25
Roberts, Neil, 59
Rockefeller Foundation, 191
Rousseauian traditions, 45, 51, 218n44
Ruin, Hans, 234n22, 238n48

Sartre, Jean-Paul, 148–49
Scarborough, Dorothy, 112

Schiller, Friedrich, 6, 14–16, 20–21, 112, 124, 167, 180, 201, 216n25, 217n37, 218n44
Scott, Clive, 228n50
Scott, Leon. *See* de Martinville, Édouard-Léon Scott
Second Reconstruction, 191, 194
Shakur, Assata, 201
Shakur, Sanyika, 146
Shepp, Archie, ix, 6
Simpson, A., 88–90, 228n50
skin: black, 35, 107, 149, 233n11; and manumission, 151; and minstrelsy, 38, 109, 116; and performance, 44–45, 105, 111–12, 130–31; and photography, 160–61
slavability, 24, 38, 51, 107, 233n11
slave community: and abolition, 36, 50, 58; and aesthetic regulation, 14; Angela Davis definition of, 33–34, 75–76; and blackness, 13, 51; and black song, 2–3, 15, 56, 60; and Douglass, 12; and George W. Johnson, 71, 73–74; and the slave society, 86; and "the slave," 45–46
slave revolts and rebellions, 5, 17, 39, 44, 46, 48, 51, 59–60, 223n47
slavery. *See* chattel slavery; emancipation; enslaved labor; plantations; slave community; slave revolts and rebellions; slave ships; slave society
slave ships, 108, 161, 164, 221n27
slave society: and aesthetic justification, 5, 19–23; and black art, 24–25, 28–29, 55, 59, 73, 99; and black music, 2, 4, 10; definition of, 214n1, 224n59; and Douglass, 34, 38, 50–51, 57, 172; and George W. Johnson, 73, 82, 107; humanization of, 13–14, 16–18, 70; imagination of, 3, 6–8, 20, 24, 39, 46; and the slave community, 86
Smith, Adam, 52, 222n32
Smith, Bessie, 61, 122
Smith, Clara, 122
Smith, Fred, 188, 241n30
Smith, Trixie, 122
Smitherman, Geneva, 200
Snorton, C. Riley, 108, 111
social death, 140, 160–61
sociogeny, 137, 143, 236n8
song (black). *See* black song

sonic technology. *See* phonautographs; phonographs
sound studies, 25, 65
South Africa, 169, 176
speculation: and aesthetics, 8, 10, 112–13; and beauty, 86; and blackness, 79; and capital, 55, 127, 186; and the imagination, 6, 11; and labor, 61, 125; real estate, 197, 204–7
Spillers, Hortense, 73–74, 108, 110–11, 131, 146
Spivak, Gayatri Chakravorty, 144, 237n22
Stadler, Gustavus, 93, 95–96
Stanley, Eric, 216n24
Sterne, Jonathan, 25, 79–80, 227n27, 228n46
Stevens, M. Charlene, 25
Stevens, Nelson, 195
Stewart, Roskin, 226n21
St. Louis, MO, 29, 173, 190–93
Stott, William, 118
structuring antagonism, 14, 216n24
subjectification, 44, 139, 144, 146, 153, 194
subjection, 17, 48, 79, 137–38, 141, 146, 149, 151
subjectivity, xv, 11, 41, 98, 128, 133, 135, 144, 149–50, 238n55; narrative, 137, 139–40
Suékama, Nsámbu Za, 146

Tate, Greg, 25, 40
Tennyson, Alfred Lord: "Crossing the Bar," 157–58
Theater Owner's Booking Association (TOBA), 110
transcendental judgment, 86, 213n3
Tubman, Harriet, 24
Turner, Nat, 24, 136–37

ugliness: and beautification projects, 205; vs. beauty, 222n33; and genre, 150; and slavery, 8, 51–53, 59, 181
"ugly hiss," 18, 96–97, 100–101, 177, 231n72
Underground Railroad, 24, 62
urban renewal/redevelopment, 170, 186–87, 190, 197–98, 199, 201, 203, 205. *See also* displacement; gentrification

Van Der Zee, James: *Harlem Book of the Dead, The*, 23, 134–35, 137, 140–41, 152–64, 170, 204
Van Der Zee, Rachel, 157–60
vaudeville, 94, 105, 109–10, 127
Virginia Serenaders, 36–37
visual hegemony, 25
voice: and Douglass, 33, 44; and jazz, 144–46, 150; Kant on, 86, 88; and mimesis, 77–79; and music, 72, 89–91; phonographic, 41, 65, 80–85, 121, 230n58

Wagner, Bryan, 97–99, 101, 122, 147, 226n17, 232n79
Walker, George, 95
Wall of Respect (OBA-C project), 194, 196–202
War on Poverty, 190, 205
"Washer Woman's Blues" (song), 121
Washington, Booker T., 55
Wedgwood, Josiah: *Am I Not a Man and a Brother*, 46–50, 118
Weheliye, Alexander, 25, 79
white aesthetics, 176–77
white family, 36, 68, 70, 73, 75, 82, 98, 172, 174
whiteness, 7, 148, 150, 171, 173, 237n19
Wilderson, Frank, 135, 142, 236n14
Williams, Bert, 95
Williams, Gerald, 195
women. *See* gender; patriarchy
Woods, Clyde, 51
Woolf, Virginia, 138
world-making, x–xi, 20, 149
World War I, 120
Wright, Richard, 154
Wynter, Sylvia: and the auto-institution, 104; and autopoiesis, 144; and black music, 8, 40, 60; and the black work of art, 22; and documentary embodiment, 117; and humanity, 86, 118, 227n25; and infrasensory ontologized, 48, 113, 221n22; and the plantation, 31, 42, 220n9, 223n47; and racial pathology, 138; and raw material, 16, 56, 223n39; and small mastery, 9; and vanished authority, 228n48

Zuhandenheit, 234n22, 238n48

www.ingramcontent.com/pod-product-compliance
Lightning Source LLC
Chambersburg PA
CBHW021340230426
43666CB00006B/359